RAYMOND CHANDLER

Born in Nebraska of Irish parents, brought up in Chicago, educated at Dulwich College, and self-taught on those 'mean streets' of Los Angeles about which he wrote, Raymond Chandler – writer, accountant, civil servant, oil executive, poet, recluse, charmer, gentleman, drunk – was as full of contradictions as his origins. This is the first authorised biography in over twenty years of the cult novelist who was described by Evelyn Waugh in 1949 as 'the best writer in America' and who inspired 'film noir' and crime writing over the next half century.

With access to hundreds of unseen personal documents, photographs and previously unrecorded accounts by those who knew Chandler, Tom Hiney has unearthed revealing new material about the man and the writer. In the light of new discoveries a much rawer, more complex, sympathetic and brilliant Chandler emerges – a man quite as extraordinary as the fiction he wrote.

TOM HINEY

Tom Hiney has written for the *Sunday Times*, the *Observer*, *Express* and *Spectator*. He was born in 1970 and lives in South Africa.

FOR FIGGY

Tom Hiney

RAYMOND CHANDLER

A Biography

VINTAGE

Published by Vintage 1998

2 4 6 8 10 9 7 5 3 1

Copyright © Tom Hiney 1997

The right of Tom Hiney to be identified as the author of
this work has been asserted by him in accordance with
the Copyright, Designs and Patents Act, 1988

Quotations from Chandler's correspondence, fiction,
notebooks and screenplays are reproduced by kind
permission of the Raymond Chandler Estate

First published in Great Britain by
Chatto & Windus 1997

Vintage
Random House, 20 Vauxhall Bridge Road,
London SW1V 2SA

Random House Australia (Pty) Limited
20 Alfred Street, Milsons Point, Sydney
New South Wales 2061, Australia

Random House New Zealand Limited
18 Poland Road, Glenfield,
Auckland 10, New Zealand

Random House South Africa (Pty) Limited
Endulini, 5A Jubilee Road, Parktown 2193,
South Africa

Random House UK Limited Reg. No. 954009

A CIP catalogue record for this book
is available from the British Library

ISBN 0 09 953351 0

Papers used by Random House UK Ltd are natural,
recyclable products made from wood grown in sustain-
able forests. The manufacturing processes conform to the
environmental regulations of the country of origin

Printed and bound in Great Britain by
Mackays of Chatham PLC, Chatham, Kent

Contents

List of Illustrations   vi

Preface   vii

Acknowledgements   x

1 From Chicago to Bloomsbury   1

2 Go West, Young Man   33

3 The Pulps   70

4 Philip Marlowe   99

5 Hollywood Days   134

6 Private Eye   167

7 The Long Goodbye   198

8 London License   220

9 Playing It Back   250

   Epilogue   276

   Notes   288

   Index   305

List of Illustrations

1. As a boy, in Ireland.
2. At Dulwich College.
3. In Freiburg, 1907.
4. During the First World War.
5. Florence Chandler.
6. In California, after the war
7. Cissy before she met Chandler.
8. On a California beach, 1920s.
9. At the Dabney oil fields.
10. Mother and son.
11. An oil industry banquet.
12. *Double Indemnity*.
13. *The Big Sleep*.
14. Cissy Chandler.
15. With Taki, the cat.
16. Dinner with Helga Greene.
17. In old age.

Preface

Who cares how a writer got his first bicycle?
(Chandler's reply to the suggestion of his British
publisher that he write an autobiography)

In 1958, the year before he died, Raymond Chandler made a short promotional tour of America with Phil Carey, the actor who had been chosen to play Chandler's hero Philip Marlowe in a TV series for NBC. Chandler was drunk throughout the tour, as he had been almost continuously since 1954. 'You could like him,' said Carey, 'but you wouldn't want to be around him.' Others disagreed. Helga Greene, the literary agent who nearly married Chandler after the tour, described him as 'a mixture of naivety and brilliance . . . he was the best company in the world'.

Raymond Chandler was otherwise described, in the course of his life, as cynical and gullible; reclusive and generous; depressive and romantic; proud and paranoid. Two things stabilized him. Being drunk, which he often was, and Philip Marlowe. Chandler tried different types of writing, but he always returned to detective fiction and to Marlowe. 'I simply cannot operate without him,' he eventually decided. It was the adventures of Philip Marlowe that made Chandler both famous and rich. In his lifetime, the Marlowe books were translated into over twenty languages and were made into six films. (Four new Marlowe adaptations have followed since Chandler's death.) They each revolve around a hard-drinking hero who combined everything that Raymond Chandler was, wished he was and feared he might be.

He had had plenty of opportunity for self-analysis by the time he came to create Philip Marlowe. He did not write his first book until he was fifty, and by then he had been variously rich, poor, drunk, teetotal, sacked, married and suicidal. He had lived in pre-Mafia Chicago, pre-telephone Nebraska, Quaker Ireland and Victorian London. Having lived in the city of Los Angeles since the age of twenty-five, he had been there long enough to witness an oil boom, two earthquakes, the Depression and an Olympic Games. 'To write about a place,' he once decided, 'you have to love it or hate it or do both by turns . . . but a sense of vacuity and boredom – that is fatal.' Chandler spent a lot of his life trying to avoid boredom, and not always successfully. He was pursued by a restless demon that haunted him most whenever he stayed still too long. He sustained no long friendships except with Cissy Pascal, his wife of thirty years, and he lived at over one hundred different addresses. To many who came into contact with him, Chandler appeared beyond eccentric.

Despite working within the disposable genre of crime fiction – and furthermore within the abrasive sub-genre of violent detective fiction – Chandler was always more than a hack entertainer. Described by Evelyn Waugh in the late 1940s as no less than 'the greatest living American novelist', he was admired by the likes of T. S. Eliot, W. H. Auden and Edmund Wilson. He continues to inspire an enormous following among both other writers and readers. In 1988, *Time* magazine suggested that 'Chandler has inspired more poses and parodies than any other writer of the century save Hemingway.'

Chandler's legacy is amplified by the work he did in Hollywood. During a five-year spell there, he rose to being not only the highest-paid screenwriter in the industry's history, but also one of the most influential. When he abandoned the studios in 1949 in order to return to his Marlowe books, the movie magazine *Sequence* estimated the impact he had made: 'Just as Chandler has many literary imitators, so has his work exercised a considerable influence on the treatment of crime and violence in the cinema. He has helped to bring healthy realism back to the cinema. What is certain is that since 1944 his work has done much to form the basis of a school of film-making as indigenously American as the Western.' Both in the movies that Chandler worked on in Hollywood, and those that were made from his books, he was central to the birth of what became known as film noir.

'I am sitting in an all-plastic motel,' once wrote the columnist S. J. Perelman to Chandler, 'overlooking another all-plastic motel which in turn overlooks the Gulf Stream, but there is no man in America (or for that matter the world) but yourself who could convey the grisly charm of the place.' Chandler's was certainly a unique talent, and a previously inconceivable one within the ranks of detective fiction. The following biography will trace the years which provoked and then nurtured that talent.

Acknowledgements

The author is particularly grateful to the following for their help: Neil Morgan; Natasha Spender; Bodleian Library (Modern Papers), Oxford; UCLA Special Collections Library, Los Angeles; Dr Judith Priestman; Michael Gilbert; Kathrine Sorley Walker; Graham C. Greene; the Raymond Chandler Estate. He would also like to thank: Albert Hernandez; Claire Paterson; Jonathan Burnham; Alison Samuel; Toby Buchan; the British Library; Dulwich College; Dr Jan Piggott; Frank MacShane; the Academy of Motion Picture Arts and Sciences (Margaret Herrick Library); James O'Brien; Sebastian Doggart; Charlotte Elston. Special thanks are due to Kay Beckett for the very generous gift to the author of Chandler's typewriter; and to Sir Gordon Reece for the loan of his house and car in Los Angeles, and for his forgiveness when the author wrecked the car.

Photographs are reproduced by permission of the Raymond Chandler Estate; illustration no. 2 is reproduced courtesy of Dulwich College, London; nos 1, 3, 6, 8, 9, 10, 11, 15, 17 courtesy of the Bodleian Library, Oxford; no. 12 courtesy of Paramount, no. 13 courtesy of Warner Bros, and both stills by permission of BFI Stills, Posters and Designs, British Film Institute, London; no. 4 courtesy of John W. Seifert Photographs, Los Angeles.

From Chicago to Bloomsbury

The swans of our childhood were probably just pigeons
(Letter, February 1954)

Raymond Chandler had different ways of remembering his childhood but the villain of the story was always the same. His father, Maurice Chandler, was a railway engineer, a lapsed Quaker and an alcoholic. He had been born to farmer parents near Philadelphia in 1859. The family was of English stock – although the word 'Chandler' is originally old French for candle maker – and had lived in the state of Pennsylvania since the 1680s.

The Chandlers had been one of several Quaker families to flee England for southern Ireland during Oliver Cromwell's persecution of the sect in the 1650s. They were among the very first of these emigrants to move on to America with the Quaker leader William Penn. Like the majority of Penn's earliest followers, they had been living as part of the Anglo-Irish Quaker community in County Waterford before sailing for the New World in 1682.

At the time of Maurice Chandler's birth, Pennsylvania was still dominated by a strong Quaker presence, even if some of the religious zealotry among members of the sect had diminished. They were the oldest group of settlers in the state and also the most prosperous. They were distinct in appearance, business methods and dynastic pride. William Penn had left his followers with stern but also openly commercial instructions:

1

Be plain in clothes, furniture and food, but clean, and the coarser the better; the rest is folly and a snare . . . diligence is the Way to Wealth: the diligent Hand makes Rich. Frugality is a Virtue too, and not of little Use in Life, the better Way to be Rich, for it has less Toil and Temptation.[1]

Maurice Chandler was a lapsed Quaker from the start. His parents had a farm outside Philadelphia, but at the age of nineteen he moved to the city. He took a room in a boarding house there and studied engineering. The University of Pennsylvania, which he attended, had been open since 1749, and was one of the few secular colleges in America. Education was not a priority for Quakers: Penn had gone as far as warning his followers that 'reading books is but a taking off the mind too much from meditation'.[2] Maurice studied at the university's science school for two years but dropped out in 1880 before finishing his course, receiving only a certificate of proficiency. Instead, aged twenty-one, he moved out to Chicago to find work on the railroads that were being built in the Midwest.

As a contract engineer, Maurice Chandler based himself in Chicago and followed the railroads wherever work was needed, chiefly in Nebraska, Kansas and Wyoming. The prairies were still considered frontier territory at this time: Nebraska had only become a recognized state in 1867 and Oklahoma was officially still 'unsafe' for settlers because of hostile Indians. The lines Maurice Chandler began work on were linking these prairies to Chicago, transforming the city into a rich grain depot and slaughterhouse. They were consequently enriching the prairies too, turning rural settlements into rail towns and speculators into local tycoons. Only a decade before Maurice Chandler arrived in the area, 'Buffalo Bill' Cody had earned his nickname after killing 5,000 buffalo as part of a contract to supply the Kansas Pacific Railroad workforce with meat.

The railroads were huge ventures, each employing up to 40,000 workers and each with its own history of speed, efficiency and unscrupulousness. Their collective effect on the region was enormous; Maurice Chandler arrived at a time that historians consider the height of American modernisation:

Railway building created and sustained hundreds of thousands of new jobs; new coal and iron mines; new coking plants; new iron and steelworks; new towns, which were also new markets; new skills; and new forms of financial and industrial organization. This was the epitome of the Industrial Revolution. It was this which began to turn the Americans into a nation of town-dwellers, and then city-dwellers; it was this which, by the demands it created, stimulated the amazing growth in production and wealth that, before the end of the century, had entirely outstripped anything the Old World could show.[3]

For seven years, Maurice worked the prairie lines as a bachelor engineer. At the age of twenty-eight, he was working in Omaha, Nebraska, when he met and married an Irish girl called Florence Thornton. Small, dark-haired and extremely pretty, Florence was in America staying with her elder married sister at a nearby town called Plattsmouth. She and her sister Grace were two of five daughters from a prosperous family in southern Ireland, all but one of whom had 'escaped' from what had been a claustrophobic home. Like Maurice Chandler, Florence was a lapsed Quaker – her parents lived in the very same Waterford Quaker community from which Maurice's own family had originated. She and Maurice were married that summer at an Episcopalian church in Laramie, Wyoming. Twelve months later Florence had a child. Raymond Thornton Chandler was born in Chicago, on 23 July 1888.

*

Chicago was a boom town at the time of Chandler's birth. Thanks to the railroads, the city had sprung from being a city of minor significance at the time of the Civil War into a metropolis of international renown. Heavy industry had added to the wealth already created from agricultural broking. Socially, the city was caught in the flux of its sudden success; though its agricultural and industrial moguls were commissioning architects to show off Chicago's importance, the power of these tycoons had not gone unchallenged. Two years before Chandler's birth, there had been vicious pitched fighting between police and strikers after a bomb killed a policeman during a union rally. Chicago's breakneck growth was turning the city into a political battleground. It was the moguls, nonetheless, who continued to hold the upper hand. In defiance of its embattled reputation, the city held a World Exposition in 1893 in order to reveal its extravagant new wealth. Twenty-eight million people visited the Exposition, which included a demonstration of the world's first petrol-run tractor.

It was not an optimism that infected the house rented by Maurice Chandler. The itinerant nature of his job meant that mother and infant son were soon spending most of their time alone. Maurice had become a hard drinker and was, according to his son, 'found drunk if he was found at all'. Alcoholism among contractual workers was a familiar problem in industrializing America. It was as a reaction against the growth of mass male alcoholism that the American Temperance Movement came into force. In 1880, the year Maurice Chandler had left Pennsylvania, the Temperance-backed Prohibition Party fought its first Presidential election.

The marriage very quickly disintegrated. Even when he was home, Maurice was drinking aggressively. The atmosphere became bitter and the couple had no more children. It was precisely the kind of marriage which, by the 1890s, was prompting an alliance between the Prohibition campaign and the Women's Suffrage Movement in America. Though there is no indication that Florence Chandler participated in any of the several rallies, petitions and campaigns in Chicago at this time, she would have known that she was not the only 'drink widow' in Chicago. And although organized crime would not emerge as a force there for another thirty years, it was already a tough city in which to be vulnerable. Chandler certainly had few romantic memories of it: 'When I was a kid in Chicago,' he later wrote, 'I saw a cop shoot a little white dog to death.'

Florence began to spend more and more time in the town of Plattsmouth, Nebraska, with her sister Grace and Grace's Irish settler husband, Ernest Fitt. The Fitt clan became a surrogate family for Florence and her son. Ernest Fitt was a boiler inspector and 'doubtfully honest' according to Chandler. Harry Fitt, Ernest's brother, ran a hardware store and drank: 'Liquor was a family vice. Those who escaped it either turned religious or went in for duck pants.'[4] Another Fitt was a local politician and was, in Chandler's memory, 'also crooked'.

4

There were other Fitts in Plattsmouth to whom the young Chandler was introduced, including one who had once ripped off a bank he had worked for in Ireland. He had escaped to Europe with the help of the Freemasons, only to be robbed himself in a hotel: 'When I knew him, long after, he was an extremely respectable old party, always immaculately dressed, and of incredible parsimony.' Another of Chandler's Nebraska uncles invented a machine which could load mail on to a train without the train stopping. He held a grand public demonstration; 'but somebody beat him out of it and he never got a dime'. In the absence of a father, Chandler enjoyed a lively and maverick wardship from the male Fitts. He was also made aware of their – and to a lesser extent his own – Irishness.

Despite its new commerce with Chicago, Nebraska was still an extremely remote place in the 1890s. Rail was the only thing that made the city, 400 miles east of Plattsmouth, seem at all close. Without the later inventions of the motor car, telephone and radio, the state was stuck firmly at the heart of a silver-and-farming northern Bible Belt. The most famous Nebraskan at the time of Chandler's boyhood was the blunt-speaking Senator William Jennings Bryan, who campaigned throughout his political career for a return to the 'plain' values of pre-industrial small-town America. He was nominated as the Democrats' presidential candidate in 1896 after winning the support of his party by criticizing city amorality and the implementation of a gold standard. Failing to beat the Republican candidate, William McKinley, in 1897, Bryan went on to devote himself to a number of 'Old America' causes, a platform which included an attack on secular education. He was later counsel for the prosecution in the infamous 'monkey trial' in Tennessee, in which a teacher was prosecuted for teaching Darwinism in breach of the state's anti-evolutionist law. Bryan was an important figure in Nebraska, and even as a small child Chandler knew who he was:

> I remember the oak trees and the high wooden sidewalks beside the dirt roads and the heat and the fireflies and walking sticks and a lot of strange insects . . . and the dead cattle and once in a while a dead man floating down the muddy river and the dandy little three-hole privy behind the house. I remember Ak-Sar-Ben and the days when

they were still trying to elect Bryan. I remember the rocking chairs on the edge of the sidewalk in a solid row outside the hotel and the tobacco spit all over the place.[5]

Compared to the progressive, if embattled radicalism of Chicago, Nebraska was a social throwback to old farming America. The boy Chandler was the exact contemporary of a fictional girl who lived in the neighbouring state of Kansas, and who also lived with her uncle and aunt. *The Wonderful Wizard of Oz,* by L. Frank Baum, would be published in 1899 and begins in the type of pre-modern setting that as a young child Chandler knew well:

> Dorothy lived in the midst of the great Kansas prairies, with uncle Henry, who was the farmer, and Aunt Em, who was the farmer's wife. Their house was small, for the lumber to build it had to be carried by wagon many miles.[6]

*

By the mid-1890s, the Chandlers' marriage was effectively over. They had given up all pretence of a permanent address, and the lease on the Chicago house had been abandoned. When Raymond Chandler caught scarlet fever in 1895, he and his mother were living in a hotel. In the same year, a divorce was obtained in Chicago and Maurice Chandler disappeared from his son's life entirely. Florence refused ever to speak of him again. With no money of her own, she decided to return to Ireland with her seven-year-old son.

The Midwest would always have a peculiar significance for Chandler. It intrigued him later in life to think what might have happened to him had he and his mother stayed there. He could not help but imagine what might have been his prospects on the prairies. The Fitts tried to persuade Florence to bring the boy up in Plattsmouth. Had they stayed on, Chandler later realized, his life would have made a very different story:

> I would have stayed in the town where I was born and worked in a hardware store and married the boss's daughter . . . I might have even got rich – small-time rich, an eight-room house, two cars in the garage, chicken every Sunday, and the *Reader's Digest* on the

living-room table, the wife with a cast-iron permanent and me with a brain like a sack of Portland cement.[7]

This thought recurred to Chandler throughout his life and in his fiction. He tried to picture what it might have been like if his father and mother had settled unhappily in the Midwest:

> . . . mother drumming on the edge of the dinner table when father tried to promote himself a second piece of pie. And him with no money any more. No nothing. Just sitting in a rocker on the front porch there in Manhattan, Kansas, with his empty pipe in his mouth. Rocking on the front porch, slow and easy, because when you've had a stroke you have to take it slow and easy. And wait for the next one. And the empty pipe in the mouth. No tobacco. Nothing to do but wait.[8]

Instead, it was to Ireland that Chandler and his mother returned in 1895. They took the train to New York and a steamer to Dublin. The Chicago Chandlers had not lasted a generation.

*

It was a dishonourable return to Waterford for Florence Thornton, whose impetuous American marriage had been even more unpopular there than her sister's unglamorous emigration with a boiler inspector. Since the early death of Florence's father, the head of the family had been Chandler's 'arrogant and stupid grandmother', guided by his uncle Ernest Thornton. Like most males in the Thornton family, Florence's father had until his death helped run the family law firm, which had offices in Waterford, Cork and Dublin. It was a rarefied Anglo-Irish world of servants and quasi-gentility; quite removed from late-nineteenth-century Nebraska. It was also a world preoccupied with both religious and social snobbery:

> My grandmother was the daughter of an Irish solicitor. Her son, very wealthy later on, was also a solicitor and had a housekeeper named Mrs Groome who sneered at him behind his back because he wasn't a barrister. The Church, the Navy, the Army, the Bar. There was nothing else. Outside Waterford in a big house with gardens . . . lived a Miss Paul who occasionally, very occasionally,

invited Mrs Groome to tea on account of her father had been a canon.[9]

The reception Florence received from her family was as stiff as she had expected. The large home in Waterford presented an atmosphere of conservatism and anti-Catholicism that left Chandler, even as a boy, with a nostalgia for Nebraska. As in Pennsylvania, the Quaker community in Waterford was an established and tight one. It was also one that shared the anti-Catholicism of other Anglo-Irish communities there; a sectarian prejudice that had outlasted the tolerant vision of the community's Quaker forefathers. There was a famous Quaker school in Waterford – 'famous to Quakers anyway' said Chandler – but Florence was insistent that her son should not be raised a Quaker. Though she was as careful in appearance and speech as any of her stock, she was no longer interested in their other ideas of propriety.

Ireland was still British in 1895, but equivocation in London over the country's constitutional future was making life extremely uncomfortable for the Anglo-Irish who lived and worked there. Despite the strongly colonial leadership of Robert Cecil, Marquis of Salisbury, the Conservative government in London was continuing to flirt with Parnell's Irish Home Rule Movement. The status and rights of Anglo-Irish communities in the southern Irish counties, including the Quaker community in Waterford, was a matter both of debate and of confusion, and would continue to be so until the 1920s. This uncertainty served to exacerbate anti-Catholic feeling among English families like the Thorntons, an atmosphere Chandler remembered clearly:

An amazing people the Anglo-Irish. They never mixed with Catholics socially. I remember playing on a cricket team with some of the local snobs and one of the players was a Catholic boy who came to the game in an elaborate chariot with grooms in livery; but he was not asked to have tea with the rest after the game. He wouldn't have accepted of course.[10]

Nor was the young Chandler immune to this religion-fuelled hostility. 'I should not like to say that in Ireland Catholicism reached its all-time low of ignorance, dirt and general degradation of the priesthood,' he later said, 'but in my boyhood it was bad enough. It does the Irish great credit that out of this flannel-mouthed mob of petty liars and drunkards there has come no real persecution of the non-Catholic elements.' It would rile Chandler when journalists later presumed that his Irishness denoted Catholicism. 'I grew up with a terrible contempt for Catholics', he explained in 1945, 'and I still have trouble with it now.'

Nevertheless, the experience of having the affable chancers of the Fitt family replaced by the self-conscious Thorntons also induced in Chandler an early suspicion of middle-class respectability. This stuffy arrogance seemed to be personified by his wealthy Thornton uncle, Ernest:

> Sometimes when the dinner did not suit him he would order it removed and we would sit in stony silence for three quarters of an hour while the frantic Mrs Groome browbeat the domestics below stairs and finally another meal was delivered to the master, probably much worse than the one he had refused; but I can still feel the silence.[11]

The Quakers were not the only proponents of British snobbery at this time. It was the neurotic self-aggrandizement of the Empire's middle classes at the turn of the century that had inspired another Anglo-Irishman, Oscar Wilde, to write his satire *The Importance of Being Ernest*. The play was first performed in 1895, the same year that Florence and her son returned to Ireland from America:

> *Cecily:* When I see a spade I call it a spade.
> *Gwendolen:* I am glad to say that I have never seen a spade. It is obvious that our social spheres have been widely different. (Act III)

*

Unable to face the prospect of staying in Waterford, Florence took her son to London, where Chandler's uncle Ernest – who worked there for much of the year – had agreed to look after them. They were temporarily installed at a house in genteel Upper Norwood, in South London, which Ernest had originally rented as a base in the capital for his mother as well as a home for his unmarried sister Ethel. Connected to Central London by a regular train service, the area was beginning to lose its leafy exclusivity and was slipping gradually down market. Ethel Thornton was scornful of Florence's intrusion and the new atmosphere was scarcely an improvement on Waterford. There were also intermittent visits to the house from Chandler's grandmother, who would humiliate Florence at every opportunity: at meals, for instance, Florence would pointedly not be served wine. The effect of this treatment from her own family and the memory of the rejection she had endured from a drunken husband was almost too much for Chandler's mother. A natural fighter, she became, more and more, a subdued presence around her son. Chandler would always be more influenced by having seen the effect of his father's neglect on his mother than he was by Florence herself. He would make little mention of her in his own adulthood, other than to say how much he wished she had remarried in London:

> I know that my mother had affairs – she was a very beautiful woman – and the only thing that I felt to be wrong was that she refused to marry again for fear a step-father would not treat me kindly, since my father was such a swine.[12]

It was a frustrated suburban atmosphere for the boy to grow up in. Florence's initial anger at having been abandoned by her husband turned into a passive unhappiness at her fate, as she and her child grew older. Ernest's guardianship was purely financial and often grudging even in that. A successful solicitor, and a bachelor, he spent most of his time mixing with London's wealthy Anglo-Irish set. Like many of that set he commuted seasonally between his interests (and residences) in Ireland and England. For all his reluctance, however, he was a crucial benefactor for Chandler. Most importantly, he now agreed with Florence that he would pay for her son's education. It was settled that when Chandler reached the age of twelve, he would go to Dulwich College, a good public school, not far from the house, which Chandler would be able to attend as a day boy. Until then, the boy would go to a local church school and spend his summers in Waterford.

There is little doubt of the coldness felt and displayed towards Florence and her offspring on their return from Chicago, for divorce was no more a Quaker institution than it was a Victorian one. In the case of Ernest Thornton it was a coldness – as Chandler later discovered – which was at least partly tempered by the knowledge of his own impurity:

> The rather amusing development in my uncle's case was that he took unto himself a Jewish mistress in London, raised her son who was an illegitimate get of a couple of Sassoons, had two illegitimate children himself, and then married her. *But he never took her to Ireland.* I could write a book about these people but I am too much of an Irishman myself ever to tell the truth about them.[13]

*

The flux of life in Chicago, Nebraska, Waterford and London (and the uncertainty that lay behind that flux) propelled Chandler into early emotional maturity. Physically, he was small yet handsome, with his mother's dark hair and bright blue eyes. But there was already an unhappy side to him – the only child among three adults, he now acquired a loathing for Sundays and Christmases that would last throughout his life. He did not read more than most children, but his structureless and nomadic childhood had left him with an early understanding that life was 'today a pat on the back, tomorrow a kick in the teeth'.[14]

The monotony of being an only child in Upper Norwood was made worse by the fact that Chandler was not encouraged to bring friends back to his uncle's house. His strange and reclusive upbringing was in danger of making him feel odd. In both suburban South London and Quaker Waterford, Chandler was an anomaly – an American-sounding boy with a pretty Irish mother about whom people, including her own family, gossiped. He was a boy raised in what other boys imagined was the Wild West, but who was now reliant on the charity of severe Quaker relatives. If dawning self-consciousness was making other pre-pubescent boys of his age feel out of step with their surroundings, then for Chandler it was not a new sensation. In late Victorian England, he was without a clear social class, nationality or male role model. Even at home, he and his mother were made to feel different.

*

School came as a relief. Dressed in Eton collar and black coat,

Chandler joined Dulwich College as a day boy in September 1900, the penultimate year of Queen Victoria's sixty-four-year reign, at the age of twelve. His school number was 5724. Dulwich College had been founded in 1619 and is five miles south of Central London, situated near the homes of middle-class families whose sons made up the majority of the school's fee-paying register. Socially, it was not in the league of Eton or Harrow, but it had a very strong academic and sporting reputation, producing middle-class boys to serve the British Empire. When Chandler joined the school it was turning out a continuous and impressive stream of scientists, generals, lawyers, academics, admirals, bishops and sportsmen.

It was a patriotic school, and particularly so during Chandler's days there. Many Old Alleynians (as former Dulwich Boys are known) were fighting in the Second Boer War when Chandler matriculated, and everyone at the school followed the campaign keenly. The fighting continued until May 1902, and was the first colonial war to be given daily and comprehensive coverage by the modernized British press. War correspondents, including Rudyard Kipling, were filing their reports by telegram. Chandler recalled there being a daily toast at Dulwich: 'To my country, right or wrong.'

Matthew Arnold had described Dulwich shortly before Chandler's arrival there as the type of school he had 'long desired, and vainly desired, to see put at the disposal of the professional and trading classes throughout this country'. The architecture echoed the school's growing reputation. Having outgrown its original Elizabethan site by the mid-nineteenth century, the school had been resited on Dulwich Common, within a comparatively giant, brand new building of red brick and white stone, designed in a hybrid of Palladian and Gothic styles by the younger Charles Barry, whose father had built the Houses of Parliament. There was a Great Hall, a Chapel, the boys' Houses, classrooms, a clock tower and playing fields – with the capacity to take 750 pupils. It was after seeing the impressive grounds from a train window that P. G. Wodehouse's father had decided, five years before Chandler's own arrival, to send two of his sons to the school. When Chandler joined in 1900, Dulwich was famous for two things: the fact that most of its boys lived at home, as opposed to boarding which was the case in most British public schools; and its charismatic head-master, A. H. Gilkes, who, by coincidence, shared Chandler's Quaker roots.

Gilkes had been headmaster at Dulwich since 1885 and was unusually central to everything that happened there. He was a talented, ascetic character who had taken a Double First at Oxford and won a Soccer Blue, and who had then deliberately rejected worldly success by working for ten years as an ostensibly lowly junior Classics master at Shrewsbury School, where he himself had been as a boy. His presence there as a teacher had been such, however, that Gilkes had effectively started running Shrewsbury from his classroom, and he had been a figure well enough known outside the school for Dulwich to appoint him Master in 1885. By the time of Chandler's arrival, Gilkes's influence on the day-to-day atmosphere of Dulwich was enormous.

An angular giant (he stood 6 feet 5 inches) with a long grey beard and a family life to which he had come only lately – he had married the sister of a Dulwich boy shortly before Chandler's arrival – Gilkes endorsed the priorities of Thomas Arnold as an educationalist. As with Rugby's famous Headmaster, morality was foremost for Gilkes; followed by Englishness; followed by intellect. He was a notorious figure both within and beyond the school grounds. 'He had a power of merciless chaff,' recalled one Old Boy, 'which I have never seen equalled in any other man . . . he was not the type of headmaster who sits apart in Olympian dignity. There can never have been a headmaster who was seen more often and more regularly by all the boys.'[15]

For the many boys at Dulwich whose fathers were overseas working within the Empire, Gilkes filled the vacuum of male authority and wisdom. This impression of patriarchy rather than tyranny was helped by the fact that Gilkes did not believe in rigorous corporal punishment. He cut a ridiculous figure among many of his masters, but appeared to command the genuine loyalty of his boys. At the turn of the century, headmasters of Britain's large schools were often public figures, quoted and referred to in the national press. Gilkes avoided such exposure, but as a published novelist he had a certain reputation; indeed H. G. Wells once attacked what he saw as a dangerous form of moral nostalgia in Gilkes's novels. These novels were dramatizations of their author's vigorous theories about tradition, gentlemanly conduct and education. Dulwich was the crucible in which Gilkes aimed to produce his distinct vision of decency and honesty. He was driven by a moral purpose that was, according to one contemporary, 'more marked in him than in any other man I have ever known'. He had, another said, 'a childlike simplicity, and a fundamental serenity of soul':

> He said such simple things with grave sincerity and opened windows to the soul. So it was, when we were reading Aeschylus or Sophocles, he would exclaim to our astonishment, 'What! Kill a King! And such a King!' or tell us how 'the Queen is very beautiful, you see, as well as wicked.' And we did see. Somehow or another he awoke our wonder, kindled our imagination, set us free for the enjoyment not of Greek and Latin only, but of many other things in later life. In all his teaching he seemed to be finding out, afresh for himself as much as for us, the beauty and the interest of what we were learning.[16]

Gilkes's relentless sense of integrity could at times be excessive. P. G. Wodehouse, who left Dulwich in the year of Chandler's arrival, remembered the Master as the sort of man who would approach him after a good cricket performance and say 'Fine innings, Wodehouse, but remember we all die in the end.' P. W. Bain, who was Captain of Athletics in Chandler's third year, confirmed that for most Dulwich boys, Gilkes's genius was only apparent after they had left: 'I think that in our youthful ignorance and arrogance we were inclined to belittle his powers as a teacher. [But Gilkes believed that] education is to supply a boy with other and better things to think of than himself – for example great men or nations or Nature – and to fit his mind properly to appreciate them ... A schoolboy doesn't think deeply enough. But later in life, realization comes.' Though Chandler would himself never make much later mention of Gilkes (nor of Dulwich in general, other than to say that he enjoyed his time there), the accounts of his contemporaries at the school suggest that Gilkes's was a presence which no boy could ever entirely shake off. Especially those pupils who had had no father figure at home. 'In my early days,' recalled one boy who arrived at Dulwich in Chandler's third year:

... he was to me an awe-inspiring figure who reminded me both by his stature and his appearance of the mythical figure of Zeus, at whose nod the heavens were supposed to thunder. As I gradually ascended the School, my awe decreased and gave way to a feeling of respect and admiration, which can be best described by the late Bishop of Zanzibar who, in a letter, said that ever since he had left Dulwich he had 'thought Gilkes and preached Gilkes'.[17]

Soon after Chandler started at Dulwich, his mother and his aunt moved in order to be nearer the school. Their new address was 77 Alleyn Park, a detached house (no longer standing) next to the college grounds, large enough to have previously housed the junior school. It was bought for them by Ernest Thornton, who was using his forced guardianship of his sisters, mother and nephew as an opportunity to invest in the fading grandeur (and prices) of South London property.

Whatever the oddities of his home life, Dulwich College offered Chandler a structure that he needed and a tradition of which he was proud. He would later join both the Public Schools Club in St James's and Dulwich's Old Alleynian Society. He would also correspond, throughout his life, with his Classics master at Dulwich, H. F. Hose. As a pupil Chandler was bright and interested – records show he ranked regularly within the top three of his class in all subjects. With the talent, but without the money, to go on to university, he followed an unusually mixed curriculum. There were two channels at Dulwich, and Chandler alternated between the two:

> In my time they had two 'sides', a Modern Side intended mostly for boys who expected to go into some kind of business, and a Classical Side for those who took Latin and Greek and expected to go to Oxford or Cambridge.[18]

The syllabus he took in his first year at Dulwich was typical in its central tenet: that the monuments of human achievement worthy of study were Athens, Rome, the Bible and the British Empire. 'English Subjects' involved a term learning about Africa and a term on Australia. 'Classics' meant Euripides, Horace, Livy, Plato, Aristophanes, Ovid and Virgil. Chandler had no intention of being a writer while at Dulwich (he planned to be a barrister), and

15

according to the ledgers from the Boys' Library for the time, his extracurricular reading was not extensive; the only novel he took out was a melodrama called *Last of the Barons*. But even if he did not imagine writing as a career for himself, Chandler would always maintain in later life that the Classics had taught him how *not* to write:

> A Classical education helps you from being fooled by pretentiousness, which is what most current fiction is too full of. In this country [America] the mystery writer is looked down on as sub-literary merely because he is a mystery writer, rather than for instance a writer of social significance twaddle. To a classicist – even a very rusty one – such an attitude is merely a parvenu insecurity.[19]

Sport was important at Dulwich. 'I played rugger a bit,' Chandler recalled, 'but was never first chip, because temperamentally I was the furious type of Irish forward and I hadn't the physique to back it up.' His nose was broken during one house rugby game, a fracture which in adulthood would give his face a tough look. In house cricket matches he was a bowler, but Dulwich had a fierce sporting reputation and Chandler never made the school teams. Public school sports results were extensively covered by the national press at this time and team places went only to serious competitors. Large crowds would turn up to watch Saturday games and top school players competed for places in Britain's international sides. Gilkes, never far from anything happening at the school, watched each game dressed in his frock coat and top hat.[20]

In his marathon tenure at Dulwich, Gilkes led a crusade against all forms of pretentiousness; to the extent of publicly reprimanding masters for that sin in front of boys. He had other obsessions. A punctual man, he one night walked a mile in the rain in order to return a boy's essay to his parents' house, having been unable to keep a prearranged appointment. His boys were expected to show similar dedication. 'There are other things a man could marry', Gilkes once wrote, 'besides a wife.' It was Gilkes who personally instructed the boys in preparation for their Confirmation vows, and in the Senior years, promising boys (including Chandler) wrote essays for him on specified themes. These essays were on general subjects such as 'Superstition' or 'Courage', and Gilkes would return them to each boy personally in his study. These were gruelling sessions for those involved, since any wordy sophistry or posing was demolished; P. G. Wodehouse described them as being 'akin to suicide'.

For all this, there was an abiding broad-mindedness about Dulwich. As primarily a day school, it had little of the infamous despotism of boarding public schools. Nor did Gilkes encourage undue rivalry within the school; indeed, he once banned the choir from performing treble solos lest it encourage hubris among soloists. Prizegiving at Dulwich was a similarly restrained affair under Gilkes's rule, to the extent of sometimes causing offence. His termly reports on the boys invariably concerned their characters rather than their achievements. Although Chandler's no longer survive, Gilkes wrote one report for P. G. Wodehouse in 1899 which, apart from being rather prophetic (given Wodehouse's later career), suggests that he was looking for integrity in his boys rather than conformity:

> He is a most impractical boy . . . often forgetful, he finds difficulty in the most simple things and asks absurd questions, whereas he can understand the most difficult things. He has the most distorted ideas about wit and humour; he draws over his books in a most distressing way, and writes foolish rhymes in other people's books. One is obliged to like him in spite of his vagaries.[21]

Each summer term during Chandler's time at the school – on the Saturday nearest to 21 June – Dulwich would celebrate Founder's Day. There was a typically Gilkesian and public school atmosphere to these affairs, as recorded by the school's annals. The day would begin with a roll call in the Victorian form rooms, followed by school prayers in the Great Hall where the lesson, 'Let us now praise famous men' from Ecclesiasticus would be read by the Captain of the School. The Founder's Day hymn, 'All people that on earth do dwell', would then be sung. At 11 am the First XI would start that week's cricket fixture, umpired by Gilkes himself and watched by the whole school. After lunch, the staff and boys would assemble in the Great Hall for Gilkes's speech:

Just before 2 o'clock the Master with Mrs Gilkes would leave his house. Lining the pathway was B Company, acting as guard of honour. Buglers and drummers sounded a fanfare to herald the Master's approach.[22]

The School Song, 'Pueri Alleynienses', was sung after which a Greek play, usually by Aristophanes, would be performed in its original language and set to music. The leading role was traditionally played by the School Captain.

After the speeches, the school would return to watch the First XI play cricket. Those with invitations would go to Gilkes's gardens: 'Here refreshments were provided – strawberries and ices', record the annals, 'and the School band, who won golden opinions for themselves.' From dusk onwards, the garden was thrown open to everyone, and the School Choir would perform:

> The last event of all was the Master's Supper in the Great Hall – for the Choir and the teams. This was a merry occasion and would close with songs, and on occasion the Master would be persuaded to sing his one song, 'Simon the Cellarer'.

*

There were other writers to emerge from Dulwich besides Chandler and P. G. Wodehouse. C. S. Forester and A. E. W. Mason (author of *The Four Feathers*) both attended the school, as did the film-maker Michael Powell, author and director of such films as *The Life and Death of Colonel Blimp*. With Chandler and Wodehouse, these Old Alleynians would form a redoubtable group of modern storytellers. Together, Chandler, Forester, Powell, Wodehouse and Mason were responsible for some of the most popular, enduring and lucrative fiction of their days. All five would go on to work in Hollywood.

Parallels between Chandler and P.G. Wodehouse, in particular, can be drawn closer still. Both grew up with absent parents – Wodehouse's mother and father lived in Hong Kong – and overbearing aunts; both would move to America after stints on Fleet Street, and both would be employed by Hollywood. Their literary trademarks would be an emphasis on character and wit and their style would be firmly non-intellectual. (Though not contemporaries, Chandler and Wodehouse shared a mutual schoolfriend, Will Townend; himself later a writer of adventure stories, and a lifelong correspondent with both men.) In Jeeves and Marlowe they created two of the most popular fictional heroes of the century. Both authors experienced their first real criticism at the hands of Gilkes, as he dissected their extracurricular essays in his study, attacking any signs of the pretentiousness he considered it his duty and vocation to exorcize.

The cultural impact of these Old Alleynians was to be enormous. Jeeves, *The African Queen*, Horatio Hornblower, *The Four Feathers* and *The Big Sleep* became widespread reference points for two generations of American and European readers and cinema goers. Each of these writers presented distinct male heroes, men of integrity, driven by a decency beyond the call of duty and fashion; and all created 'middle-brow' modern protagonists lacking in pretensions but possessed of a sense of honour that got them repeatedly in (and out of) trouble. Their fictional heroes, whether consciously or not, would be in line with the vision of benign patriarchy spelt out by Gilkes's own novels, one of which was titled *A Day At Dulwich*:

> The noblest thing in the whole world is man, and the world will be saved by developing the noblest thing in it – the manliness in man. Sanitation, great production, great power of locomotion do not necessarily benefit man; they may even greatly harm him because they make it more difficult for him to be unselfish – that is to obey the highest law within him. A return to the old ideal is a necessary thing, to the ideal realized in theory, and in fact also, by the Greeks – the idea of the self-sacrifitic.[23]

The idea of the 'self-sacrifitic' male hero was embodied for the school by the most famous old Dulwich boy of all. In 1901, while Chandler was in his second year at the school, Ernest Henry Shackleton was trying to reach the South Pole with Captain Scott. Shackleton was only eight years Chandler's senior and, like Chandler, he was Anglo-Irish.

*

Chandler picked up several prizes towards the end of his time at

Dulwich. He was outstanding at mathematics. (This was a proficiency Chandler shared with the two other most famous crime writers of his generation: Georges Simenon and Dashiell Hammett. In the 1940s, while trying to dry out, Hammett used to do algebra to pass the time.) No prizes, however, could alter the fact that Chandler was not bound for university. Although he still wanted to become a barrister, his uncle's financial patience was running thin, and such a lengthy apprenticeship was out of the question. The young man was expected to find himself a job and start supporting Florence, and so it was decided by Ernest Thornton that he should sit the Civil Service examination.

Chandler was withdrawn from Dulwich a year early in 1904 at the age of sixteen. In lieu of this lost year, his uncle was prepared to make one final contribution to his nephew's education and agreed to pay for him to spend a year on the Continent, half of it in France, and the other half in Germany, before he returned to London to sit his examination. Knowledge of modern languages was now considered essential for those applying to the Civil Service and Chandler was to receive private tuition in both countries. It meant twelve months away from the matriarchal gloom of South London, and Chandler agreed to his uncle's plan.

*

In retrospect, 1905 was an exciting year for a dilettante to be in Europe. Apart from the tangible modernization that was dramatically changing the communications and cities of Europe, many European writers, artists and musicians were at their most influential in that year; Freud, Strindberg, Strauss, Debussy and Matisse were all in their prime. Marcel Proust was shortly to embark on his epic *Remembrance of Things Past* and Einstein's *General Theory of Relativity* was published in Paris in 1905. Politically, and again with hindsight, it was also a year that marked the continuing instability which would lead towards the outbreak of the Great European War. In Russia, the first anti-Tsarist revolution took place in 1905. By that year, too, the governments of France and Germany were becoming publicly wary both of one another and of the strange new pressures being released domestically by a cramped urban population. Chandler, however, was not a radical, and neither politics nor anti-bourgeois culture interested him: 'I was a young man,' he remembered, 'and very innocent, and was very happy wandering around, with very little money, but a sort of starry-eyed love of everything I saw.'[24]

In Paris, he stayed at a cheap *pension* on the Boulevard St-Michel, close to the cathedral of Notre-Dame, and attended a business college where he studied commercial French. In the end, though, very little information about Chandler's time in Paris survives, other than the fact that he clearly learnt French with some ease. His time on the Continent encouraged a life-long fascination with language, and with slang in particular:

> I have always been a great admirer of French colloquial slang. I think it's the only body of slang that can compare with ours. German is pretty good too. There is a wonderful precision and daring about French slang. I don't think it has quite the reckless extravagance of ours, but it seems to have more endurance.[25]

Having been brought up to the sounds of Irish English, American English and public-school English, Chandler had never taken language for granted. His own accent after Dulwich was a mid-Atlantic drawl, and would in adulthood grow to sound like that of the actor Jimmy Stewart. For his proficiency in languages – a proficiency which would be demonstrated beyond doubt when he came to sit his Civil Service exam – it would seem that Chandler again owed something to Gilkes, who had taught him Classics in his last year at Dulwich. A fellow Gilkes pupil, J. T. Sheppard, who went on to become Provost of King's College, Cambridge, insisted that 'no one who had the fortune to learn Latin prose and Greek verse from Gilkes could fail to acquire a mastery of languages.'[26] Having had to give up his initial vocation, the Bar, Chandler considered another while on the Continent in 1905:

> For God's sake save your people the anguish and expense of sending me 8 Finnish translations. Four would be more than enough . . . I once hoped to be a comparative philologist (just a boyhood fancy no doubt) and dabbled in such strange lingos as Modern Greek, Armenian, Hungarian, besides the simpler and more obvious Romance tongues and the Germanic group. I slept with a chart of the 214 key ideographs of the Chinese Mandarin language pinned

to the wall at the head of my bed in the Pension Narjollet, 27 Boulevard St. Michel, au cinquième. But Finnish, hell it's worse than Turkish.[27]

Away from the constraints of South London, Chandler was later annoyed with himself for passing up opportunities to lose his virginity in Paris. His looks were becoming increasingly striking, with his dark hair swept back from a broad forehead, and what he used to describe as 'my smiling Irish eyes'; he held himself impressively and was always smartly dressed. At 5 feet 10 inches, Chandler was a little above average height. His most distinctive feature was his broad mouth, which could alternately draw his face into a huge and friendly grin or pull it into an unsettling scowl. When mixing with other people, he had the outward-going nature of an only child used to striking up conversation with strangers. Sexually, on the other hand, he was entirely innocent. During one of his Confirmation lessons at Dulwich, Chandler had revealed that he had never masturbated, nor really understood what it meant; had he been to a boarding school, he might not have been so innocent. As he had no brothers or father or old childhood friends to consult, however, he had preserved a remarkable naivety about sex. Instead, in the space created by this innocence, had been instilled the image of what pain his father had caused. Florence Thornton was a broken woman, frightened to remarry, and he was determined not to repeat this damage in his own life. 'One does not love', he would later say, 'in order to hurt and destroy':

I do not, and I hope I never shall, admit that sex is a thing to be treated as if it were of no great consequence. You can make all sorts of jokes about it, mostly lewd (I've made them myself) but at the bottom of his heart every decent man feels that his approach to the woman he loves is an approach to a shrine.[28]

Chandler later realized the extent of his naivety in Paris, recalling how two of the women boarding at his *pension* were clearly prostitutes, but that he failed to recognize their advances at the time. But even without such bedroom conquests, he enjoyed the freedom of living by himself. After six months in Paris, he moved to the Bavarian capital of Munich and then on to the university town of Freiburg in the Black Forest where he studied business German and had a photograph of himself taken for his mother at a studio. Chandler said later that he would have happily stayed on there ('I did like the Germans very much, that is the South Germans') had it not been 'an open secret' that Britain and Germany would soon be at war. 'There was never any question of whether it would happen,' he explained. 'The only question was when.' Germany, which in 1905 had been a single united nation for only thirty-four years, was simply too jealous of the overseas colonies of France and Britain to be satisfied with its own industrial wealth.

Although Chandler never properly recorded his year in Europe, he would later jokingly romanticize it. On reading a potted biography of himself, he noted no mention of his eighteenth year:

> What about the time I spent under the shadow of the Saint Sulpice in that short but intoxicating affair with a demoiselle from Luxembourg – the one that afterwards became known the world over – but no, this is dangerous ground. Even in Luxembourg they have libel laws – in three languages as a matter of fact. And what about that six lost months I spent in the Hollenthal trying to persuade a funicular railway to run on the level? [29]

Chandler enjoyed meeting Americans in Europe. His own Irish American accent had been modified by the time he left Dulwich, but it had been pronounced enough while he was there for him to have been made aware of his 'Yank-ness'. He was in Paris fifteen years before the mass influx of young Americans to the Left Bank in the 1920s, but he liked those whom he met:

> I had no feeling of identity with the United States, and yet I resented the ignorant and snobbish criticism of Americans that was current at that time . . . most of them seemed to have a lot of bounce and liveliness and to be thoroughly enjoying themselves where the average Englishman of the same class would be stuffy or completely bored. [30]

Chandler's confused nationality presented practical as well as potentially symbolic problems. On returning from Europe to sit his Civil Service exams, he had first to take advantage of a law covering the children of divorced British women in order to obtain British citizenship. Following the death of her mother, Florence was now living alone in a smaller house which Ernest had bought in Streatham, South London. The address was 35 Mount Nod Street; it was a pleasant enough street, but was surrounded by long bleak rows of small, similar workers' houses. Streatham was an unlovely and insalubrious suburb in 1907. Despite his un-glamorous new address, however, and his complete lack of a private income, Chandler continued to dress as impeccably as he had been taught to at Dulwich. It was soon after arriving back from Germany, in fact, that Chandler bought himself a silver-topped cane.

It was in the space between his return from Freiburg and the impending examination that the well-dressed, trilingual eighteen-year-old composed his first poem one Sunday 'while in the bath' in Streatham. Called 'The Unknown Love', this poem has been described by at least one critic as having 'no merit whatsoever':[31]

When the evening sun is slanting,
When the crickets raise their chanting,
And the dew-drops lie a twinkling on the grass,
As I climb the pathway slowly,
With a mien half proud, half lowly,
O'er the ground your feet have trod I gently pass.[32]

As poetry it was, in Chandler's later opinion, 'Grade B Georgian', though he said he was proud that he had never subscribed to what he called the 'I-dare-you-not-to-understand-what-I-am-talking-about' school of poetry. The poem excited him enough at the time to make him decide to become a writer. He was aware that the Civil Service might offer an ideal day job – there was a precedent in such an arrangement among British writers without private incomes, very few of whom could support themselves on the proceeds of what they published.

Chandler passed third out of the eight hundred candidates who sat the Civil Service exams in 1907, and came top in the Classics paper. He was offered a post at the Admiralty as Assistant Stores

Officer, a job which involved seeing to the movement of, and accounting for, naval supplies, including ammunition. Despite the easy hours – work stopped at four o'clock – he hated the job and walked out after six months, to the horror of his uncle and mother. 'I had too much Irish blood in me', he said, 'to be pushed around by suburban nobodies.'[33]

Through his old Classics master, H. F. Hose, Chandler was taken on to do some part-time teaching at Dulwich. This lasted only a term, but it meant that he was able to add 'schoolmaster' to his lengthening curriculum vitae. Fascinated by his new vocation as a writer, Chandler started to attend public lectures in London:

> As a very young man, when Shaw's beard was still red, I heard him give a lecture in London on Art for Art's Sake, which seems to have meant something then. It did not please Shaw of course; few things did unless he thought of them first.[34]

Chandler's early poetry, with few exceptions, is most remarkable for the fact that he managed to have it published – for payment – in reputable magazines. Though deeply unimpressed by his nephew's decision to leave the Civil Service, Ernest Thornton again provided a lifeline. Through an acquaintance within London's Anglo-Irish fraternity, Roland Ponsonby Blennerhasset, he arranged an introduction for Chandler to the editor of the *Westminster Gazette*. The *Gazette* had several distinguished contributors at the time, including Hector Hugh Munro ('Saki'), and was imaginatively edited by J. A. Spender, Stephen Spender's uncle:

> Spender bought a lot of stuff from me: verses, sketches and unsigned things such as paragraphs lifted from foreign publications. He got me into the National Liberal Club for the run of the reading room . . . I got about three guineas a week out of all these but it wasn't enough. I also worked for a man named Cowper who succeeded Lord Alfred Douglas (Oscar Wilde's fag) in ownership of the *Academy* [magazine], and did a lot of book reviewing for him, and some essays which I still have. They are of intolerable preciousness of style, but already quite nasty in tone.[35]

For four years, poems by 'R. T. Chandler' appeared every few weeks in the *Gazette* and the *Academy*. Their style rarely changed:

> The world expends its useless might,
> The heaving nations toil and fight,
> The dizzy thinker peers for light,
> The day doth follow day and night,
> Is there no rest from anything?

Those of his early poems which lacked this grandiose gloom usually compensated for it with esoteric Classical allusions. Raymond Chandler, who had now moved again, with his mother, to 148 Devonshire Road in Forest Hill, was holding nothing back in his bid for early poetic immortality: 'There is no thought born in man's brain,' runs another poem, 'Which I have never known.' The semi-detached house in Forest Hill was a better investment for Ernest Thornton, for though not far from Streatham, the area had preserved more of a village atmosphere.

Since Chandler did not try writing again for publication until he was well into his forties, this four-year period of juvenile versifying can be viewed as much as a career in itself as it was the foundation for another. In later years, Chandler saw the experience as a good one, believing that it exorcized any desire that he might have had in his later writing to be clever and imitative. 'I was an elegant young thing', he said, 'trying to be brilliant about nothing':

> What though some monster's bloodstained foot
> Crush me in his chaotic race?
> Stamp out my being to the root? –
> I laugh in his frenzied face.

Chandler's essays and book reviews from this time, on the other hand, do give some indication of what was to come. The *Westminster Gazette* generally prefaced his essays with a disclaimer, explaining that the views stated were not necessarily those of the editors. The situation was ideal, since it effectively allowed Chandler to be the token 'young voice' for one of Britain's most prominent weeklies. His book reviews were no less arrogant. A typical notice was one he gave a novel called *The Reason Why* by Elinor Glyn in the *Academy* in December 1911. The piece closes with a brief description of the novel's ending, followed by the reviewer's verdict on the author:

> Tristan becomes wilder and wilder, loses all taste for his food, suspects her of infidelity, and departs for the Soudan. But the financier, meantime reformed by the softer passion, allows Zara to explain matters which she promised to conceal, and she reaches Tristan's rooms in London just in time to fall into his arms and murmur, 'Tu sais que je t'aime'.
>
> Mrs Glyn writes with an enormous amount of sensuous zest, which suggests that she really believes her work to be worth doing. It is this quality that lifts her out of the sea of bad fiction to a position of some notoriety, but to the critical reader it only condemns her, in a literary sense, the more securely.

In an essay Chandler wrote in September 1911 called 'The Remarkable Hero', he suggests that the upper-class hero in British fiction has been replaced by a new breed of cardboard aristocrat:

> Satirized out of his old, honest, matter-of-fact reverence for rank and wealth, the commonplace reader has to satisfy his inborn humility by looking up to an intellectual superior. Forbidden to act the flunkey to the aristocrat, he allows himself to adore the prima donna, the brilliant statesman, the swaggering freebooter, or the subtle master of intrigue. As he can no longer delight in the conversation of the duke, he accepts instead the conversation of an eminent house-breaker. And seeing that, however slight his knowledge of the aristocratic circles might have been, his acquaintance with men of genius is even slighter – he is seldom able to spot the fraud which is so often played upon him.[36]

Perhaps most interesting of all, though, was an essay called 'Realism and Fairyland', written by Chandler, then aged 23, in which he criticizes the idea that art should be either realistic or fantastic. He evaluates the relative natures of both fantasy and reality. 'Fairyland', depending on the dreamer in question, could be a scene of 'perfect nature' or a codeless place 'where people love or hate on sight'. For another it may mean 'an anarchy of the beautiful touched with terror'. Rather than fantasy being detached from the time in which it is written, Chandler suggests that 'the spirit of an age is more essentially mirrored in its fairy-tales than in the most painstaking chronicle of a contemporary diarist'. He attacks the new pessimists like Emile Zola, who 'inform us that we must look dull facts in the face if we would see the truth, that we must not delude ourselves with rosy dreams or golden castles in Spain. By way of showing us how to proceed, they rake over the rubbish heaps of humanity . . . unpleasantness becomes associated in their minds with truth, and if they wish to produce a faultlessly exact portrait of a man, all they need do is paint his weaknesses.'

Realism of this sort, says the young Chandler, is really just 'the mood of every man's dull and depressed hours'. Anyone, he maintains, can describe a dull house dully, but the challenge is to write about real things magically. Those who can do this respond to a far nobler and more profound human impulse: '. . . any man', he says, 'who has just walked down a commonplace city street at twilight, just as the lamps are lit, can reply that such artists are not realists, but the most courageous of idealists, for they exalt the sordid to a vision of magic, and create pure beauty out of plaster and dust.'

Having tasted domestic independence on the Continent, Chandler moved into a cheap boarding house (9s 6d a week for bed and breakfast) near Russell Square in Bloomsbury in order to pursue his early career in letters. Though he never recorded the exact location, the house was no doubt similar to one described in 'English Summer', an unpublished story he worked on in the 1950s. It was one of only two stories Chandler ever set outside California (the other, 'The Bronze Door', was also set in London). The action takes place in Bloomsbury in the early years of the century, at the time Chandler was living there:

> Not too early I reached a railway station and rode it to London. I knew where to go, a small lodging house in Bloomsbury, north of Russell Square, a place where no one was what he should be or what he wanted to be, and no one cared, least of all the old slattern who called herself the landlady.
>
> Breakfast, a cold, greasy mess on a tray outside your door. Lunch, ale and bread and cheddar, if you wanted it. Dinner, if you

were in the dining class, you went out and foraged for. If you came home late at night, the white-faced spectres of Russell Square haunted you, creeping along where the iron railings had been, as though the mere memory of them brought some shelter from the policeman's lantern. They haunted you all night with the ache of their 'Listen, dearies' and with the remembrance of their pinched lips, gnawed thin from within, their large, hollow eyes in which a world was already dead. There was a man at the digs who played Bach, a little too much and a little too loud, but he did it for his soul. There was a lonely old man with a poised, delicate face and a filthy mind. There were two wooden butterflies who thought themselves as actors.[37]

The details of this account seem too particular not to have had some basis in Chandler's own time spent among the cultured grifters of Bloomsbury. Rather than living with his mother, he clearly relished the rarefied squalor and bohemian authenticity of renting a room near the British Museum. Central London was still a menacingly dirty place. With motor cars rare in 1910, horse-drawn carriages were – together with trains – still the predominant means of transport. 'The muddy slime of the city streets' (as Chandler remembered it) was closer to the grime of Dickens's London than it was to later descriptions of the city by E. M. Forster or Evelyn Waugh. In fact, Chandler's time in London can be most accurately sensed in the writing of Arthur Conan Doyle. The fictional career of Sherlock Holmes spanned from 1887 to 1917 and captured a city that Chandler knew at first hand. 'London,' says Holmes in *A Study in Scarlet*, 'that great cesspool into which all the loungers of the Empire are irresistibly drained.' Chandler read little of Doyle's work until much later on in his life, but he was instantly able to recognize the London of which Doyle wrote.

Raymond Chandler may have been enjoying a false spring as a writer, but he was at least proving himself full of confidence. This was true in person as well as in print. One of his tactics as a freelance writer, in order to win commissions with which to pay his Bloomsbury rent, was to announce himself at the offices of a magazine and express an interest in buying the publication. This he had tried at the *Academy* and did again at a magazine called *Tit-Bits*, both times with equal success. At the latter he was 'received most courteously by a secretary, definitely Public School, who regretted that the publication was not in need of capital, but that my approach had at least the merit of originality'. Chandler also managed to find employment as a news reporter at the *Daily Express* in 1911, but it was a short apprenticeship since he 'kept getting lost' when sent off to cover a story.

*

Eventually, in 1912, the twenty-four-year-old Chandler decided to forget writing and leave London. The problem was not the poverty of his self-imposed lifestyle, or the meanness of his quaters, but the lack of real prospects in London to support either himself or his mother. In just over four years he had published twenty-seven poems, eight essays and four book reviews, but the money he had earned had been barely enough for him alone. Ernest Thornton insisted that he now take over responsibility for his mother, and Chandler was part of an imperial generation taught to look abroad for prospects if there were none in Britain. Like many Europeans at this time, Chandler chose America. He still felt an emotional attachment to the country of his birth, despite having no immediate family or professional contacts there: 'America,' he said, 'seemed to draw me in some way.' He borrowed £500 (at 6 per cent interest) from the exasperated Ernest Thornton and booked his passage. He was embarking for the New World, he said, with 'a good suit and no money' – and undaunted by the sinking of the New York-bound *Titanic* in April of that year, at the cost of 1,490 lives.

Wherever Chandler had decided to find his fortune, the plan had always been for Florence to follow him there once he had found employment. He had come of age, and as far as Ernest Thornton was concerned, that meant that he must now fulfil one immediate filial obligation. Chandler had to take over support of his mother.

*

Though Chandler's decision to emigrate in 1912 meant that he would narrowly miss the cultural wave of modernism that was about to begin in London, with Bloomsbury as its nerve-centre, he did write one final poem which shows the influence of that movement. Written more in dejected pastiche than seriousness, as his early efforts at immortality came to an overdrawn and under-inspired halt, 'Free Verse' is unlike the formalized and derivative poetry Chandler had been writing until then. Nor is it too far removed from the style of T. S. Eliot, who had arrived in London just twelve months prior to Chandler's departure.

I'd flatter my ideas by even
Calling them
Moods.

A little twist of phrase or thought
This way or that
To give it an air of meaning such a lot
More than it says.
A mere trifle of nervous reaction
From the sound of the elevated
Or too much coffee,
Or a bad night smoking till 2AM

This stuff of mine is pure inspiration,
It's as easy as falling off a log,
The only difficulty is to know where
To stop . . .

And words themselves mean such a lot,
The cute little things,
Take 'mauve' for example,
What a lot that simple word seems to mean,
So much more than one can say.
I like to put a word like that down
And just look at it
With my head on one side,
And run around it,
Around and around it,
Until I get a bit dizzy,
And then I sit down and babble a bit.

Lots of people are talking quite seriously
About our American intellectual Revolutionists.
And I wouldn't want it to get about everywhere
That we're only intellectual

Bankrupts,
With a nice sense of the discords
Of a cracked fiddle
When fiddled by a rather indifferent performer
At the conflagration
Of a rather more than indifferent
Universe.

Rather than seeing this way of writing poetry as the keystone of a new modernist form of art, Chandler saw it as the end of his own attempts to be part of the great tradition of English poetry. Modernism meant nothing to him, and he opted instead to leave Europe and start a career. Always keen to add retrospective melodrama to his story, he later recalled his decision to emigrate with a scene of suitably impulsive resolve. In 1912, he was offered, by a newspaperman called Horace Voules, the chance to write serial romances for six guineas a week:

> Imagine me then in a blue-chalk striped flannel suit cut by a West End tailor, wearing an old school tie band on a natty straw hat, carrying a cane and gloves, and being told by this elegant fellow to write what appeared to me then to be the most appalling garbage ever slung together in words. I gave him a sickly smile and left the country.[38]

2

Go West, Young Man

Funny thing civilization. It promises so much and what it delivers is mass production of shoddy merchandise and shoddy people

(Letter, November 1940)

It was the autumn of 1912 when Chandler returned, by himself, to America. He had not been in the States since the age of seven. Even as a boy he had not been outside the Midwest, except on the return to Ireland with his mother, when they had sailed from New York. He had been schooled in Britain, had become a British citizen and had worked for the British Admiralty. In America, he knew no one outside Nebraska, and he had certainly not come back to look for his father. He had had no communication with Maurice Chandler since the age of seven, and would at no point in his adult life make any attempt to find his father's whereabouts. Beyond giving him automatic entrance into the USA, the fact that Chandler had been born in the United States offered no guarantees for the success of his move there.

Nor was he sure precisely where he planned to settle. His voyage to America at the age of twenty-four was a gesture of impulse rather than the result of much planning; Chandler knew only what he was leaving behind in Britain. He said that he was through with being counted among the 'worn intellectuals with cigarette coughs and no money in the bank'. The forwarding address he had left in London was the Fitts' house in Plattsworth, Nebraska.

33

Having stopped growing, Chandler was 'an inch under six feet when dressed for the street'. His dark brown hair was short-cropped and parted in the centre. His most distinguishing feature was still the broad mouth, the set of which could completely change his expression. Photographs from this period of Chandler smiling and Chandler frowning are almost unrecognizable from each other. Only the bespoke linen and flannel suits are consistent.

The return started well. Alone on the steamer to New York in 1912, he was befriended by one of the wealthiest families in Los Angeles. The Lloyds, who were returning *en famille* from one of their regular trips to Europe, were all struck by the young ex-poet. In return, they represented everything that Chandler was now looking for in America: hard cash (from oil, in their case) and intelligent company. The Lloyds and their circle were East Coast-educated, avant-garde and generous. Warren Lloyd, father of the family, had a doctorate in philosophy from Yale, and his wife was a talented sculptress. They urged Chandler to consider moving to LA, offering him introductions to employers and to people in society there.

Southern California was not an obvious destination for him. Several Dulwich boys had moved to anglophile New York – there were Old Alleynian dinners held in the city – but few had thought of going west. The population of Los Angeles was relatively small at the turn of the century, and neither Wall Street nor Washington were yet entirely convinced of the city's potential. On disembarking at New York, Chandler left the Lloyds. With no money to his name other than that lent to him by his uncle he could not stay there unless he found a job in New York immediately, and passage to California was too much of a risk until he had more money. Nor did Chandler have time to explore: Florence was waiting to join him in the States as soon as he had settled with an income. With the Midwest as a point of some familiarity, Chandler took a train to St Louis, Missouri. Since he knew no one there, he put himself up at a boarding house and found work as a clerk. His immediate plan was that of many educated but effectively penniless immigrants: to find manual or clerical work while educating himself in the evenings for a profession. On the basis of his short apprenticeship at the Admiralty and his proficiency at mathematics, Chandler decided on accountancy. It was now the early winter of 1912, and bitterly cold in Missouri.

St Louis proved a short stop. Chandler's English public school airs were provocative to those he had to work with – they nicknamed him 'Lord Stoppentakit' – and the weather was more bleak than he had anticipated. It was a rude awakening for the young and self-confident Chandler, and after less than a month in the city he got himself into trouble. Disgusted at how everyone in the Midwest seemed to spit, Chandler told his boss how revolting he thought the habit. 'The crusty old boy informed me with a great fraudulent dignity that the American gentleman did not spit. I said, Good, perhaps I'll meet him some day.' He left his job and St Louis, and moved on to the Fitts in Nebraska.

If adolescent nostalgia had lent something of a cheerful pastoral tint to Chandler's childhood in Nebraska, a job at his uncle Harry's hardware store was not something that the Dulwich boy, with contemporaries in the City, the Indian Civil Service and at Oxford, was at all ready for. He was too recently out of class-ridden London not to feel snobbish towards his in-law employer:

> Since I was fresh out of England at the time and a hardware store was 'trade' I could hardly be expected to get on terms of anything like familiarity with him. Boy! Two stengahs, chop chop![1]

He stayed with his aunt and her husband, Ernest Fitt, who played the piano. 'He used to come home in the evening,' Chandler remembered of Ernest, 'put the paper on the music rack and improvise while he read.' Though Chandler was not a heavy drinker at this time, his brief stay with the Fitts does include an ominous account of the homemade way in which the Fitt males were managing to beat Prohibition:

> They had a sour mash corn whisky which topped them all. It was delivered in flat pints by a greasy but honest character who produced about 14 pints from various pockets. The stuff tasted so awful that it had to be leaded with lemon and ginger ale and sugar and even then you were apt to throw it across the room until your nervous system was paralysed enough to kill the reflexes.[2]

After two months with the Fitts, Chandler decided to try

California. He travelled, by the rail system his father had helped build, to San Francisco.

*

Midwesterners moving to California for work were not a novelty in early 1913, and no fanfare awaited Chandler. They were part of what Charles Fletcher Lummis, later editor of the *Los Angeles Times*, described as 'the least heroic migration in history':

> Hard working farmers who'd sold their land; ne'er do well salesmen looking to score; small-town lawyers, dentists, and schoolteachers; the tubercular; the invalid; the wealthy widow or pensioned spinster; the speculators in stock and real estate.[3]

Nor, clearly, did Chandler feel in a position to announce himself immediately at the Lloyds' house in Los Angeles. Impeccably dressed throughout these early months in America, he considered himself a young gentleman rather than a case for further charity. Lacking, in any case, the professional experience that would enable him to benefit from nepotism, Chandler decided to begin in San Francisco instead of Los Angeles. For the time being, he needed a job rather than a career and San Francisco was still the larger of the two cities. He worked initially on an apricot ranch, where he was paid 20 cents an hour for a 10-hour day, and then found employment with the Spalding sports company, stringing tennis racquets for $12.50 a week, 54 hours a week.[4] With no capital other than that lent to him by Ernest Thornton, and no one in America from whom he could borrow more money, Chandler had to keep earning by any means necessary.

While supporting himself through monotonous jobs, Chandler attended a night book-keeping course in San Francisco. He lived in a succession of boarding houses, places that he would later recall in his fiction. In *The Little Sister*, Philip Marlowe rummages around old beach-front boarding houses in search of a young man who has recently arrived in California from the Midwest with the intention of improving his lot:

> No. 449 had a shallow, paintless front porch on which five wood and cane rockers loafed dissolutely, held together with wire and the

moisture of beach air. The green shades over the lower window of the house were two-thirds down and full of cracks. Beside the front door there was a large printed sign 'No Vacancies'. That had been there a long time too.[5]

There is no doubt that the character of Philip Marlowe was fleshed out in these resolute, if friendless and moneyless, months in Californian boarding houses. Of his hero, Chandler wrote a month before his death that he always saw him 'in a lonely street, in lonely rooms, puzzled but never quite defeated'. Like Marlowe, Chandler in 1913 was intelligent but without immediate prospects. Solitary Christmases, Sundays and birthdays also tortured him afresh. But Chandler, like Marlowe again, was starting to develop a self-deprecating wit with which to deal with his loneliness:

I knocked the cold ashes out of my pipe and refilled it from the leather humidor an admirer had given me for Christmas, the admirer by an odd coincidence having the same name as me.[6]

Despite his impoverished circumstances, he continued to present a well-groomed front to the world. It was during these months in San Francisco that he met up with Will Townend, the former Dulwich boy with whom both he and Wodehouse were to correspond, who was travelling through the city on his way to Canada. Townend recalled the meeting:

We were both wearing straw hats – everyone did in those days – with Alleyn Club ribbons and got acquainted . . . Raymond asked me to lunch at one of the expensive restaurants and I firmly said no. He was hard up and I was hard up, so I said we had better have a meal at a fairly cheap place, which we did. He was then working for Spaldings, the sports outfitters, stringing tennis racquets and not making much money. I went up to British Columbia and while I was there I heard from Raymond again. He was then employed in the office of an ice-cream manufacturer in Los Angeles.[7]

Within five months of odd-jobbing in and around San Francisco, Chandler had managed to teach himself basic accountancy: 'As I knew nothing about bookkeeping,' he said, 'I went to a night school and in six weeks the instructor asked me to leave; he said I had done the three years' course and that was all there was.'[8] Having by now presented himself to the Lloyds in Los Angeles, he was already using their address to receive mail from London. Finding the family as friendly and encouraging towards him as they had been on the steamer to New York, he decided to move to Los Angeles permanently. The Southern Pacific Railway ran a daily service between the two cities, and by it Chandler left San Francisco for Southern California.

In 1880, Los Angeles had had 12,000 inhabitants and ranked as only the 187th largest city in the country, but it had grown massively since then, both in terms of population and of economy. A census in 1911 put its population at 350,000. One history of the city quotes a near-contemporary account of the LA Chandler arrived in:

> Here is an artificial city which has been pumped up under forced draught, inflated like a balloon, stuffed with rural humanity like a goose with corn . . . endeavouring to eat up this too rapid avalanche of anthropoids, the sunshine metropolis heaves and strains, sweats and becomes pop-eyed, like a young boa constrictor trying to swallow a goat. It has never imparted an urban character to its incoming population for the simple reason that it has never had any urban character to impart. On the other hand, the place has retained the manners, culture and general outlook of a huge country village.[9]

Through a friend of Warren Lloyd, Chandler secured a job as a book-keeper at the Los Angeles Creamery, specializing in the ice-cream accounts, and was able to rent a cheap furnished apartment downtown on Loma Drive. He began to spend time with the Lloyds and their circle. There were musical evenings, readings and even seances, attended by the city's small group of wealthy bohemians. He got on particularly well with Dr Lloyd, with whom he shared a cynical sense of humour. One of their pranks was to go to cinemas showing tragic melodramas. They would sit one on each side of the audience and, at an arranged moment, each would start laughing as if it were a comedy. The idea was to see whether the rest of the audience would begin laughing too, which they often would. Lloyd had written a book called *Psychology Normal and Abnormal*, and shared with others in his circle a fashionable interest in the occult. Ouija boards and the spiritualist experiments of Madame Helena Blavatsky (the Russian-born founder of the Theosophical Society) were popular at this time, both in America and Britain, and Chandler attended such experiments at the Lloyds'. Young, bold and bright, he was a welcome addition to their bohemian set, and there was soon talk of him being groomed to marry their youngest daughter, Estelle.

In contrast to the Lloyds' set, however, Los Angeles was a puritanical place in 1913. Prostitution, gambling and street vending were illegal, and a law in 1906 had put a limit on the number of bars in the city. In the year of Chandler's arrival, the Los Angeles City Hall passed a law banning sex between people not married to each other. There was an Anti-Saloon League, an Anti-Racetrack Gambling League and a Sunday Rest League.[10] The city had 'a stupid censorship', said a New York journalist in 1913: 'Los Angeles is overrun with militant moralists.' There was a sense of panic behind this moral policing. The city's population was growing so rapidly that there was a feeling of impending chaos among LA's Protestant civic leaders. The city prided itself on being a last bastion of the values held by the Founding Fathers.

Loma Drive, where Chandler now lived, was within earshot of central Pershing Square and close to where the Lloyds lived on Bonnie Brae. It was an urban mixture of spacious New World gentility and cheap city housing. Within two decades, wealthy families would start to move out to the hills around LA, but in 1913 the area offered Chandler both cocktail intellectualism with the Lloyd set as well as proximity to the street where the boxer Kid McCoy had recently shot his estranged wife. Chandler had a gun of his own, a Smith and Wesson .38 Special, as did many of his neighbours. It was a square mile of early oil money and, increasingly, organized crime. Although the City Hall continued to sell Los Angeles to America as a clean city, the cracks were starting to show. 'From 1915 to 1923', a history of the city confirms,

. . . eight police chiefs served four scandal-plagued city administrations. During those years, mayors, DAs, and city councilmen had been taking campaign money and sometimes payoffs from madams, bootleggers, and gamblers.[11]

It was a palpably relaxed coastal city, none the less, and, after he began his job at the Creamery, Chandler decided to stay. Soon, Florence – now in her early fifties – joined her son in California. Although his book-keeping job at the LA Creamery was in no way exhilarating, it earned him a regular wage and served to support both him and his mother. Life for the two of them began to achieve a degree of stability. Florence, who also got on well with the Lloyds, was content to look after her son's house. For three years, Chandler continued to work as a book-keeper.

As the months passed, however, the initial satisfaction of finding a means of income began to give way to exasperation. The rumours that he might marry Estelle Lloyd came to nothing, and Chandler himself no longer felt like a young man with prospects. The need to support Florence offered him little chance for manoeuvre; he grew bored, watching his twenties vanish in a job he was stuck to. The little poetry that he wrote during this time was still 'Grade B Georgian' in quality, but its theme of lost dreams and opportunities was now more heartfelt:

Song of the Boatman on the River Roon

Hear now the song of the boatman,
The boatman on the River Roon,
Playing his antique zither
To a long melodious tune,
Leaning his side to the tiller,
Weeping a furtive tear,
With his back to the land of the sunrise
And his eyes to the vanish'd year

Telling of the dew of kisses
On the lips of ravish'd love,
Telling of a cold dim requiem
Sounding from a haunted grove,
Telling of the flowers of longing
That are weeds in a tarnish'd pool,
And the song of a vanish'd singer,
And the jest of a vanish'd fool.

Hear now the song of the boatman,
The boatman on the River Roon,
Playing the antique zither
To a long melodious tune.
I would that my voice could sing it,
But down in the heart it lies
Where never a voice can reach it,
In the dim dark house of sighs.[12]

By 1917, Chandler was twenty-eight years old and restless. The fortune he had intended to make in America was evading him. He was earning only enough money to support himself and Florence, and he was not sufficiently motivated by his profession to seek promotion. He knew few people outside the Lloyd circle, which was itself beginning to bore him. He had neither a past nor a future that inspired him. He was an accountant living with his mother and desperate for a change of scenery.

In the summer of 1917, however, he found an honourable way out of Los Angeles. He decided to join the Canadian Army and fight in Europe. The war against Germany and her allies had been going on for almost three years by then, and Chandler, aware that many of his Dulwich classmates were already in the trenches, chose to join them. Dulwich records show that a large number of former pupils who died in the First World War had returned from outside Europe to fight. It was the proper thing for Chandler to do, even if he was no longer strictly a subject of the British Empire. It also absolved him of any guilt he might otherwise have felt at leaving his mother alone in Los Angeles.

Chandler, accompanied by another young member of the Lloyd set, Gordon Pascal, went north in August 1917 to join the Canadian Army at Victoria in British Columbia. Unlike the United States, which had joined the war in the spring of that year, Canada (as part of the British Empire) had been fighting with the Allies from the start, and had been heavily engaged on the Western Front since the war's escalation in 1915. 'It was still natural for me to prefer a British uniform,' said Chandler, though it was also a fact that the Canadian government, in contrast to the American, offered an allowance to the dependants of conscripts, in Chandler's case Florence. In Victoria, he joined the Gordon

Highlanders, and was issued with a kilt as part of his uniform. It gave another twist to his national loyalties, as he once explained to a Canadian correspondent:

> I am an American citizen by birth. Educated in England, Anglo-Irish mother. Strong pro-British feelings and also pro-Canadian, since I served in the CEF [Canadian Expeditionary Force] and spent months at Victoria . . . If I called Victoria dull, it was in my time dullish as an English town would be on a Sunday, everything shut up, churchy atmosphere and so on. I did not mean to call the people dull. Knew some very nice ones.[13]

Having enlisted at the end of the summer of 1917, Chandler was trained, equipped and shipped to Europe by the end of November. He landed at Liverpool as a private soldier and was seconded to the British Columbia Regiment at Seaford, on the Sussex coast. Details of his movements after this come from war records, since he never recorded them himself. By March 1918, he was in France with his regiment, which formed part of the Canadian forces under the command of the British Commander-in-Chief Field Marshal Sir Douglas Haig, whose armies in turn came under the overall command of the Allied Supreme Commander Marshal Ferdinand Foch. It was a trench deployment near Arras; Chandler was joining men who had fought in the battles of Vimy Ridge and Passchendaele, where – in the latter battle alone – the British and Dominion casualties had numbered 400,000 men. The fatalities from wounds and vermin-spread disease by the time of Chandler's arrival in 1918 meant rapid promotion for those still alive. 'Once you have had to lead a platoon into direct machine-gun fire,' Chandler said, 'nothing is ever the same again.'

Chandler's Canadian battalion had a normal strength of 1,200 men and had suffered 14,000 casualties since its deployment in France in 1915, having been repeatedly made up to strength by drafts of replacements and reinforcements. It was this gruesome turnover that found Chandler, only two months after arriving in the trenches, promoted to non-commissioned rank and given command of a platoon of thirty men. Although fierce fighting continued on the Western Front throughout those spring months of 1918, as the German army forced a final offensive under

General Ludendorff, the war had almost exhausted itself. Nearly ten million soldiers' lives had already been lost and twice as many had been wounded. Neither Britain nor Germany or their allies were anxious to face another winter campaign. Chandler therefore saw sporadic trench warfare rather than the attritional carnage that had characterized the worst battles. The action he saw was terrifying none the less:

> If you had to go over the top somehow all you seemed to think about was trying to keep the men spaced, in order to reduce casualties. It was always very difficult, especially if you had replacements or men who had been wounded. It's only human to want to bunch for companionship in face of heavy fire.[14]

In June 1918, Chandler was knocked unconscious when German shells bombarded his battalion's trench position. He was concussed and taken behind lines. The bombardment had so depleted his own outfit that it was disbanded and survivors, including Chandler, were transferred back to England; to the Royal Air Corps at Waddington, near Lincoln, in order to learn how to fly the Allies' new military aircraft. It was an abrupt end to his twelve-month career as an infantryman.

It was during his four months' training in Waddington – 'a hell of a place to spend a Sunday' – that the shell-shocked Chandler discovered his taste for alcohol. He had never seriously drunk before the war:

> When I was a young man in the RAF I would get so plastered that I had to crawl to bed on my hands and knees and at 7.30 the next morning I would be as blithe as a sparrow and howling for my breakfast. It is not in some ways the most desirable gift.[15]

When the war ended in November 1918, Chandler was moved down from Waddington to Seaford, there to await repatriation to Canada. He had learned how to fly a plane, but the war had finished before he had been required to go back into combat. He had made the rank of sergeant and, like all surviving Allied servicemen, was awarded both the 1914–1918 Star and Victory Medal for his service. There was a month's gap between the armistice and his embarkation, but if he tried to make contact with his remaining London friends, there is no record of it. He had been luckier than many. Three hundred and fifty former Dulwich boys had been killed in the war and Gilkes, deeply depressed by what had taken place, had resigned his headmastership in order to become ordained as a parish clergyman.

Waiting for embarkation to Canada, Chandler wrote a short description of the trench bombardment he had experienced. It is unclear whether he meant it for publication but it marks, nevertheless, a profound shift in the way he wrote. Clever explanations (being 'brilliant about nothing', as he had described it) were being replaced by an eye for tangible detail. More obviously, though, the piece marks a creative shift for Chandler, from poetry to prose:

Trench Raid

The strafe started a lot heavier than usual. The candle stuck on the top of his tin hat guttered from something more than draught. The rats behind the dugout lining were still. But a tired man could sleep through it. He began to loosen the puttee on his left leg. Someone yelled down the dugout entrance and the beam of an electric torch groped about on the slimy chalk steps. He swore, retied his puttee, and slithered up the steps. As he pushed aside the dirty blanket that served for a gas curtain the force of the bombardment hit him like the blow of a club at the base of the brain. He grovelled against the wall of the trench, nauseated by the din. He seemed to be alone in a universe of incredibly brutal noise. . . .Time to move on. Mustn't stay too long in one place. He crawled round the corner of the bay to the Lewis gun post. On the firing step the Number One of the gun crew was standing to with half of his body silhouetted above the parapet, motionless against the glare of the light except that his hand was playing scales on the butt of his gun.[16]

The solitary experience of pain – actual physical pain, rather than the symbolic and intellectual anguish of his poetry – recurs constantly in Chandler's later books. Philip Marlowe is frequently beaten unconscious:

Mine was the better punch, but it didn't win the wrist watch, because at that moment an army mule kicked me square on the back of my brain. I went zooming out over a dark sea and exploded in a sheet of flame.[17]

In some of the stories Chandler would write for pulp magazines in the 1930s, he invented scenes that were gut-wrenchingly explicit, even by pulp standards:

Big Chin's face was a mess of blood. I couldn't see it as red, but I had put the eye on it a time or two and I knew it was there. His hands were free and what the kick to the groin had done to him was long ago, on the far side of oceans of pain. He made a croaking noise and turned his hip suddenly against De Spain and went down on his right knee and lunged for the gun.

De Spain kicked him in the face. . . . He twisted the foot quickly, with both hands. Big Chin's body seemed to leap in the air and dive sideways, and his shoulder and face smashed into the ground, but De Spain held onto the foot. He kept on turning it . . . Big Chin screamed like a dozen sheets tearing.[18]

Chandler could not help but absorb the details he had witnessed in wartime France; from the way a man's eyes look just after death to the viscosity of blood that seeps from a fatal head wound. These observations he would use in his later fiction. It would seem that he had also decided that the way to deal with such sights, apart from dulling their memory with drink, was to keep himself as distant from the events as possible. In 'Trench Raid' are the first signs of the detachment with which increasingly he chose, in both life and fiction, to deal with unsavoury realities.

*

Once back in Canada, and officially discharged in Victoria, BC, on 20 February 1919, Chandler was in no rush to return to Los Angeles. He stopped for a while in Seattle with an army friend called Smythe who was a barber; 'a great rogue and a comedian'.[19] A year and a half in the ranks had helped to erode the class snobbery which Chandler had picked up as a boy in post-Victorian London. Drinking was also a strong leveller. The North-Western Seaboard appears occasionally in Chandler's later writing, most notably in a screenplay called *Playback*, which is set on the Canadian/American border. At one point the heroine is asked by a man on a train whether she would like to see the Seattle paper: 'No thanks,' she replies, 'I've seen Seattle.'

Another screenplay Chandler would later write, *The Blue Dahlia*, begins with three friends returning from war in Europe. They head for a bar, where one of them orders 'Bourbon, with a bourbon chaser'. Two of the characters rent a temporary apartment together, something Chandler and Smythe the barber may have done in Seattle. One has a plan to get his mother out of Chicago, where she is married to a drunkard, but he is too shell-shocked to manage anything constructive at all.

The flow of Chandler's writing from florid intellectualism to rugged irony was not entirely smooth. It was during his stop in Seattle that he tried to sell a pastiche of Henry James, whom he greatly admired at the time. None of the magazines to which he sent it were interested, however, so he began looking for work again.

He was still reluctant to return to Los Angeles (least of all to his old job at the Creamery) and tried instead to find work in San Francisco, a city he said he liked for its 'go-to-hell attitude'. When he did briefly return south to LA, to spend Christmas of 1919 with his mother, Chandler found the atmosphere too depressing to stay. Florence was living with the father and stepmother of Gordon Pascal, the man with whom Chandler had left LA to join the Canadian Army in 1917. She was no longer well and was spending an increasing amount of time in bed. In a short poem Chandler wrote over that Christmas, he spoke of 'the secret and silence and the perfume . . . in the quiet house of all the dead'.[20] Back in San Francisco, in the New Year of 1920, he tried another and again unsuccessful stint as a reporter, working for the West Coast desk of his former employers, the *Daily Express*. But Chandler lacked the patience to start a new career, and his job with the *Express* lasted only a week. He then found work at two banks in the city: the Anglo and National Paris Bank, and the Bank of British North America. It was the kind of sensible career move that his uncle had tried to force on him in London, but Chandler was growing averse to making sensible decisions:

> Common sense is the guy who tells you that you ought to have had your brakes relined last week before you smashed a front end this

week. Common sense is the Monday morning quarterback who could have won the ball game if he had been on the team. But he never is. He's high up in the stands with a flask on his hip. Common sense is the little man in a grey suit who never makes a mistake in addition. But it's always someone else's money he's adding up.[21]

Chandler moved back to Los Angeles. Now thirty-one, he was an unlikely looking rebel, maintaining as he did the Edwardian panache he had affected since Dulwich. The reason for his return, however, was far from orthodox. He had finally fallen in love, and the object of his desire was Gordon Pascal's forty-year-old step-mother. Cissy Pascal was not an obvious lover to choose. She was still married to her second husband, Julian Pascal, a pianist of some international repute who was an integral part of the Lloyd set. (Cissy was herself an accomplished pianist.) The Pascals had looked after Florence in their house on South Vendone Street while Chandler had been fighting in Europe, and were still doing so.

Cissy had been born Pearl Eugenie Hurlburt in Perry, Ohio, and had moved to New York in her twenties. There she had changed her name to Cecilia (which in turn became 'Cissy' or 'Cissie') and had worked as a model while living in Harlem; rumour had it that she had been part of a high-life opium set while in New York. She once showed Chandler nude photographs of herself from her modelling days in New York. Her first husband had been a 'salesman' called Leon Porcher, whom she married in 1897 at a church on East 29th Street infamous for shotgun weddings, known as 'The Little Church Around the Corner'. She had divorced him after seven years and married Julian Pascal (whose real name was Goodridge Bowen) in 1911. It was during Chandler's stay with the Pascals over Christmas 1919 that he had written Cissy one of his 'Grade B Georgian' love poems. It was a poem of which one presumes her second husband and Chandler's mother were unaware. One verse is particularly revealing:

The touch of lips too dear for mortal kisses
The light of eyes too soft for common days
The breath of jasmine born to faintly lighten
The garden of ethereal estrays.[22]

Beyond her eroticism, Cissy remains almost as much of an enigma now as she would do in later life to most of Chandler's friends. All her letters to him he destroyed after her death. The one early photograph that survives confirms her to have been breathtakingly beautiful, with almost perfect features and an air of wistful nonchalance. She was no less perfect, Chandler decided, in character. On one occasion, he was in a car with her when she ran over a policeman's foot. Flustered, she put the car into reverse and ran over his foot again. Her charm was so natural, said Chandler, that even the policeman smiled:

> When she was younger she used to have sudden and very short-lived tempers, in which she would throw pillows at me. I just laughed. I liked her spirit. She was a terrific fighter. If an awkward or unpleasant scene faced her, and at times we all face that, she would march right in, and never hesitate a moment to think it over. And she always won, not because she deliberately put on the charm at the tactical moment, but because she was irresistible without even knowing or caring about it.[23]

Chandler believed that Cissy understood him. Having grown bored of the Lloyd set, he saw in her someone of like mind and, most importantly, without the fragility he was wary of in women. Her colourful past had given Cissy both a cynicism towards convention and an independent spirit. Having married twice, she had a wit and resourcefulness that Florence Thornton had never quite managed in the face of bad luck. Cissy was a worldly and beautiful woman whom Chandler could talk to on equal terms without worrying that her feelings might be easily hurt, or that she would be in need of constant reassurance. She may have been older than he was, and twice married, but Chandler seemed glad to be able to forgo a conventional courtship. Nor, at thirty-one, was he himself so young any more.

Falling in love with Cissy in 1919 lifted his spirits immeasurably. He now had a partner and a soul mate. He wrote her another poem, called 'Ballad to Almost Any Goddess (A Gentleman of Leisure addresses the Venus Anadyomene)' in which their shared sense of humour is obvious:

I bowed down to your feet with reckless words,
Sipping the tea, sipping the god-damned tea,
And no one heard but you, and no one smiled,
They were not there. They died before their death.

I have not called you Beauty, nor yet Woman,
Disliking as I do, the capitals.
They say you are immortal. What a bore.

Lacking the grand style what more can I say?
Down the forgotten night,
Down the dim night that has no date, no time,
No requiem, no elegy, no romance.
In the soft violet of the nameless stars,
We wander hand in hand. A pretty image
For those who like that sort of thing, but I
Immensely loathe it.
Is it possible
That you will be at leisure about eight
Of this most god damn gorgeous evening?
  So I thought.[24]

Given the peculiar circumstances of the courtship, Chandler's engagement to Cissy was arranged with surprising ease. The Lloyd circle took such pride in their avant-garde attitude towards social mores that a meeting was arranged between Cissy, Julian Pascal, Chandler and Dr Lloyd. Cissy explained at this meeting that she loved her husband but that she loved Raymond Chandler more, and it was decided by consensus that she should file for divorce. This was obtained by the end of 1920. It was the same year in which Washington passed the Nineteenth Amendment giving all women in America the right to vote; for Chandler it meant he now had two women to support and no income.

Florence was furious at her son's planned marriage. Having been looked after by Julian and Cissy throughout 1918 and 1919, she felt bitterly defensive about Julian Pascal, believing that he was being abandoned by Cissy in the same way that she herself had been by Chandler's father. Worse still, the persistent illness that had been plaguing her since 1918 was now diagnosed as cancer. Following the diagnosis, her resolve hardened as her condition rapidly worsened. Florence's refusal, from her deathbed, to condone the marriage meant a morbid wait for Cissy and Chandler until she died. The delay was particularly frustrating for Cissy, who was lying about her age and would do so on her eventual marriage certificate. Rather than being forty at the time of her divorce from Julian Pascal, she had in fact been born in October 1870 and was fifty. Chandler would not realize this until after their marriage – Cissy was, it seems, even more capable of looking after herself than he had bargained for.

In the four-year gap between Cissy's divorce and Florence Chandler's death, Chandler supported the two women in different houses in Los Angeles. Both lived in cheap apartments in mixed neighbourhoods south of the city: Cissy on Hermosa Beach; Florence in South Catalina Street on Redondo Beach. Badly overstretched, Chandler desperately needed a regular job and some luck.

He found both with a small oil syndicate, in which Dr Lloyd had an interest, and started work there in 1920. In America as a whole, it was a much better time than it had been in the pre-war years for educated men on the make like Chandler. Cheap migrant labour and a federal government bent on tycoon economics had paved the way for a boom. In 1921, Congress repealed the wartime excess profits tax, eliminated luxury taxes, lowered corporate taxes and cut the top-bracket income tax rate from 65 per cent to 32 per cent. These changes were implemented by Treasury Secretary Andrew Mellon, whose own personal tax reduction consequently exceeded that of the entire population of Nebraska.[25] Every American city caught boom fever but Southern California had special reasons to anticipate prosperity: oil and land.

With support from Washington, Los Angeles continued to be sold to the rest of America throughout the 1920s. 'Los Angeles is not a mere city,' noted one commentator at the time. 'On the contrary, it is, and has been since 1888, a commodity; something to be advertised and sold to the people of the United States like automobiles, cigarettes and mouthwashes.'[26] The city's population was mushrooming, towards an estimated 1.5 million by 1930. For LA's civic leaders, the success of their advertising meant nothing without business. As a massive influx of new citizens, Chandler among them, moved to find its feet in the city, emergency measures were taken to protect and consolidate the growth of the economy.

The two priorities of City Hall at this time were to maintain law and order and to encourage further investment in the city. The 'militant moralists' of LA's pre-war years had now given way to a new breed of militant financiers. The best policy to protect the city's expansion often proved to be no policy at all: a blind eye was collectively turned on both strong-arm policing and dubious financing, since both appeared to serve the city's booming economy. Neither was considered as dangerous to the city's health as obstructive unions and vagrancy. It was time for fast, raw power-broking, and not necessarily one for overscrupulousness. 'Don't be a hero, young man,' Marlowe would later be told in *The Long Goodbye*. 'There's no percentage in it.'

Just as the 1920s were an ideal decade in which to be male, educated and white in Los Angeles, Chandler's own move into the oil industry could scarcely have been more timely. Southern California was on the brink of an oil bonanza. The syndicate he began working for was one of several quickly set up to exploit the high-risk, high-return oil reserves around the Los Angeles basin. Such syndicates were constantly being merged, closed down, renamed and split; it was not at all inevitable that the one Chandler joined, the Dabney Oil Syndicate, should have prospered so early on. There was never any guarantee that oil would be found on an area of prospection, or that the reserves struck would be of a sufficient quantity or quality to justify the colossal investment that further exploration involved. But the Dabney Syndicate – later renamed the South Basin Oil Company – had fortuitously moved into part of Signal Hill on Long Beach. Within two years of Chandler starting work, Signal Hill and its two immediately neighbouring oilfields were producing twenty per cent of the world's oil.[27] The domestic market for this oil was massive, thanks both to the growth of American industry and the development of cheap internal combustion engines: Henry Ford alone sold 15 million motor cars in the United States between 1907 and 1926.

Cash poured into the syndicate. Joseph Dabney himself became a millionaire several times over, and Chandler found that he was ideally placed as a junior accountant. Luck then struck again: in the disorder of the syndicate's sudden fortune, its chief accountant was arrested for embezzlement. This was the direct result of sleuth work by the firm's new recruit: 'I found him out', said Chandler, 'and at his trial I had to sit beside the Assistant DA and tell him what questions to ask.'[28] When the culprit's successor then suddenly died of a heart attack, Chandler was brought up from the ranks to replace him, with an immediate pay rise of 100 per cent. He was now to be paid $1,000 a month as right-hand man to one of the biggest players in the Californian oil boom. This was 'the Roaring Twenties' and Chandler, miraculously, was a part of it:

> I was an executive . . . a director of eight companies and a president of three, although actually I was simply an overpriced employee. They were small companies but very rich. I had the best office staff in the Los Angeles area and I paid them higher salaries than they could have got anywhere else, and they knew it. My office door was never closed, everyone called me by my Christian name, and there was never any dissension, because I made it my business to make sure there was no cause for it. Once in a while, not often, I had to fire someone – not someone I had picked myself, but someone who had been imposed on me by the big man – and hated it terribly, because one never knows what hardship it may mean to the individual. I had a talent for picking out the capabilities of people. . . .There was a lawyer on salary who was very acute but also very unreliable, because he drank too much. I found out just how he used to use his brain, and he said often and publicly that I was the best office manager in Los Angeles and probably in the world. (Eventually he crashed into a police car and I had to get him out of jail.)[29]

Finding himself in a position of some power at Dabney's, Chandler began to enjoy his work. He took pleasure in the rawness of the industry, and discovered that he had a taste for getting into fights with those he thought were trying to hoodwink the syndicate. He judged most lawyers, for instance, to be crooked: 'Of course the lawyers always back each other up,' he once explained, 'because they know that if they don't hang together they'll hang separately.'[30] Insurance companies were another enemy:

> I remember one time when we had a truck carrying pipe in Signal Hill (just north of Long Beach) and the pipe stuck out quite a long

way, but there was a red lantern on it, according to law. A car with two drunken sailors and two girls crashed into it and filed actions for $1000 a piece. They waited almost a year, which is the deadline here for filing a personal injury action. The insurance company said, 'Oh well, it costs a lot of money to defend these suits, and we'd rather settle.' I said, 'That's all very well. It doesn't cost you anything to settle. You simply put the rates up. If you don't want to fight the case, and fight it competently, my company will fight it.' 'At your own expense?' 'Of course not. We'll sue you for what it costs us.' He walked out of the office. We defended the action, with the best lawyer we knew, and he proved that the pipe truck had been properly lit and then we brought in various barmen from Long Beach (it took money to find them, but it was worth it) and proved that they had been thrown out of three bars. We won and the insurance company paid up immediately about a third of what they would have settled for, and as soon as they did I cancelled the policy, and had it re-written with another company.[31]

Chandler was good at his job, and he began to take an interest in how other businesses ran. He was fascinated by the new corporate giants like Du Pont, Alco and Standard Oil. Once a private enterprise had acquired a large enough labour force, he decided, governments in fear of mass unemployment would never prosecute or inspect them for anything serious. They could do anything. They could 'even afford to be benign, charming, friendly and full of charity' to their staff, since they were 'too intelligent to think that fear can make men creative; it can only make them assiduous'.[32] He considered them, none the less, to be dangerous to a country's economy, since they ended up 'destroying the very thing they purport to represent – free competition'. Chandler had no time, however, for any communist alternative to big business: 'I think a bunch of bureaucrats can abuse the power of money just as ruthlessly as a bunch of Wall Street bankers, and far less competently.'[33]

Even on the domestic front, Chandler was now on the lookout for corruption. He refused to be intimidated by those institutions he believed prospered on the public's ignorance. When Cissy suffered a bout of pneumonia, he received an enormous medical bill. It was, he believed, fraudulently high: 'I wrote that I considered it exorbitant and explained why. The next thing I knew

I was served by a collection agency. Well, it just so happened that one of the lawyers we used at the time (I was in the oil business then) volunteered to represent me, and refused my fee. The attorney immediately moved for a dismissal and we got it.'

*

Chandler's mother finally died in January 1924. The date of Florence's birth is unknown, but it would seem that she was certainly under sixty at the time of her death. Her son was thirty-five, and well on the way to a personal fortune. He and Cissy were married two weeks later on 6 February 1924. It has been suggested that Chandler never knew Cissy's real age, and although it is unlikely that a man who would go on to write detective stories could fail to notice discrepancies in his own wife's life story, Cissy certainly did not look fifty-three in 1924.[34] Having never had children of her own, she had kept her model's figure and, according to Chandler's colleagues at Dabney's, had the sexual presence of a thirty-year-old. Indeed, for the first years of her marriage to Chandler, she even used to do the housework naked. That the marriage was always likely to be childless (however old he thought Cissy was) did not seem to bother Chandler. Having a family of his own had never been a serious plan. 'I love hearing the patter of little feet,' he once said, 'running away from me.'

In many ways, Cissy and Raymond Chandler were made for each other. She dressed with panache, looked twenty years younger than she was, and liked to make the house look elegant; Chandler dressed like the Edwardian abroad he never quite was, and had no interest in furniture, nor owned any of his own. Cissy was East Coast, witty and intentionally enigmatic about her past; Chandler was British-educated, cultured, and with an unusual background of his own. Cissy pronounced her new surname 'Chond-lah', with a mock flourish, and thought Chandler's poetry was funny. The two of them would take afternoon tea together and listen to the classical music programme on the radio; and they also went dancing, the waltz being Chandler's favourite. For each wedding anniversary, Chandler would fill the house with red roses and the two of them would drink champagne together. It was a chivalrous marriage that baffled and amused many observers and neighbours. Cissy called Chandler 'Raymio' because he was so romantic and she was a good foil to his erratic daydreams. He sometimes drew up lists of his future plans, including making so much money that he could take Cissy back to live in England. 'Dear Raymio,' wrote Cissy at the end of one of these lists, 'you'll have fun looking at this maybe, and seeing what useless dreams you had. Or perhaps it will not be fun.'[35]

Chandler once offered a friend eight rules for a happy marriage. For 'however perfect the honeymoon', he explained, 'there will come a time, however brief it is, when you will wish she would fall downstairs and break a leg, and vice versa':

1. Ride her on a short rein and never let her think she is riding you.
2. If the coffee is lousy, don't say so. Just throw it on the floor.
3. Don't let her change the arrangement of furniture more than once a year.
4. Don't have any joint bank accounts unless she puts in the money.
5. In case of a quarrel, remember it is always your fault.
6. Keep her away from antique shops.
7. Never praise her girlfriends too much.
8. Above all never forget that a marriage is in one way very much like a newspaper. It had to be made fresh every damn day of every damn year.[36]

*

By the late 1920s, Raymond Chandler's life had turned around. With a loyal wife, a job at which he was successful and a brand-new Chrysler, he was an ex-tennis racket stringer turned oil executive who had succeeded in fulfilling most of his material New World ambitions. He played tennis at friends' houses and swam regularly. He even mastered high-board diving. The oil business had produced more intriguing and sharp-witted colleagues than had the LA Creamery, and Chandler had new friends: hard-working, hard-drinking friends who appreciated his wit and irreverence, among them a lawyer named 'Red' Barrow, and Milton Phileo, a colleague at Dabney's. By now he had lived in Los Angeles for longer than he had anywhere else, and he had become fond of it. He liked the energy and the rudeness of the city, as he would later describe it in his books:

It was one of those clear, bright summer mornings we get in the early spring in California before the high fog sets in. The rains are over. The hills are still green and in the valley across the Hollywood hills you can still see snow on the mountains. The fur stores are advertising their annual sales. The call houses that specialize in sixteen-year-old virgins are doing a land-office business. And in Beverly Hills the jacaranda trees are beginning to bloom.[37]

Some instability prevailed: Chandler insisted on moving house annually; there was always something, or someone, that prevented him from renewing a lease. Landlords were as open to suspicion as lawyers and insurance companies. He loved feuds, and he could not help himself spotting well-concealed errors:

> I am having a feud with the gardener. I am having a feud with the man who came to assemble a Garrard changer and ruined several LP records. . . . Let's see who else – oh skip it. You know Chandler. Always griping about something.[38]

Despite his rising salary, Chandler was determined to save money in case something untoward should happen; but he did not consider property a priority. 'I was living that year on Yucca Canyon in the Laurel Canyon district,' Marlowe says in the opening of *The Long Goodbye*, ' . . . the rent was low partly because the owner wanted to be able to come back on short notice, and partly because of the steps.' The succession of houses did move slowly up market, but never into the swimming-pool bracket that Chandler could now afford. The addresses that still stand today are quiet, anonymous Spanish-style houses around Echo Park and Silver Lake, in the hills just north of downtown Los Angeles. Immediately after the wedding, the couple moved to a semi-detached house at 2863 Leeward (on the corner of Magnolia). Subsequent addresses where they stayed for any length of time during Chandler's oil days include 700 Gramercy Place (on Melrose Avenue), 2315 West 12th Street and 1024 South Highland Street. There was a plan to buy land and build a house, so as to cap his New World success, and the Chandlers nearly did this in Huntington Palisades, south of the city, but the scheme fell through because he decided it would be too 'bleak and windy'.

Chandler's wariness about being ripped off by Angelino real-estate brokers and landlords was partly born of paranoia about being poor again, and partly a reaction to the scam-ridden local economy. The huge and virtually unregulated growth of billboard, newspaper and radio advertising in 1920s California had found a deeply sceptical observer in Chandler. He was both fascinated by the fraudulence of most advertising claims and determined not to fall victim himself. He had been observing the Angelino land industry with particularly careful scrutiny, and now that he had the money to buy property he was extremely suspicious of anyone selling it.

It was a cynicism compounded by his inside knowledge of the oil business, one of the biggest of all advertisers in the state. Most Californian oil ventures were funded by the sale of shares to the public, advertised in city newspapers and at 'picnic' open days. With the exception of ventures by Standard Oil and Shell, Wall Street was keeping a wary distance from LA oil speculation. Some advertised ventures would be deliberately over-issued and some were fraudulent from the start, with shares sold in fields that were known beforehand to be 'dry'. It was a maverick-led industry, but no amount of scandal seemed capable of dampening the public's fever to speculate. J. Tygiel's history of the Californian oil boom records countless episodes of double-crossing among the hustlers who operated behind the industry. It is worth bearing in mind, when considering the sums of money involved in these incidents, that Chandler's highest salary as a vice-president at Dabney's never exceeded $3,000 a month:

> When Alvin Frank, a mainstay of the Bennett operations, attempted to collect on two loans totalling $75,000, Bennett instructed his messenger to return at four in the afternoon. At 3.00pm Bennett departed, leaving Frank and the others in the lurch. Three hours later he reportedly boarded the Santa Fe Chief at Union Station and headed east. Around his waist was a money belt allegedly holding an estimated $625,000.[39]

Joseph Dabney, who lived in a vast mansion on South Lafayette Place, was himself taken to court by the Lloyds at one point for misappropriating oil revenues. The most extravagant scandal of all, however, involved the Julian Petroleum company. For almost two years it was the biggest story in LA, and it was not only unfolding on the front page of the newspapers Chandler saw each day, but within his own industry. C. C. Julian was the original scam artist, an ex-milkman who had arrived in LA from Winnipeg with little to his name other than the mining qualifications and family background he had invented. Julian's genius as a speculator was in raising money from the public. He took out a permanent advertising space in the *LA Daily News* in which he would personally write rabble-rousing daily updates on his latest venture. Julian would quote Kipling and Shakespeare and cleverly use self-parody in order to win the confidence of newspaper readers. When his syndicate eventually began to fall under the scrutiny of the authorities, Julian used the column he paid for to present himself as a hero of the people, fighting bureaucracy in order to bring money to the homes of California. The following advertisement appeared in the *LA Daily News* on 5 January 1924:

'RED BLOODED
AMERICANS'
I'M CALLING ON YOU
TODAY

'The Powers aligned against me', after months of vicious attack from every possible angle, have finally thrown every control into the breach, in a last desperate attempt to annihilate the 'Julian Petroleum Company'.[40]

Julian gave his articles banner headlines like: 'LET ME BE YOUR SANTA CLAUS', 'JUST ONE DAY LEFT' or 'FAINT HEART NE'ER WON A LADY'. He was as cunning as he was gushing. The greatest response to any column he wrote was for speculation in Santa Fe in 1922. His headline had read:

JULIAN REFUSES TO ACCEPT YOUR MONEY UNLESS YOU CAN AFFORD TO LOSE! WIDOWS AND ORPHANS, THIS IS NO INVESTMENT FOR YOU!

Julian organized enormous free picnics, transporting potential small investors out to the oilfields by chartered trains. These occasions were news events in themselves and over the 1920s Julian became a society figure and a frequent guest at Hollywood parties. His celebrity only fuelled his apparent bankability, and many of the city's luminaries became involved with his company. When the bubble finally burst on him in 1927 – Julian stock had by then been over-issued by more than 1,000 per cent – every section of LA society had been affected. Apart from the thousands of small investors, Louis B. Mayer, Cecil B. De Mille and Charlie Chaplin all lost money. The scandal turned to drama when Motley Flint, a movie financier involved with Julian, was shot dead in a downtown courtroom. The District Attorney was himself tried for taking bribes and attempting to scupper the case against the scam's perpetrators. The scandal ended with Julian, a flamboyant and handsome man, fleeing eventually to Shanghai, where he killed himself. The sequence of events surrounding his downfall has more than one scene that must have appealed to Chandler:

> That night, as Julian worked with Julian Petroleum vice-president Jack Roth, an anonymous caller warned he would be killed before morning. Julian and Roth left the office and drove to Julian's Los Feliz mansion. His chauffeur detected a taxi following them. . . . Shortly before 1.00am, as Julian and Roth dove for cover, a shot crashed into the wall. The closely grouped bullets, fired from thirty feet away, formed a close circle of holes in the window.[41]

Following Julian's flight, the city's new DA sent private detectives to Europe to track down one of the fraudster's chief accomplices. They followed his trail through France, Italy and Austria, before finding him in an 'elaborately furnished apartment' in Paris. But partly because of the initial trial's sham prosecution, and partly because no jury could be found whose members fully understood the complicated workings of the fraud, no proper convictions were ever obtained. The case provoked US Senator Gerald Nye to comment that the Julian Petroleum scandal was 'emphatic evidence that you cannot convict a million dollars in the United States'. It was a cynicism towards Californian justice which Chandler shared – the only difference between crime and business in LA, Marlowe would later decide, was capital.

*

Throughout this time, Chandler continued writing his poems. Working on them late at night, he addressed most to Cissy and would leave them on the kitchen table for her to find in the morning. They grew increasingly restless in theme; as the excitement of his new profession started to wear off, the big plans he had once had were – as Cissy had predicted – no longer fun for him to remember. Though better paid, he felt that he was wasting his thirties at Dabney's, just as he had wasted his twenties at the LA Creamery. Chandler again became impatient with his life, and began to suffer from insomnia: '2.30am,' he wrote at the top of one poem. 'A silly way to spend the night I suppose, but better than moping.' He had now conceded that his poetry was the hobby of an overactive mind, rather than a true vocation: 'Lady, please waken, I long to kiss/Those gentle answering lips', started one poem; 'Ye echoes of old songsters dim, forlorn/And plaintive magic', ran another.[42]

Some of his poems from the 1920s provide a more specific insight into his state of mind as he continued to work in the LA oil business:

Nocturne From Nowhere
There are no countries as beautiful
As the England I picture in the night hours
Of this bright and dismal land
Of exile and dismay.

In fact, the best poetry Chandler ever wrote was in forms furthest removed from classical metre; though one piece, which could hardly have differed more from the verse he had produced in London, was remarkable more for its content than its form:

Song At Parting
He left her lying in the nude
That sultry night in May
The neighbours thought it rather rude
He liked her best that way

He left a rose beside her head
A meat ax in her brain
A note upon the bureau read
'I won't be back again.'[43]

*

With no children, Chandler once again began to spend a lot of time on his own. Cissy's physical stamina was not proving equal to her strength of character. She suffered another bout of pneumonia and was often tired. Chandler still had the friends he had met through the oil business, but by the summer of 1927 he was thirty-nine and most of his male colleagues were busy having families. He seemed to be trapped in a position identical to the one in which he had been in 1917, working at a job he found uninspiring in order to support a woman who was no longer healthy. In 1917, the war had provided Chandler with an escape out of Los Angeles. He now started to use different ways to escape tedium in the city: he was drinking regularly and heavily, and he also began to look elsewhere for love. In the regular company of secretaries and friends' wives – and possibly aware for the first time of Cissy's real age – Chandler became restless:

> You know how it is with marriage – any marriage. After a while a guy like me, a common no-good guy like me, he wants to feel a leg. Maybe it's lousy, but that's the way it is.[44]

Through the late 1920s and early 1930s, the drinking got heavier still and less controllable. Chandler moved out of the house into a hotel room, and continued binge drinking. He was sporadically separated from Cissy throughout this period. His main friends became those who were as hell bent on drink as he was:

> I can remember sitting around with two or three congenial chumps and getting plastered to the hairline in a most agreeable manner. We ended up doing acrobatics on the furniture and driving home in the moonlight filled with music and song, missing pedestrians by a thin millimetre and laughing heartily at the idea of a man trying to walk on two legs.[45]

There were weekend trips to football games in San Francisco that would start with drink and would sometimes never get as far as the stadium. With his friend from Dabney's, Milton Phileo, Chandler would charter a small aeroplane and pilot and fly down the coast towards Mexico. On one occasion, he undid his seatbelt and tried standing up in the open cockpit. It was more than just a prank. Chandler was growing occasionally manic in his drunkenness, and made a series of suicide threats from hotel rooms. Friends would drive to whichever LA hotel he had called from, to find him in his room, drunk and alive.

There was a secretary at Dabney's, never named, with whom Chandler had an affair, according to his old colleagues, and with whom he would disappear out of Los Angeles at weekends. The two of them drank so much together on these jaunts that Chandler would have to cover for his lover when she failed to appear at the office on Monday mornings. Then he, too, stopped appearing on Mondays, and eventually neither party was turning up until Wednesday.

*

Chandler experienced blackouts, or alcohol-induced amnesia, when he drank heavily. He would sometimes remember details of previous blackouts when drinking again. This was not unusual, as Professor D. Goodwin writes in his study of alcoholism. For instance, 'alcoholics often report hiding money or alcohol when drinking, forgetting it when sober, and having their memory return when drinking again. During blackouts, the person is conscious and alert. He may appear normal. He may do complicated things – converse intelligently, seduce strangers, travel. A true story:'

> A 39-year-old awoke in a strange hotel room. He had a mild hangover, but otherwise felt normal. His clothes were hanging in the closet; he was clean-shaven. He dressed and went down to the lobby. He learned from the clerk that he was in Las Vegas and that he had checked in two days previously. It had been obvious that he had been drunk, the clerk said, but he hadn't been very drunk. The date was Saturday 14th. His last recollection was of sitting in a St Louis bar on Monday the 9th.[46]

In one of the pulp-magazine stories he would later write, Chandler created an LA hotel detective called Steve Grayce. Offered a drink, Grayce turns it down. Pushed as to why, he explains: 'I'm an occasional drinker, the kind of guy who goes out for a beer and wakes up in Singapore with a full beard.'[47]

There would be an intense blackout scene involving amnesia and usually alcohol in every one of Chandler's Marlowe novels, as well as in one of his Hollywood screenplays. In fact, the blackout scene became a distinct trademark of Marlowe's adventures. These scenes were given such prominence and space throughout Chandler's writing that they beg at least two clear biographical correlations. First, the German bombardment that left Chandler unconscious during the First World War and ended his infantry career. Second, the blackouts that he experienced when he drank heavily; specifically, the sustained binge he embarked on at Dabney's.[48]

There are of course other, less subtextual, reasons why Chandler may have detailed so many blackouts. Like other serial heroes, Marlowe must fight villains, but he can never die. One way in which his survival could retain any sort of credibility is for him to receive regular non-fatal blows. That said, few action writers can ever have given the head injury so much attention, or lavished upon it as much imagery, as did Chandler.

Although censorship meant that his work in Hollywood contained neither as much drink nor as much violence as his books, there is a pertinent passage in the screen notes which he wrote to his film *The Blue Dahlia*. The story, he said, 'is about three discharged soldiers. Let us say they are the last survivors of a bomber crew that made too many missions.' One of the three, whom Chandler initially intended as the murderer, has a silver plate in his skull, having been hit by a bullet: 'He gets headaches and loud noises bother him, and once in a while after excitement, he blacks out. He can't remember what happened. Some people do this from drinking too much.'

On one occasion, Chandler drove out to play tennis with Milton Phileo and his wife. Arriving drunk, he learnt that Phileo's wife was ill and would not be playing. Chandler went upstairs and tried to drag her out of bed until he was stopped by Phileo, who told him to go home. Presuming him to have gone, Phileo went back downstairs to discover Chandler pointing a gun he had found at his own head. He was becoming unfathomable. Meeting him, as another friend said, was sometimes like 'landing at an interesting place but finding it wrapped in fog'.

Though Chandler made scant direct record of, or reference to, these lost years, it was a period in his life on which, in his later books, he would draw more heavily than any other. The age and circumstances of his fictional character, Philip Marlowe, would be very similar to those of Chandler during the last four years of his oil career. Both men were lonely drinkers working in Los Angeles. Both were good at jobs which they found distasteful and both, to some extent, were addicted to physical danger.[49] The unique atmosphere of early 1930s Los Angeles would also figure more strongly in Chandler's fiction than that of any other period, for his own instability around 1930 was mirrored by the situation in which LA found itself following the Wall Street Crash of 1929.

As the cataclysmic effects of the Depression swept the United States after 1929, one in four American men found themselves without jobs. A large number of them also lost their homes. 'Without unemployment insurance, social security, or federal welfare benefits,' as one historian has put it, 'the Depression caused the transformation of 2 million Americans into homeless, jobless, wandering vagabonds routinely and often violently routed from town to town.'[30] Many of them were heading for Los Angeles. In 1931, 2,000 were arriving a week, forcing the police to set up 'bum blockades' on roads leading into the city. On top of this influx were the 600,000 citizens that LA had absorbed during the boom years of the 1920s. Law and order was growing ever more difficult to enforce in Chandler's adopted town.

Even before the start of the Depression, the Los Angeles crime rate had risen noticeably enough to have the city's power-brokers worried. The metropolis had simply grown too quickly to be controlled. In 1926, a group known as the 'Breakfast Club', consisting of Senator Samuel Shortridge, Louis B. Mayer, Henry Chandler (owner of the LA Times) and Guy Barham (who represented William Randolph Hearst in LA), as well as various real estate tycoons, financiers and industrialists, had decided to confront the spread of lawlessness. Between them, the Breakfast Club already controlled City Hall appointments, and in April of 1926 they appointed as Chief of Police James Edgar Davis, a man famous for wanting to fingerprint every resident of Los Angeles or, failing that, 'all the domestics'.

The effects of the Depression on the Los Angeles job market

only increased the amount of power Police Chief Davis was allowed by his power-broking sponsors. His targets were not the organized crime racketeers, who were themselves now power-brokers, but vagrants, union leaders and critics of City Hall. Raymond Chandler, with everyone else in the city, was all too aware of the strong-arm and unscrupulous tactics being used by the LAPD. In 1929 an outspoken critic of the police force, councilman Carl Jacobson, was publicly arrested in a hotel on charges of 'lewd conduct' after being found with a prostitute. When Jacobson demanded a public trial, it was revealed that he had been framed by the LAPD: the 'prostitute' was in fact the sister-in-law of a vice detective who had paid her $2,500 to get Jacobson into her bed. The revelation was followed in the press by another in 1929:

> Harry 'Bathhouse' McDonald, who had been paying vice squad commander Max Berenzweig and his men $100,000 a year to be permitted to run his large bootleg operation, was arrested and, once in custody, started to talk. As a result, both Berenzweig and one of his detectives, James Howry, were indicted and skipped town to avoid prosecution.[51]

While racketeers operated under the eyes of the authorities, more visible threats to public order were stamped down on with the full weight and venom of the emergency powers granted to the police. While Chandler never admitted whether his own drunken exploits ever brought him into contact with this viciousness, his knowledge of police brutality certainly seemed to go beyond intuition. One of the LAPD's martial law-type measures during the instability of the Depression was to place hundred-man dragnets across a dozen major city roads with orders to stop and search any 'suspicious characters':

> Here in California . . . the cops decide who is or who is not a material witness. He might simply be a man who refused to go down and be grilled about his movements for the last twenty-four hours. If you don't want to go – and you don't have to go according to the law – they take you away, by force if necessary, in handcuffs if they want to.[52]

It was a dangerous moment in the city's history to be embarking on an alcoholic binge. One of the most autobiographical characters in Chandler's later books, Roger Wade in *The Long Goodbye*, certainly knows the inside of LA County's infamous drink tank at Lincoln Heights: 'No bunk, no chair, no nothing. You lie there on the concrete floor. You sit on the toilet and vomit on your own lap. That is the depth of misery. I've seen it.'[53] In another book, *The Lady in the Lake*, Marlowe annoys a policeman, who in retaliation simply follows his car, pulls him over, pours whisky over him and arrests him for driving under the influence.

Chandler knew how intolerable he was becoming at Dabney's, and realized, too, the extent to which drink had got the better of him. Like many alcoholics, he did not suffer hangovers; nor did he need them to feel remorse. By deserting Cissy in order to hit the bottle, he was precisely repeating the sins of his hated father. Every self-loathing mention of alcohol by Marlowe in the later novels would have biographical resonance for Chandler:

> I smelled of gin. Not just casually, as if I had taken four or five drinks of a winter morning to get out of bed on, but as if the Pacific Ocean was pure gin and I had head-nosed off the boat deck. The gin was in my hair and eyebrows, on my chin and under my chin. I smelled like dead toads.[54]

It was the start of a self-imposed reclusiveness that Chandler would never entirely shake off, nor fully understand.

*

Chandler was not the only American to be drinking heavily through the years of Prohibition. 'The Noble Experiment', which Roosevelt finally repealed in 1933, had not only proved an unenforceable piece of legislation from the start, but also a detrimental one. The Amendment to ban the 'manufacture, sale, or transportation of intoxicating liquors', introduced as a patriotic gesture, had passed through Congress in the last months of the First World War, and had become law early in 1919. The Prohibition movement had enjoyed some lobby power in Washington since 1880, but it was the fact that most brewers were of German origin, and that American corn was needed for the Allied war effort, which had allowed the movement to rally a Congressional majority in 1918.

Successive federal budgets after 1918 failed to make available the funds necessary to enforce the ban, and (according to one estimate) '$2,000,000,000,000 worth of business was simply transferred from brewers and bar-keepers to bootleggers and gangsters, who worked in close co-operation with the policemen and politicians they corrupted.'[55] With the rise of organized crime, America never recovered from the effects of Prohibition. In New York, almost 90 per cent of cases involving breaches of the ban of alcohol were dismissed for insufficient evidence. In cities like LA, drink was easily available, but at extortionate prices. What Prohibition encouraged was a binge mentality amongst those who continued to drink – more alcohol was consumed in total in America during Prohibition than had been consumed in an equivalent period before the ban. Thanks to its proximity to the Mexican border, Los Angeles came to resemble Chicago – which had the equally permeable Canadian border – in the size of its gangster drink economy. Prohibition undermined the whole concept of legality, as Chandler later remembered:

Few Americans except bluenoses and fanatics ever believed in Prohibition. Most of us went to speakeasies and bought bootleg liquor quite openly, the 'most of us' including judges, police officers and government officials. . . . I remember that in one night club in Culver City, two policemen were always on duty – not to keep you from getting liquor, but to keep you from bringing in your own instead of buying it inside.[56]

Illegal binge-drinking was nowhere more evident in Los Angeles than within the city's movie industry. In 1921, the plumber's assistant turned comedy star Fatty Arbuckle had been sensationally tried for manslaughter, following a two-day party in a hotel room. The prosecution claimed that Arbuckle had perforated an actress's bladder with a glass bottle; the girl had died a few days later. The indignation created by the press (though Arbuckle was eventually acquitted) towards this and follow-up exposures of debauchery in Hollywood forced the movie industry into introducing self-regulated censorship. As a result, the major film companies set up the Motion Pictures Producers and Distributors of America, known as the Hays Office after its first head Will Hays, in 1922 – the year after the Arbuckle case – in order to try to distinguish in the public's mind the difference between the films that were being made and the 'debauchery, riotous living, drunkenness, ribaldry, dissipation and free love'[57] allegedly being practised by those making the films. As further scandals of Hollywood's decadent and drunken private life hit the press through the rest of the 1920s and early 1930s, however, mounting criticism of the industry continued to blur that distinction. By 1934, Hollywood finally found the controls of censorship decisively snatched by the American Roman Catholic Church. Mae West and gangster films were replaced by drink-free musicals and romantic epics; a sanitization which would last until the early 1940s.

As well as drinking with other law-breakers in Los Angeles, Chandler had started to drink alone. There would always be the occasional friend who was able to see through his irascibility, but by 1932 Chandler did not really want to see anyone. 'I am sorry if [I have] managed to irritate you,' a friend once wrote to him, 'but I think I see a very nice guy behind that forbidding exterior . . . since you ask us, we will come by some time, provided you don't act so startled when you open the front door. Maybe you'd better specify the exact hour and date, in writing, so we can call the cops up if necessary to gain entrance.' Chandler objected to the well-established LA custom of people turning up at friends' houses without warning. Not only would he often refuse visitors admission, but if they did stay, he would make no bones about suggesting their quick departure. On one occasion, a guest proved so impervious that Chandler simply left the room and returned in his pyjamas. Studies in alcoholism suggest that chronic addiction usually leads to solitary drinking and subsequently to reclusivity. Drinking now both exacerbated, and was a symptom of, Chandler's loneliness.

*

Since Californian oil was one of the few industries from which Wall Street had kept its distance in the 1920s, the Crash of 1929 did not damage the LA oil business as badly as did the Depression which followed it, and which radically reduced the country's gasoline consumption. Nevertheless, it was for his alcoholism, rather than because of the economy, that Chandler was fired by Dabney in 1932. Regularly absent or drunk on the job, he was no longer employable.

His career in the oil business had been something that he had alternately enjoyed and despised. A group photograph taken at an oil industry dinner before his sacking shows him sitting gloomily aloof. One colleague said that Chandler would frequently end such evenings making a 'nuisance' of himself, grotesquely drunk and holding forth loudly and pathetically to 'a bevy of showgirls'. He had no direction or ideals left on the day he was fired in 1932; he no longer considered himself to be a gentleman, and his paranoia about being without money again seemed about to be realized.

Chandler would never quite forgive the oil industry for the humiliation he deserved. The beginning of his first book, *The Big Sleep*, would have as its setting a house in Los Angeles that overlooked an old oilfield:

> The Sternwoods, having moved up the hill, could no longer smell the stale sump or the oil, but they could still look out of their windows and see what had made them rich. If they wanted to. I don't suppose they wanted to.[58]

The novel ends with Marlowe standing on the same oilfield and deciding that when one was dead, 'Oil and water were the same as wind and air to you. You just slept the big sleep, not caring about the nastiness of how you died or where you fell. Me, I was part of the nastiness now.'

3
The Pulps

'I like you,' she said. 'You look like the kind of guy who was almost a heel and then something stopped him – just at the last minute.'

('Mandarin's Jade', November 1937)

Being fired from his career of almost thirteen years was a severe enough signal to jolt Chandler out of his self-destruction. He retreated alone to Seattle, where he stayed with his army friends for two months, during which he managed to stop himself drinking. On hearing that Cissy had again fallen ill with pneumonia, however, he returned to LA. Despite his having no job or property – or immediate prospect of either in 1932 – Cissy, once she had recovered, agreed to take him back. Chandler was still in no mental condition to look for re-employment, but he was now detachedly aware of the effects drink had on him. The dawning of this sober self-consciousness about alcohol would be obvious in the books he was soon to begin to write:

> I went back to the office and sat in my swivel chair and tried to catch up on my foot-dangling. There was a gusty wind blowing in at the windows and soot from the oil burners of the hotel next door was being draughted into the room and rolling across the top of the desk like tumbleweed drifting across a vacant lot. I was thinking about going out to lunch and that lunch was pretty flat and that it would probably be just as flat if I took a drink and that taking a drink alone at this time of day wouldn't be any fun anyway.[1]

The fear of financial insecurity that had always haunted Chandler – and which had stopped him from indulging in an executive-level lifestyle when at Dabney's – now saved him. For although he had no property to his name, he had enough money to support himself and Cissy for the immediate future. With no parents, brother or cousins in existence who might offer potential life-lines in time of disaster, Chandler had always been very conscious of how little stood between himself and Skid Row; particularly once he started drinking. There was no one in the city on whom he could count to bail him out, or even give him a room in which to stay. Cissy had no money of her own and he had successfully insulted most of the friends who might previously have helped.[2] There had not been the security in the back of Chandler's mind – during the course of his breakdown – that if everything collapsed, as it now had, there was someone he could rely on, or somewhere he could go as a last resort. He could hardly return to Ireland and there was a limit to what more he could ask of the Lloyds. There is nothing like losing your money, Chandler later said, in order to see who your friends are. And by 1932, at the age of forty-four, Chandler had none.

Bolstered by a fresh surge of self-confidence following his physical rehabilitation, Chandler listed himself as a 'Writer' in the Los Angeles telephone book. This was now his plan. He and Cissy would have to move out of central Los Angeles to the cheaper rents of Santa Monica, but for the time being they could survive on what they had while he tried to earn money by writing fiction. It was a precarious career move for someone in his mid-forties who had never written any fiction before but Chandler was optimistic, and he soon hit upon the type of fiction he would write:

Wandering up and down the Pacific Coast in an automobile, I began to read pulp magazines, because they were cheap enough to throw away and because I never had any taste at the time for the kind of thing which is known as women's magazines. This was in the great days of the *Black Mask* [a pulp crime magazine] and it struck me that some of the writing was pretty forceful and honest, even though it had its crude aspect. I decided that this might be a good way to learn to write fiction and get paid a small amount of money at the same time. I spent five months over a 18,000 word novelette and sold it for $180.[3]

71

Chandler decided to approach fiction more methodically than he had approached his earlier poetry career. He was business-minded enough – and patient enough – to believe that he had first to learn the mechanics of fiction in order to sell whatever talent he had. Just as he had done to learn accountancy, Chandler enrolled in a local evening course and bought books on the subject. The course was called 'Short Story Writing 52AB' and he received a grade 'A' for the following piece about a ship mutiny:

> One-eyed Mellow glanced at the braid, once no doubt gold, that adorned the outer edges of his sleeves. He smiled insidiously, and his hand, with a movement very familiar to his men, began to wander towards the pistol stuck in his sash. As he freed it, coolly and without haste, from the broad band of dirty silk, the little dark sailor made an abrupt but very graceful movement. One-eyed Mellow's face turned rapidly at his elbow, and he perceived his pistol hanging by the trigger-guard on the blade of a slim dagger.
>
> 'Very pretty,' he drawled at length, when the silence threatened to become unbearable. 'Very pretty work indeed.' His Adam's-apple moved restlessly under the skin of his lean throat.
>
> The little dark sailor slipped around the head of the table and plucked his dagger from the wall.
>
> 'Your pistol, I believe, Captain,' he remarked in a mincing tone, and politely held out the weapon to its owner.
>
> 'Thank'ee, my man,' said One-eyed Mellow, a little wearily.[4]

Chandler considered fiction to be far more demanding than poetry, and set himself to the task of learning how to carry a prose scene. 'I could hardly get his hat off,' he said of one early exercise. He would later calculate that it was two to three years before he could get a character out of a room convincingly; longer before he could control a scene involving more than two people. Writing was, none the less, a form of discipline that the reforming alcoholic enjoyed. Chandler grew fascinated by the mechanics of fiction, and even experimented with the physical process of typing: he began using narrow yellow pieces of paper which he would feed into his typewriter with the long edge horizontal. Each sheet was about the size of a small paperback book laid on its side, and allowed him room to write only twelve to fifteen lines. It was a trick, he discovered, which forced him to put 'a bit of magic' on to each small sheet; be it an image, description or wisecrack. It also meant that he was less reluctant about starting a page again, even if he was near the bottom of the page he wanted to rewrite. Closer to a screenwriting method, it was also a discipline that worked well with the dialogue-based fiction demanded by pulp magazines. Chandler was never to abandon this approach, and after further experiments he also decided never to try to revise weaker scenes, but instead rewrite them from the start.

He bought a small pocket address book in which he started to collect (alphabetically) character names that occurred to him. He considered names to be as important as titles, both of which he thought were crucial to a story's quality. In another notebook he collected potential titles, many of which he went on to use – those that would not be later chosen included 'Guys With Guns', 'The Black-Eyed Blonde', 'Party Before Danger', 'Twenty Inches of Monkey', 'Tough On Women', 'All Guns Are Loaded' and 'Party Girl'.[5] In the same book he collected one-liners to use in stories: 'If you don't leave I'll get someone who will'; 'Goodnight, goodbye and I'd hate to be you'; 'As fancy as a Filipino on Saturday night'; as well as one telling description of a man in need of a drink: 'He wanted to buy some sweetness and light and not the kind that comes through the east window of a church.'

In the same methodical vein, Chandler began to make detailed notes of clothes that he had either seen people wearing or had read about. He also started collecting slang expressions he had heard, though he said that he suspected that half the slang used on American streets had been taken from pulp magazines and films in the first place. Some had not, and those he collected included 'grape' and 'eel juice' (liquor), 'lip' (lawyer), 'under glass' (in prison) and 'Chicago lightning' (gunfire). Under a separate heading for Narcotics Squad slang, he had 'cecil' (cocaine), 'black' (opium), 'joy pop' (occasional user), 'pearl diver' (dish washer), 'mojo' and 'mary' (both morphine). The only exception to his careful planning was plot; the best way to stop the reader guessing the end of a story, he decided, was not to know how it ended yourself.

Despite his diminishing capital, Chandler continued to bide his time through the end of 1932 and the beginning of 1933. Before trying to write anything for publication, he concentrated on writing pastiches of other writers' stories. He would take a story he admired, try to rewrite it and then reread the original. By doing this he found that he could spot structural weaknesses in his own writing, and found, too, that he was beginning to understand some of the invisible effects seasoned writers managed to create without the reader noticing. At this time, he considered Hemingway to be 'the greatest living American novelist', and wrote a pastiche of his writing:

> Hank put the toothpaste down and looked around. There was a bottle of alcohol on top of the built-in drawers where the towels were kept. It was grain alcohol. Velma hated rubbing alcohol with its harsh irritants. Her skin was sensitive. She hated almost everything. . . . Hank's face in the mirror wavered like a face behind thin smoke. It was a face drawn on grey silk by unscrupulous shadows. It was not a face at all.
>
> 'The hell with it,' he said. 'She shouldn't have done it.'[6]

Having decided to concentrate on detective fiction, Chandler practised the same method on established crime writers. He took a story by the most successful crime writer of the day and rewrote it. Erle Stanley Gardner, who would eventually become a friend and correspondent of Chandler's, was an ex California lawyer whose crime stories – many of them starring his hero Perry Mason – have to date sold 300 million copies. A year younger than Chandler, he had been expelled from school as a child for punching a teacher. He had gone on to study law and was admitted to the Californian bar in 1911, once successfully defending a client 'by getting several Chinamen to exchange identities and thus confuse a key prosecution witness'. Having retired from the bar in 1933 he began writing full time – using a dictating machine, he had once managed to write a book in three days. Compared to Chandler's eventual Marlowe novels, Gardner's are conventional, dry and contrived, but he had the mechanics of plot and structure honed to perfection. He could generally finish a book in three weeks, and by the time he died in 1970 he had published some one hundred and fifty novels. Other writers may have proved to be more of an inspiration for Chandler's detective writing, but Gardner's work was his early source of technique. In a letter to Gardner in 1939, Chandler spelled out his debt:

I learned to write a novelette on one of yours about a man named Rex Kane, who was the alter-ego of Ed Jenkins and got mixed up with some flowery dame in a hilltop house in Hollywood who was running an anti-blackmail organization. You wouldn't remember. It's probably in your file No. 54276-84. I made a detailed synopsis of your story and from that I rewrote it some more, and so on. It looked pretty good.[7]

*

Chandler wanted to make money from his writing, but he was also genuinely intrigued by detective fiction and the likes of Dashiell Hammett and Gardner. American crime fiction had, since the 1920s, been throwing off the polite shackles of the genre's English originators.[8] The result was a tough, 'hard-boiled' and instantly popular new sub-genre. It was also a sub-genre that had found, in *Black Mask*, both a new platform and a mass market.

Black Mask was a pulp magazine which had been set up by two New York editors in 1920 to support the loss-making but prestigious literary magazine *Smart Set*. The connection with *Smart Set* – whose most famous contributor was Scott Fitzgerald – was an ironic one for Chandler. The magazine for which he was now planning to write was effectively subsidizing an American equivalent of the London magazines he had written for as a precocious twenty-year-old. *Smart Set*'s cover subtitle, 'A Magazine of Cleverness', was an uncanny symbol of the type of writing he had now rejected:

I have at times a futile urge to explain to whoever will listen why it is that the whole apparatus of intellectualism bores me. But you have to use the language of intellectualism to do it. Which is bunk. . . . Thinking in terms of ideas destroys the ability to think in terms of emotions and sensations.[9]

Hard-boiled fiction Chandler saw as having an 'honesty' that neither Arthur Conan Doyle nor contemporary intellectual fiction possessed. Without quite claiming that if Shakespeare were alive he would have been writing for *Black Mask* – he did later say he thought the playwright would have been working in Hollywood – Chandler genuinely believed that this new crime writing he had stumbled upon, because of its lack of both pretension and tradition, provided an opportunity for writing at its unfettered best. Detective fiction was conceivably, Chandler decided, the only honest fiction left for an age incapable of art's traditionally greatest theme – love:

> The love story and the detective story cannot exist, not only in the same book – one might also say the same culture. Modern outspokenness has utterly destroyed the romantic dream on which love feeds. . . . There is nothing left to write about but death, and the detective story is a tragedy with a happy ending.[10]

Black Mask had been launched in April 1920 by H. L. Mencken and George Jean Nathan, after the financial success of another pulp money-spinner of theirs called *Parisienne*, which itself had been followed by an erotic stablemate called *Saucy Stories*. Mencken was a well-known literary journalist and sometime poet; Nathan a drama critic. Keeping *Smart Set* solvent was always their priority, and there had initially been plans to follow up *Saucy Stories* with 'an all-Negro pulp'. These plans were scrapped in favour of *Black Mask*. It was a purely commercial venture, in direct contrast to *Smart Set*, and its first issue was not even devoted exclusively to crime. In an open attempt to cater for as wide a readership as possible, *Black Mask* initially offered 'Five Magazines in One: The best stories available of Adventure, the best Mystery and Detective Stories, the best Romances, the best Love Stories, and the best stories of the Occult'. The few pages devoted to detective stories offered little that was special; it was all standard, English-influenced mystery. Some of the early stories defied parody:

> 'My dear inspector,' protested the Professor. 'You surely don't expect me to believe that a mere monkey . . .'
> 'That monkey threw Madame La Tournette into uncontrollable hysterics,' Inspector Donaldson insisted. 'Fifteen years ago, while on a hunting trip to Africa, her husband was crushed to death in the arms of a giant gorilla. . . .'[11]

Despite the poor quality of *Black Mask's* early issues, Mencken and Nathan quickly made a return on their initial $500 investment. Eight issues after its successful launch, they sold the magazine to its publishers for $12,500. After their departure, *Black Mask* was colonized by a new school of tough crime writers, under the direction of an imaginative and inspired new editor, 'Cap' Joseph Shaw.

A national fencing champion and East Coast gentleman, Shaw was an unsuccessful adventure story writer who was appointed editor of *Black Mask* in 1926. He had until then been serving with the army in Europe as one of the American enforcers of the Versailles Peace Treaty. Through nepotistic contacts in New York, he was placed in charge of a magazine with which he said he had 'not even a bowling acquaintance' [sic]. The bachelor ex-soldier nevertheless approached his task with vocational verve. His editorial agenda demanded clarity and plausibility: 'We always held,' he said later, 'that a good story is where you find it regardless of author-fame or medium of publication. It has been said that with proper materials available, a good mouse-trap can be built anywhere.' The recollections of Lester Dent, a *Black Mask* contemporary of Chandler's, suggest striking parallels between Shaw's editorship of the magazine and Gilkes's headmastership at Dulwich:

> Cap was gentle with his writers. You went in to Black Mask and talked with him, you had feelings of stature, you felt you were doing fiction that was powerful. Cap gave this strength to his writers. He could, because he was so convinced it was the truth. . . . Cap himself was the personification of English culture. This was so sincere in him that it was almost a spiritual garment he wore. . . . Here was a cultured man editing a pulp . . . a man who could breathe this pride of his into a writer. Cap didn't think I was a pulp hack . . . [he] used his horse whip in strange gentle ways. He would start discussing his writers, their skill, and before you knew it you would find some Hammett or Chandler in your hands along with a blue pencil and Cap would be asking, 'Would you cut that somewhere. Just cut a few words.' The idea, of course, was that there was no wordage fat. You could not cut. Every word had to be there.[12]

Shaw often wrote editorials for the magazine on subjects such as the jury system and gun control. He believed strongly in the moral responsibilities of crime fiction. Specifically, he believed that crime fiction could promote the ideal of justice on the increasingly lawless streets of America. It could show criminals for the spineless villains they were, and restore the tarnished image of law enforcement.

The reason so many of *Black Mask*'s fictional law enforcers were private detectives rather than policemen was more than partly due to a growing public distrust of the police. A stream of news stories exposing the corruption and ineffectiveness of the American police during Prohibition prompted *Black Mask* writers to create alternative champions of the law. Shaw regularly used his editorials to attack the state of the nation's justice system and police forces. Real-life American private detectives had an image problem of their own, however; apart from their 'peeper' tag, they were best known in the 1920s for breaking strikes by infiltrating workforces on behalf of industry bosses. Since they took no oaths, though, they had never been seen as hypocrites. In some celebrated instances, they had even proved heroic: Allan Pinkerton, the Scotsman who had set up America's first private detective agency in 1850s Chicago, made such a quick name for himself in solving a series of railway robberies that President Lincoln appointed him head of the Union's Secret Service during the Civil War. The FBI had been set up in the 1920s on explicitly Pinkerton lines. He may have become better known before his death in 1884 as a mercenary strike-breaker to the coal industry, but Allan Pinkerton was an honourable enough precedent to justify *Black Mask*'s fictional replacement of the policeman and sheriff with the private detective.

Although it was Cap Shaw who nurtured the realistic detective element in *Black Mask*, it had been before his ten-year tenure, in the issue of 15 May 1923, that the magazine had published what is considered to be the first ever tough private detective story, 'Three Gun Terry' by Carroll John Daly:

> I have a little office which says 'Terry Mack, Private Investigator,' on the door; which means whatever you wish to think it. I ain't a crook, and I ain't a dick; I play the game on the level, in my own way.[13]

Daly had followed Terry Mack up with a detective called Race Williams, and it was this violent and wisecracking character who really set up the prototype for the 'hard-boiled' sleuth. The detective stories appearing in *Black Mask* grew more violent, the style harder, the dialogue blacker and the wit dryer: 'My bullet cracked home,' ran a subsequent Carroll John Daly story. 'There was a tiny black hole in the whiteness of his face. . . . If hell wasn't all filled up here was another customer.'

Under Shaw, this crude but immediately successful type of story was made a priority. Having been appointed editor in 1926, Shaw spent a week reading through *Black Mask* back issues. He decided that the best writers were those producing detective stories, and as a result decided to drop most of the rest. The only other stories he printed were westerns and adventure stories, and even they were fillers until Shaw could find more crime talent. In 1927, he wrote an editorial in which he outlined his plans for *Black Mask*: '. . . detective fiction, as we see it, has only commenced to be developed . . . all other fields have been worked and overworked [but detective fiction] has barely been scratched.' In another editorial, which appeared in the same 1933 edition as Chandler's first published story, Shaw wrote that he wanted to see characters who bled when they were wounded – 'when they are hurt, you feel it'.[14] He proceeded to puff that issue's stories, trailering Chandler's first effort, 'Blackmailers Don't Shoot': 'A private dick out of Chi sees how the Coast lags play the big game.' By the time of this issue, December 1933, the magazine was publishing nothing but crime stories, and its national circulation had risen from 66,000 when Shaw had taken over to 103,000. Its cover price was 20 cents.

The focus of inspiration for Shaw, Chandler and the readers who backed this new-look *Black Mask*, was Dashiell Hammett. He alone seemed to have first realized the full potential of hard-boiled detective fiction beyond its gunslinging appeal. An ex-Pinkerton detective turned self-taught writer, Hammett was uniquely qualified to give his characters the three dimensions of which other writers of the tough detective story were largely incapable. Until he drank himself out of contention in 1934, Hammett was the champion: his 'Continental Op' series was a favourite among *Black Mask* readers, editors and co-contributors. When he threatened to leave the magazine in the late 1920s unless he was paid more, Erle Stanley Gardner offered to subsidize Hammett's rates from his own fee cheques.

By the time Chandler came to write his first story, Hammett's full-length books were being widely read in both America and Europe. The novelist William Faulkner (later to win the Nobel Prize for Literature) was a drinking partner of Hammett's, and people who did not normally read crime fiction knew who he was. He had gone on from his *Black Mask* success to write novel-length detective fiction (*The Maltese Falcon*, *The Thin Man*), which was published in hardback by a prestigious New York publisher, Alfred Knopf.

What was even more inspiring for Chandler was that, despite his respect for Dashiell Hammett (he met him once at a *Black Mask* dinner in LA, and had liked him), he did not consider Hammett to be an especially good writer: 'What he did he did superbly,' decided Chandler, 'but there was a lot he could not do.' By 1933, Hammett had given private detective stories a huge following, but by then he was also an alcoholic mess. In the last months of that year, he was writing what would prove to be his last book, *The Thin Man*; Chandler, meanwhile, was writing his very first story – and felt himself ready to take over.

*

It took Chandler five months to write his first story, and he rewrote it five times; a work-rate which immediately revealed his ambition. Though many *Black Mask* writers had college educations (Chandler and Hammett being exceptions), few took time to work to improve their styles. Many used up to three pen-names in order to maximize their income, and almost all were writing for other magazines at the same time. A motley crew of ex-newspapermen, ex-lawyers, ex-cops and failed Hollywood screenwriters, the men who wrote most for *Black Mask* did not have time to take too much care over their work. It was a much bandied statistic among the pulp fraternity that in order to support himself, a pulp writer had to write 1 million words a year. With an editor in Cap Shaw who took a blue pencil to anything he disliked, most contributors to the magazine, besides not having the time, did not have the inclination to experiment with the way in which they told their stories. It was in this spirit of consistency that Erle Stanley Gardner would dictate a Perry Mason novel to his secretary in three weeks; and it was in the face of this attitude that Chandler took nearly half a year to write his first story.

Raymond Chandler may have acquired anti-intellectual views of his own since leaving London, but now he had to put that philosophy into practice. In order to be published, and earn money, he had first and foremost to tell a good story. Any literary embellishments that he managed to get past Shaw's blue pencil were a bonus. Even so, as the opening paragraph of his first story demonstrated, Chandler was not going to give up these bonuses without a struggle:

> The man in the powder-blue suit – which wasn't powder blue under the lights of the Club Bolivar – was tall, with wide-set grey eyes, a thin nose, a jaw of stone. He had a rather sensitive mouth. His hair was crisp and black, ever so faintly touched with grey, as by an almost diffident hand. His clothes fitted him as though they had a soul of their own, not just a doubtful past. His name happened to be Mallory.

'Blackmailers Don't Shoot' – 'a goddamn pose' Chandler would call it later – has an almost completely indecipherable plot. It is possible to read the story half a dozen times without understanding what has taken place. This was partly arrogance on Chandler's part – his refusal to map out plots was largely because he considered them superfluous to the new realistic spirit of detective fiction. He believed that English-style twist-in-the-tale mystery stories were anathema to decent writing, because 'to get the surprise murderer you fake character. . . . If people want to play that game, it's alright by me. But for Christ's sake let's not talk about honest mysteries. They don't exist.'

Chandler wanted to create strong, melodramatic characters at the expense of ingenious plots. In trying to achieve this in 'Blackmailers Don't Shoot', however, he fell between two stools. The plot proved to be a mess, and he was not yet sufficiently good a writer to create characters convincing enough to compensate for this. The story concerns a Hollywood starlet called Rhonda Starr who is being blackmailed, and Mallory, a Chicago private investigator who is brought in to sort things out. There are nine characters in the story and seven of them are killed, while every character is double-crossed or beaten up at least once. In the end,

Mallory and Rhonda Starr are the only characters left alive, and the story closes with the starlet explaining to the detective that the blackmail had been a scam to get publicity.

The story would be less confusing if the detective were the narrator, but 'Blackmailers Don't Shoot' is written in the third person. Chandler would experiment with different types of narrative in his *Black Mask* stories before finally settling for the 'I' that would become his trademark. Even the recurring 'powder-blue suit' of the first paragraph of 'Blackmailers Don't Shoot' would fit better by the time he came to reuse it, five years later, in the opening of his first full-length book, *The Big Sleep*:

> It was about eleven o'clock in the morning, mid-October, with the sun not shining and a look of hard wet rain in the clearness of the foothills. I was wearing my powder-blue suit, with dark blue shirt, tie and display handkerchief, black brogues, black wool socks and dark blue clocks on top of them. I was neat, clean shaven and sober, and I didn't care who knew it. I was everything the well-dressed private detective ought to be. I was calling on four million dollars.[15]

*

While Chandler started work on his second *Black Mask* story in 1933, he and Cissy continued to exhaust his savings. The $180 he received from Shaw for *Blackmailers* was a nominal amount for five months' work, even during the Depression. Chandler, who had been earning almost $3,000 a month before he left Dabney's, hated not having money and felt no sense of dignified poverty about his situation. He disagreed entirely with the idea that struggling writers were more creative the closer they were to the breadline. He and Cissy were almost on that now, and he hated it. He kept a passage in his notebook from a book he had read called *South Wind,* by Norman Douglas, which echoed his own views at this time on the supposed artistic 'purity' of poverty:

> A poor man is always denying himself this or that. One by one his humane instincts, his elegant desires, are starved always by the stress of circumstance. The charming diversity of life ceases to have any meaning for him. To console himself he sets up perverse canons of right and wrong. What the rich do, that is wrong. Why? Because he does not do it. Why not? Because he has no money. A poor man

(and a pure one) is forced into a hypercritical attitude towards life, debarred from being intellectually honest. He cannot pay for the necessary experience.[16]

Chandler insisted that he once went for five days on a single bowl of soup. 'I never slept in the park,' he said, 'but I came damn close to it . . . it didn't kill me, but neither did it increase my love of humanity.' Self-deprivation was almost natural to a man who had just painfully forced himself out of a drink addiction. There was, however, the guilt of not being able to look after Cissy properly, as well as the guilt of having brought such a situation upon himself. Cissy's patience with, and continued love for Chandler over this time won his eternal respect. Living as reclusively as they did in their Santa Monica apartment, the two of them became inseparable and fell back in love again. He wrote her a poem in October 1935, called 'Improvisation for Cissy':

You who have given me the night and the morning,
(What have I given you?)
Lean years slinking by at the edge of the dusk,
Gaunt with memories, hollow with old pain. . . .

This is what love is, this is what love is.
When love is this, how can there be despair?[17]

Resolute in his new vocation, Chandler did not consider seeking regular employment once the Depression began to ease up in 1934. He continued writing, and his stories got better and better. Eight months after the publication of 'Blackmailers Don't Shoot' came 'Smart Aleck Kill', featuring a private detective called Johnny Dalmas and a lot of gratuitous gunplay:

He slipped the magazine out and ejected the shell that was in the breech, picked it up, and pressed it into the magazine. He forked two fingers of his left hand over the barrel, held the cocking piece back, twisted the breech block, and broke the gun apart. He took the butt piece over to the window.

The number that was duplicated on the inside of the stock had not been filed off.[18]

Even in this, Chandler's second story, the distinct style of his later books was already coming more sharply into focus. *Black Mask* readers thought they wanted action, Chandler decided, but the things that really hooked them was not that a man got killed, 'but that in the moment of death he was trying to pick up a paper clip off the polished surface of a desk'.[19] They also wanted wit and, in 'Smart Aleck Kill', Chandler's own dry humour was starting to come through. There is the doorman at Carli's nightclub who had 'given up trying to look as if it mattered who came in'. In another club, a drunkard greets Johnny Dalmas from the foyer: 'Everybody's here but the Pope's tomcat – and he's expected.' The story also finishes with what would become another Chandler trademark; the downbeat ending. Dalmas has only solved the case after annoying almost every police officer in Los Angeles. By the end he is forgiven, and sits down with Captain Cathcart for a drink: 'What'll we drink to?' asks the Captain. 'Let's just drink,' says Dalmas.

In October 1934, Chandler's third – and his first memorable – story was published. Called 'Finger Man' and written in the first person, the story marked Chandler's break. He had held his own in the two earlier stories, but now he was starting to do something really different, and with confidence.[20] 'Finger Man' starts with one of Chandler's downbeat openings: 'It was a good crowd for a Tuesday but nobody was dancing.' The characters are less stilted and two-dimensional than previously, notably the story's heroine, Miss Glenn, who 'was something more than pretty and something less than beautiful'. Chandler's imagery was also getting punchier. A promise made by one character is described as being 'thinner than the gold on a week-end wedding ring'. By relaxing his pace, and using a first-person narrative, Chandler was finding his rhythm:

> I mixed myself a drink, swallowed half of it and began to feel it too much. I put my hat on, changed my mind about the other half of my drink, went down to my car.[21]

Before deciding to step up his rate of writing stories, so as to earn something approaching a living wage, Chandler continued to submit only two titles a year to Shaw. Despite this, or more probably because of it, he enjoyed quick promotion in the course of 1934 and 1935 within *Black Mask*'s pecking order. Each issue would feature five or six stories, one of which would be illustrated on the magazine's garish cover. Shaw was so impressed by Chandler that he was giving his detectives star billing from 'Finger Man' onwards – the arrival of a new Chandler story was becoming a selling point for Shaw's Madison Avenue office.

As the stories went on, distinct characters emerged in Chandler's writing. Some, like the Angelino cops Violets M'Gee and Bernie Ohls, reappeared in different stories. In other cases it was a question of recurring types: the rich mobster who invariably looked 'like a bouncer who had come into money'; the tough girl in trouble ('You're down and out and knee deep in nothing, baby'); and the honest guy out of his depth in a tarnished city ('He was a big, handsome brute with eyes like a cow and something innocent and honest in them'). The honest characters in Chandler's stories are almost always heavy drinkers. Another recurring type was the 'two-bit porch climber', a lean criminal failure who tries to pull off a big job on his own, only to find the cops and the hoods after him.

There were other characters who became familiar to early Chandler followers. The hotel night porter who has given up on life; the cigarette girl pretending to be bored with her job as she flirts with the hero; the outsize henchman who relishes every working day; the wisecracking and unshockable cab driver; the vicious quack psychiatrist; the death-wish gigolo; the tired newspaper hack; the drunken widow; the paranoid millionaire; the millionaire's wife; and, always, the bastard cop. They were all exaggerated caricatures culled both from Chandler's experiences in LA and from staple pulp familiars. There was no time in a *Black Mask* story to unravel a character, Chandler decided; they all had to be colourful, instantly recognizable and melodramatic from the start.

Chandler never passed up an irrelevant scene in his pulp stories if it meant the chance to expand on his minor characters. In a 1939 story called 'Trouble Is My Business', for instance, the detective tries to reach someone on the phone. Although the person he speaks to is almost entirely superfluous to the story, we are told that 'the voice that answered was fat. It wheezed softly, like the voice of a man who had just won a pie-eating contest.'[22] In another story, 'Mandarin's Jade', the detective sets out to look for a small-time racketeer called Lou Lid. He starts in a bar that Lid is known to frequent. The bar, like the pie-eater on the telephone, is in the story only as an excuse for Chandler to add atmosphere; it never features again. While most other *Black Mask* contributors were making only cursory and dutiful references to the setting of their tales, Chandler and his early detectives were noticing everything. As he had told Shaw, it was the atmosphere rather than the story that he was interested in:

> The barman was playing the pin game on the house's money and a man stood with a brown hat on the back of his head reading a letter. Prices were scrawled in white on the mirror back of the bar.
>
> The bar was just a plain, heavy wooden counter, and at each end of it hung a frontier .44 in a flimsy cheap holster no gunfighter would ever have worn. There were printed cards on the walls, about not asking for credit and what to take for a hangover and a liquor breath, and there were some nice legs in photographs.
>
> The place didn't even look as if it paid expenses.
>
> The barkeep left the pin game and went behind the bar. He was fiftyish, sour. The bottoms of his trousers were frayed and he moved as if he had corns. The man on the stool kept right on chuckling over his letter, which was written in green ink on pink paper.
>
> The barkeep put both his blotched hands on the bar and looked at me with the expression of a dead-pan comedian, and I said 'Beer'.[23]

*

The pulp magazine stories that Chandler wrote during the 1930s – twenty-one in all – would invariably start, or end up, in Los Angeles. One reason for the popularity of tough American crime stories was the rise in hard-boiled crime itself, and this was certainly true in Southern California. Adventure stories, westerns and tales of the occult no longer seemed quite so exciting when, on a daily basis, local newspapers were full of real-life dramas involving larger-than-life characters. Chandler had considered writing westerns – many *Black Mask* writers moonlighted under pseudonyms for western pulps – but decided against them: 'I guess the trouble with Westerns as a species,' he said, 'is a kind of appalling solemnity about such elementary things.'[24]

Nor did polite murder stories have much relevance any longer to a public which had become fascinated by the fast, ruthless growth of Italian and Irish mobs, as well as by the heavy press coverage given to motiveless killings. The likes of Hercule Poirot, whom Agatha Christie had first introduced in 1920, could hope for little purchase on the imagination of city-living Americans in the Depression. As Chandler would later put it, 'It's not that kind of story . . . it's not lithe and clever. It's just dark and full of blood.'[25] The Hollywood movie industry, in these early years before tightened censorship, seemed to agree. The director Howard Hawks's portrayal of Al Capone in his 1932 film *Scarface* had capped a string of popular, tough gangster pictures made in the early 1930s.

In their coverage of crime, Californian newspapers revelled in the explicit. Photographs of mutilated homicide victims were as commonplace as pictures of the detectives leading celebrated cases. In Los Angeles, incumbent District Attorneys enjoyed more press inches than most movie stars, and no detail of the crimes they came up against was too minute for examination by the press. At one point, Chandler began to wonder whether even hard-boiled murder stories were not going to seem 'a bit on the insignificant side' for the Angelino reader, considering the publicity given to real-life urban homicide.

This publicity was especially weighty in cases where the police themselves were put on trial. In 1937, a Los Angeles private detective called Henry Raymond was badly injured by a car bomb. He had been preparing to go into court to give evidence proving that one of the Mayor's aides had received money from two mobsters during the mayoral campaign of 1933. Raymond had been hired by a local watchdog group known as CIVIC, the Citizens' Independent Vice Investigating Committee. It was subsequently revealed that the Intelligence Squad of the LA Police Department had been keeping him under twenty-four-hour surveillance, as well as other journalists and politicians critical of the Mayor or the LAPD. A Greek vegetable dealer who lived next door to the private detective identified a member of the Intelligence Squad as having been in Raymond's garden the night before the bombing. The officer and his lieutenant were convicted and sent to

St Quentin jail, and Mayor Shaw was voted out of office the following year.

Another sensational crime – and one that took place only a mile away from where, in Santa Monica, Chandler was writing his *Black Mask* stories – was the unsolved murder of film star Thelma Todd. In December 1935, Todd was found dead in her car near her Pacific Coast Highway house. Her corpse was still dressed in 'a mauve and silver evening gown and a $20,000 mink coat; her neck and wrist were covered with jewels'[26] – all of which seemed to rule out robbery as a motive for the killing. Public interest in the case prompted a huge police inquiry. Todd was initially deemed to have died of poisoning, but then the wife of Wallace Ford, another Hollywood actor, came forward claiming she had spoken to Todd twelve hours after she was supposed to have been killed. Rumours of blackmail and further Hollywood intrigue abounded, though the case remained unsolved.

Another front-page story of the time was that of a Santa Monica doctor called George Dayley, who was tried for the murder of his wife five years after she had been reported as having committed suicide. The prosecution claimed that Dayley had drugged his wife in 1935 and then carried her into the garage, starting the car's engine so that she died from exhaust fumes. Witnesses testified to having heard Dayley brag that he had committed the perfect murder, but no evidence was found and he was acquitted. Chandler, who was living in Santa Monica when the case reopened, would later use the story in the sub-plot to one of his novels.[27]

The LA press pandered to a glorified new breed of cops and robbers in the 1930s. Picture editors used shots of mobsters in their best suits, and reporters noted each courtroom wisecrack. It was not difficult to create flamboyant fictional criminals when known hoods like Bugsy Siegel were regularly mixing with Hollywood's glitterati, and when the mobsters themselves seemed so intent on celebrity. The same was true of the cops: Police Chief James Edgar Davis never missed an opportunity to steal the limelight, until his sacking in 1938 after the Henry Raymond bombing. Joe Domanick, historian of the LA Police Department, confirms this:

James Davis loved being chief. He loved the respect. He loved the authority. He loved playing the role and the women it gave him. He loved greeting VIPs. He loved the spit and polish and the way the Mexican federales would send their generals up to Los Angeles to observe *his* troops.[28]

Davis's obsession with the limelight included police shooting demonstrations, open to the public, at which he would snuff out candles with a well-aimed bullet. (As both Davis and the policeman who set up these demonstrations apparently knew, any bullet passing within a foot of the flame would create enough tailwind to blow out the candle.) The Police Chief would entertain important Angelinos in the beautifully landscaped grounds of LAPD headquarters:

> Each week came different faces who were otherwise interchangeable: rich downtown businessmen who ran the city, their power-broking attorneys, well-connected real estate speculators, small-time entrepreneurs, film-industry executives and movie stars as famous as little Shirley Temple and Freddie Bartholomew. Anyone who James Davis thought might be even remotely useful to him or to the department's image was welcome.[29]

The other side to celebrity was, of course, notoriety; and the history of the LAPD during the 1930s only gives weight to Chandler's crooked fictional cops. In 1937, a federal grand jury investigation discovered that no less than 600 brothels and 18,000 unlicensed bars were operating under the noses of LAPD officers. It also confirmed in its report that 'a portion of the underworld profits have been used in financing campaigns of city and county officials in important positions. . . . The District Attorney's office, Sheriff's office, and the Los Angeles Police Department work in complete harmony and never interfere with . . . important figures in the underworld.' This was particularly well illustrated in 1937 by the murder of gambling kingpin Les Bruneman at the order of Bugsy Siegel. Everyone in the press and police knew that Siegel was trying to take control of LA gambling and had ordered the murder, but no attempt was made to prosecute him. Similar protection was provided to police officers who ran into trouble. Following his own scandalous fall from grace, James Edgar Davis was made chief of security at Douglas Aircraft.

Lawlessness in 1930s LA was a fact. Guns were ubiquitous and, following the repeal of the Prohibition laws, organized rackets were moving further into drugs, gambling and prostitution. The Depression had pushed thousands of men on to the streets without any form of welfare payment from the state, many of them prepared to do occasional work for the city's well-run criminal organizations. But the lawlessness was also liable to be exaggerated. Hollywood, the press and local pulp writers were so fascinated by what was happening that they could not help but over-dramatize it. It was both the fact and fiction of the city's criminality that contributed to the atmosphere of intimidation felt by Angelinos during this time; and it was the atmosphere – as much as the rise in crime itself – that made 'noir' such a pertinent and lasting tag for the fiction and movies that would arise out of this period. *The Smell of Fear* was the name Chandler would later give to an anthology of his pulp stories. In an introduction to the book, he put *Black Mask* stories (not just his own) within the context of this permanent edginess:

> Their characters lived in a world gone wrong, a world in which, long before the atom bomb, civilization had created the machinery for its own destruction. . . . The streets were dark with something more than night.[30]

*

The Los Angeles police feature in almost all Chandler's pulp-magazine stories, and can be divided into two types: the overstretched, almost-honest workhorse and the amoral sadist. Neither really refutes Chandler's claim that 'law is where you buy it in this town', and Chandler featured more than one police murderer in his stories. But although his private detectives invariably get more hindrance than help from the police, he would always acknowledge (through his occasional 'good cop' characters) the near-impossible task that faced an honest police officer in LA:

> It's like this with us baby. We're coppers and everybody hates our guts. And as if we didn't have enough trouble, we have to have you. As if we didn't get pushed around enough by the guys in the corner

offices, the City Hall gang, the day chief, the night chief, the chamber of commerce, His Honour the Mayor in his panelled office four times as big as the three lousy rooms the whole homicide staff has to work out of. As if we didn't have to handle one hundred and fourteen homicides last year out of three rooms that don't have enough chairs for the whole duty squad to sit down at once. We spend our lives turning over dirty underwear and sniffing rotten teeth. We go up dark stairways to get a gun punk with a skinful of hop and sometimes we don't get all the way up, and our wives wait till dinner that night and all other nights. We don't come home anymore. And nights we do come home, we come home so goddam tired we can't eat or sleep or even read the lies the papers print about us. So we lie awake in the dark on a cheap street and listen to the drunks down the block having fun. And just about the time we drop off the phone rings and we get up and start all over again.[31]

Chandler often qualified the criticisms that were starting to seep into his depiction of contemporary Los Angeles. He was writing from the start about real streets in an actual city, so his own opinions about the running of his home town were bound to appear in the crime stories he wrote. He thought the LA police to be riddled with corruption, but he had a loathing far deeper for the hypocrites who criticized the police without admitting how crooked America was. They were usually the same people, he said, who used the prostitutes and patronized the off-shore gambling ships which had made the mobs so rich in the first place. How, he once asked, could people not expect the average policeman to be cynical in a country that could not convict Al Capone?

*

While achieving growing recognition and earning larger fees – though still never more than $350 – for his *Black Mask* stories, Chandler continued to live in low-rent Santa Monica. Even writing five stories a year, as he did in 1936, only earned him $1,500. In contrast to the grandeur of nearby Beverly Hills, Santa Monica contained thousands of small wooden houses on near-identical streets that were spread either side of Pico Boulevard. At its commercial centre were apartment blocks, and it was here that Cissy and Chandler lived. In the 1930s it was still a mostly white area renowned for its low-to-middle income conservatism; white, reactionary, safe and gossipy. Chandler, mindful of the fact that living there at all was a daily reminder of the humiliating state of his finances, detested it from the start.

In particular, he loathed the way that Santa Monica prided itself on being a community of Old American values, while allowing gambling ships to operate visibly off its beaches. He was convinced that the town was only as quiet as it was because the entire police force was in the pocket of mobsters. He once considered writing a non-fictional exposé of Santa Monica, after being encouraged to do so by a magazine editor who had read his stories, but instead he settled for repeatedly insulting it in his fiction, under the name 'Bay City':

> The other day I thought of your suggestion for an article of studied insult about the Bay City (Santa Monica) police. A couple of DA's investigators got a tip about a gambling hell in Ocean Park, a sleazy adjunct to Santa Monica. They went down there and picked up a couple of Santa Monica cops on the way, telling them they were going to kick in a box, but not telling them where it was. The cops went along with the natural reluctance of good cops to enforce the law against a paying customer, and when they found out where the place was, they mumbled brokenly: 'We ought to talk to Captain Brown about this before we do it, boys, Captain Brown ain't going to like this.' The DA's men urged them heartlessly forward into the chip and bone parlour, several alleged gamblers were tossed in the sleezer and the equipment seized for evidence (a truckload of it) was stored in lockers at local police headquarters. When the DA's boys came back next morning to go over it everything had disappeared but a few handfuls of white poker chips. . . . Nothing will come of it. Nothing ever does. Do you wonder I love Bay City?[32]

Chandler hated Santa Monica's law-abiding image far more than the open vices of downtown LA. Many of its blue- and white-collar inhabitants were subscribers to 'good-citizen' movements like Moral Rearmament. Originally called the Oxford Group, this was an international movement for spiritual and moral renewal. Chandler considered such associations pompous and hypocritical. 'If Bay City is a sample of how it works,' he once said of Moral Rearmament, 'I'll take aspirin.'

His criticism of Santa Monica was not based on the sort of

research that could ever have legitimized a non-fictional exposé. It was suspicion confirmed by anecdote, aggravated by a gut resentment at having to live there in the first place. Chandler would always be cavalier about research. He said that he agreed with Robert Louis Stevenson; namely, that as far as writing about the world was concerned, 'experience is largely a matter of intuition'. And it seemed to work for him. 'It is quite extraordinary to me', he once boasted, 'how many letters I have received from police officers and former police officers of all kinds. One man, 28 years in the LAP force, offered to identify every police character I ever used in a story.'[33]

But Chandler had a magpie eye for detail. He was fascinated by the way other people did things – like the look on someone's face when they were writing their own name, or the way someone played with a glass. He knew he was good at it, and would sometimes show off, remarking, for instance, on a tie someone had worn two months previously. 'His eyes', wrote a journalist years later, 'seem to miss nothing.' This talent was something Chandler appreciated in other writers. He read C. S. Forester's Hornblower novels, and found that what he liked most was 'the detail of the handling of the ships, the manoeuvres for battle and all that sort of thing [which] seems to me quite fascinating and wonderfully exact'. Similarly, while he was writing stories for *Black Mask,* he cut out the following satire of a Beverly Hills delicatessen which he found in the *LA Times* on 4 October 1936:

Sugarless jam and jellies and vintage marmalade from Oxford; honeys from Greece, Smyrna, Portugal, Syria and the Ionian Islands; turtle soup from the Caribbean and marrons glacés from France; escargots, neatly tinned from the same country; goose liver in port wine from Strasbourg; Bar-le-Duc currant jelly . . . Norwegian trout in jelly; caviar kept at 28 degrees ever since it was torn from the mother sturgeon in Russia; bird's nest and shark's fin soups from China; also fried rice birds in tins from China; poppadums from India, made of meal, that, when dropped into hot butter, curl into fancy shapes; from Turkey preserves of bergamot blossoms and rose petals; yerba maté from South America with a gourd and bombilla to sip it through.[34]

Together with his love of similes, Chandler's own curiosity in detail became more and more pronounced as his pulp stories continued. Observation was central to his writing, as the opening of his story 'Smart Aleck Kill' had shown:

> It was raining outside the Delmar Club. The liveried doorman helped Hugo Candless on with his belted white raincoat and went out for his car. When he had it in front of the canopy he held an umbrella over Hugo across the strip of wooden matting to the kerb. The car was a royal blue Lincoln limousine, with buff striping. The licence number was 5A6.[35]

Though it was serving him well in his writing, this permanent scrutiny of his surroundings was not always an advantage for Chandler as a person. It was a heightened form of self-consciousness that made it very hard for him to relax or accept anything at face value. It was a sort of purgatory; the inability to switch off unless comatose with drink, which was an option that he was trying not to consider any more.[36] Relentless observation was of course the quality needed by a private detective, even a fictional one, in order to survive and profit. If Chandler could not help spending so much of his energy spotting the minutiae of phoney components that lay behind modern California, then it at least served his detective characters well. His heroes were trained to see the 'neon slum' beneath the bright lights of LA. That was their job, just as it was their author's obsession.

The Los Angeles that began to emerge from these early stories was one where all institutions were to be instinctively distrusted, all witness accounts doubted, and everything straightforward ignored. In the majority of Chandler tales, the story told to the detective by the person who hires him turns out to be deceitful. Equally, there are no easy denouements in Chandler's *Black Mask* stories – the identity of the murderer often seems the least baffling of questions raised in the course of a story's events. Ultimately, the only person the detective can trust to be telling the truth is himself, and without any reliable facts he can usually only work with his impressions.

In this, Chandler differed from other *Black Mask* writers, including Hammett and especially Gardner, who had both continued to work within relatively neat 'good guy/bad guy' parameters. However hard-boiled their style, they were still using the traditional mystery formula of disguised premeditation rather than impulse. Chandler rejected this from the start:

> The boys with their feet on the desk know that the easiest murder case in the world to break is the one somebody tries to get cute with; the one that really bothers them is the murder somebody only thought of two minutes before he pulled the trigger.[37]

One of Chandler's favourite ways of distancing his early stories from the join-the-dots tradition of mystery writing was his use of the offbeat ending. These he employed to puncture the clichéd climax of having to reveal 'whodunit', which every *Black Mask* story was still duty bound to deliver. This is illustrated by comparing the ending of a *Black Mask* story Chandler wrote in 1937, 'Red Wind', with one by Hammett from 1924 called 'The Golden Horseshoe'. In the former, the detective ends the story at the edge of the Pacific, throwing fake pearls into the water. The last line reads: 'They made little splashes and the seagulls rose off the water and swooped at the splashes.' This was something altogether new for *Black Mask*. Chandler was not simply being pretty (the same story contains the line 'I'm going to vomit if you don't take the gun out of my throat'); he was merely trying to give the story some resonance beyond the fictional mystery just solved – he did not want people to be reading his story in order to know who had killed whom to win the pearls. The latter, however, is pretty much what Hammett was still catering for in 'The Golden Horseshoe', a story that ends with the following wrap-up:

> I can't put you up for the murders you engineered in San Francisco; but I can sock you with the one you didn't do in Seattle – so justice won't be cheated. You're going to Seattle, Ed, to hang for Ashcroft's suicide.
> And he did.[38]

Whatever experiments Chandler was making with detective fiction in *Black Mask*, he also had to continue to provide the staple ingredients of hard-boiled writing, which he listed as 'brutality, sadism, sex and blood'. And for all his efforts at redeeming something significant from crime fiction, he never had too many problems filling this quota. A typical story in this respect was 'The King in Yellow', published in 1938. In it, Chandler manages to deliver what pulp readers required of him – sensationalism – while also stamping his own identity on the story through the language he uses. Though the bare plot could have come from any other pulp crime writer, the style in which it is told is already distinctly Chandler's.

The story concerns a hotel detective, Steve Grayce, and his hunt for the murderer of a black jazz trombonist called King Leopardi. It opens with Leopardi making a disturbance on the eighth floor of the low-rent hotel in which the detective works. Grayce, who actually likes Leopardi's music, goes up to stop the noise: 'Put that bazooka down big stuff.' The trombonist, who is in his room with two floozies, ignores the order and Grayce is forced to square up: 'If you want trouble, I come from where they make it.' The two of them have a fight, the details of which Chandler shares explicitly with the reader. The fight ends when Leopardi has finally sagged 'blindly to his knees and vomited'.

Inexplicably, Grayce is sacked by the hotel after this incident and angrily senses something crooked. He goes to an apartment address he has seen scribbled down in Leopardi's room. There he finds a dead girl whose condition Chandler details: 'Garters and skin showed at the top of her stockings, and a blue rose on something pink. She wore a square-necked, short-sleeved dress that was not too clean. Her neck above the dress was blotched with purple bruises.' Grayce questions the Italian who runs the apartment building, but he too is killed, shot when he momentarily leaves Grayce to answer another query. The detective then goes to the club where Leopardi is playing and has another fight with him, this time coming off the worse of the two: 'Blood oozed from Steve's lip and crawled down the line at the corner of his mouth and glistened on his chin.'

Grayce is helped out by a stunning nightclub singer, whose hair is 'the colour of brush fire seen through a dust cloud'. Later that night, she rings Grayce and asks him to come over to her house. He is met at the door by a black maid in 'short skirts, sheer silk stockings, and four-inch spike heels'. Leopardi is dead in the house and the singer does not know how he got there. Grayce suspects the maid – who has returned home – and drives to her house, finding her also dead, strangled, in a car. Again the reader gets the X-rated detail for which pulp stories at the time were notorious: 'In the reflected moonlight her mouth was strained open. Her tongue stuck out. And her chestnut eyes stared at the roof of the car.'

The end of the story is typically rushed; once more Chandler was not as interested in plot as the atmosphere in which the plot takes place. Grayce returns to the hotel where he used to work and asks an old colleague there to find out whether Leopardi had ever stayed at the hotel before. He had, two years previously, and one of his floozies had killed herself on that occasion – the hotel's last suicide case. Grayce now remembers the incident and, acting on a hunch, drives up to the mountains outside LA, where his former boss at the hotel is holed up with his brother. They admit all – it was their younger sister who had killed herself two years earlier, driven to suicide by Leopardi, and they have now taken their revenge. The brother is shot by Grayce, who then gives his old boss an hour to escape in return for a full written confession. The culprit writes the confession and then drives his car off a cliff. The convoluted but entertaining story ends with Grayce reaching the scene of the crash: 'Eight hundred feet below, what was left of a grey sedan lay silent and crumpled in the morning sunshine.'

Although gratuitously gory, 'The King in Yellow' shows how Chandler managed to fulfil his pulp duties as a sensationalist while also achieving something more lasting. Pulp eroticism and violence sit next to original wordplay and dialogue – a blueprint for all his crime stories. Moreover, Chandler was no longer writing just for *Black Mask*. There was now a rival publication – which paid better – called *Dime Detective Magazine,* whose launch had been prompted by *Black Mask*'s success, and he had begun to write for it after Shaw's resignation from *Black Mask* in 1936. All this was serving to ease the financial strain on Chandler and Cissy by the end of the 1930s, but he was still not producing stories quickly enough ever to reach the million words a year that a pulp writer needed to turn out in order to achieve a decent income. *Dime Detective* paid Chandler $400 per story, but that was not enough to enable him and Cissy to move out of the Santa Monica apartment.

The break came in 1938, when a New York literary agent called Sydney Sanders showed some of Chandler's pulp stories to the publisher Alfred Knopf. Knopf was impressed, and told Chandler that he would be interested in seeing a novel.

Now that he was aged fifty, Chandler's luck seemed to be changing again. He had salvaged his life from the point of disintegration at which it had been when he was sacked by Joseph Dabney, and had brought it to a point of anticipation. In 1932 he had been a man bitter with the world, guilty about his treatment of Cissy, and desperate to recover his self-esteem through writing. He had promptly become the best pulp writer in America. But he had done so at a cost: for five years he and Cissy had cut themselves off from the world while he wrote, and this seclusion had hurt him. His complexion had paled, he suffered from rheumatism in his right arm, and he had become almost totally reclusive. 'Most writers,' he later said, 'sacrifice too much humanity for too little art.' It was now time for Chandler to resolve, with his first novel, whether his own sacrifice had been worth while.

4

Philip Marlowe

'You're Marlowe?'
I nodded.
'I'm a little disappointed,' he said, 'I rather expected
something with dirty finger nails.'
'Come inside,' I said, 'and you can be witty sitting
down.'

(*The High Window*, August 1942)

The Big Sleep was written in Chandler's Santa Monica apartment
over the summer of 1938. The setting was again Los Angeles and
the framework of the story was a collage of his best *Black Mask*
plots. It was the book's hero, Philip Marlowe, which distinguished
it from anything Chandler had previously written. Named after
Marlowe House at Dulwich College, the novel's narrator and hero
was thirty years old and single: 'I'm unmarried because I don't like
policemen's wives.' It was soon obvious that Marlowe was no
ordinary pulp private detective. He played chess by himself, and
often felt paranoid:

> My mind drifted through waves of false memory, in which I seemed
> to do the same thing over and over again, go to the same places,
> meet the same people, say the same words to them, over and over
> again, and yet each time it seemed real, like something actually
> happening, and for the first time.[1]

But nor was Marlowe too vulnerable. He was a well-dressed and
streetwise hero who, despite his intelligence, was still a man's man:
'I went out to the kitchen and drank two cups of black coffee . . .

You can have a hangover from other things than alcohol. I had one from women. Women made me sick.' It was this boorish quality that lent credibility to the character's self-conscious flourishes. If Marlowe was an idealist, said Chandler later, 'he hates to admit it, even to himself'. He confronts physical danger, 'since he thinks that is what he was created for'. Here was a tough, independent character with an acute and almost constant sense of life's absurdity. He was also driven, on the surface at least, by a traditional pulp-detective morality:

> The place was horrible by daylight. The Chinese junk on the walls, the rug, the fussy lamps, the teakwood stuff, the sticky riot of colours, the totem pole, the flagon of ether and laudanum – all this in the daytime had a stealthy nastiness, like a fag party.[2]

At the start of *The Big Sleep,* Marlowe is called to the downtown mansion of the invalid General Sternwood. The General's two spoilt daughters have fallen in with a gang of highlife racketeers. While the elder one, Vivian, has been running up gambling debts, Carmen, the younger, is hooked on opium. Carmen has also been posing naked for photographs, negatives of which the gangsters are offering to return to the General for money.[3] Sternwood tells Marlowe that he is too old to protect his daughters; nor is he prepared to pay off such crooks. He does not know who they are, but he wants Marlowe to smash them. He also tells Marlowe that Vivian's Irish husband Sean Regan (of whom the General was very fond) has disappeared, though he refuses to believe that Regan is involved with the extortion attempt.

Marlowe rummages through criminal LA, buying information and being pistol-whipped as he goes. He discovers the man behind the Sternwood scam to be an LA casino owner called Eddie Mars, who seems to have a hold on the sisters, and enough gunmen around him to stop Marlowe getting close enough to find out what that hold is. The gambling debts are settled and the pornographic negatives destroyed by Marlowe, but the consequence seems to be that Mars's control over the girls grows even stronger. Vivian and Carmen themselves are busy either drunkenly trying to seduce Marlowe, or to feed him false clues, but their father – by now on his deathbed – urges the detective to persevere. Marlowe is unsure how to proceed. He continues to get knocked about and shot at, without much idea as to what he is supposed to be looking for any more. It seems that Sean Regan is involved somehow, but the detective cannot find him. When he finally works out the bond between Eddie Mars and the Sternwood girls, Marlowe is glad that the General is too ill to understand: on one of her opiate binges (before the start of the book) Carmen had shot Regan, who had refused to sleep with her. Eddie Mars helped the sisters hide the body and any traces of the man or the killing. In return, Mars is now blackmailing both of them.

In writing novel-length fiction, Chandler had found himself free to experiment with crime writing in ways he had been unable to do in the pulps. Though the violence and the stock characters are still present, he was able to reduce the mystery element of his story in order to concentrate on atmosphere and character. The last page of *The Big Sleep* is less about the discovery of a villain than it is about Philip Marlowe himself:

> What did it matter where you lay once you were dead? In a dirty sump or in a marble tower on top of a high hill? You were dead, you were sleeping the big sleep. . . . On the way downtown I stopped at a bar and had a couple of double scotches. They didn't do me any good.

To end a murder story questioning the significance of death was a new departure for a crime writer. The book had not been about who had done what, so much as what Marlowe had made of it all. ('What the hell happened', Chandler said, 'rather than whodunit.') The suspense was still there, but it was there as atmosphere rather than in hidden clues. Not even Hammett had risked going this far with his detectives; nor had Hammett developed the vision of crime fiction that Chandler was now developing. For him, detective stories should be about the detective first and the story second:

> Down these mean streets a man must go who is not himself mean, who is neither tarnished nor afraid. The detective in this kind of story must be such a man. He is the hero, he is everything. He must be a complete man and a common man and yet an unusual man. He is a lonely man and his pride is that you will treat him as a proud

man or be very sorry you ever saw him. . . . If there were enough like him, I think the world would be a very safe place to live in, and yet not too dull to be worth living in.[4]

In Philip Marlowe, Chandler had created a combination of his own character and the traditional pulp hero. On the surface, Marlowe was as lonely, unsociable and self-persecuting as was Chandler, but beneath that lay a sense of honour and of humour, as well as sensitivity. By writing in the first person, Chandler could show that it was the world and not innate bitterness that had made Marlowe a loner and an alcoholic (which he is, in all but name). The character of Philip Marlowe was therefore a way in which Chandler might explain his own eccentric reclusivity.

Mindful of not being too self-indulgent with his hero, however, he had also made Marlowe his own man. Whatever the similarities between Marlowe's and Chandler's outlook on life, several details of their lives were different. The writer once explained his hero's imaginary history. Marlowe had, he said, been born in Santa Rosa, fifty miles north of San Francisco. He had spent two years at college in Oregon and then gone to work as an investigator for an insurance company. This had been followed by a stint as a detective for LA's District Attorney. At 'slightly over six foot' he was a little taller than Chandler, at thirty younger, and unlike his creator (who smoked a Dunhill pipe), Marlowe generally smoked cigarettes: preferably Camel, but 'almost any sort of cigarette will satisfy him'.

The same imaginary biography, nevertheless, also revealed plenty of links between the two men. Like Chandler, Marlowe never spoke of his parents, 'and apparently he has no living relatives'. As to why the detective had ended up living in Los Angeles, Chandler said that he had no answer to that, 'except that eventually most people do'. Like Chandler, Marlowe first became self-employed after being fired: 'The circumstances in which he lost that job are well known to me but I cannot be very specific about them.' Chandler also confirmed that his hero 'will drink practically anything that is not sweet'.

If it was the Raymond Chandler side of Philip Marlowe that made the detective so much more three-dimensional than other pulp heroes, then it was equally Marlowe who brought out the best in Chandler. Chandler had never achieved anything of creative note until he began writing hard-boiled detective stories. The genre helped him to focus the too-clever jumble of his poems and, increasingly, his correspondence. *Black Mask* had drummed the self-indulgence out of his writing, so that by the time he came to start his first novel he had decided that the role of a novelist was 'to outwrite the reader without outthinking him'. Philip Marlowe was the middle ground between Chandler the self-indulgent English poet and Chandler the production-line American pulp writer. Each, on the evidence of *The Big Sleep*, seemed ideally capable of curbing the clichés and excesses of the other.

Chandler considered the book to be such a departure from his earlier work that he felt no qualms about adapting material from his old pulp stories. The outcome of *The Big Sleep*, therefore, would not have been surprising to anyone who had read his story 'The Curtain' in the September 1936 issue of *Black Mask*. The pornography racket sub-plot of *The Big Sleep* was similarly lifted from 'Killer in the Rain', a story published in *Black Mask* in 1935. Equally, many of the fight scenes in *The Big Sleep* had been pulled almost verbatim from earlier *Black Mask* efforts. The following two passages illustrate this; the first is from 'Killer in the Rain', the second from *The Big Sleep*:

> The blonde took her teeth at my hand and spat my own blood at me. Then she threw herself at my leg and tried to bite that. I cracked her lightly on the head with the barrel of the gun and tried to stand up. She rolled down my legs and wrapped her arms around my ankles. I fell back on the davenport again. The girl was strong with the madness of fear.[5]

> The blonde spat at me and threw herself on my leg and tried to bite that. I cracked her on the head with the gun, not very hard, and tried to stand up. She rolled down my legs and wrapped her arms around them. I fell back on the davenport. The blonde was strong with the madness of love or fear, or a mixture of both, or maybe she was just strong.[6]

Chandler felt justified in this process of 'cannibalization' (as he called it), and did not care that it could spoil the mystery element for some readers. With the space that the novel form allowed him, he believed that he was rewriting disposable stories into enduring fiction.[7] This change in his writing was most obvious in the novel's wit. Like other pulp writers, Chandler had used one-liners in *Black Mask* as a matter of course; wisecracks had, by the 1930s, become a central part of the private detective genre. But in a *Black Mask* story there had always been too much action to describe in too little space for Chandler ever to exploit fully his acute eye for the absurd. The greater wit of *The Big Sleep* followed as a result of its greater length. Examples of this use of 'space' were the extended passages of dialogue – often incidental to the plot – which Chandler could now get away with. Although Marlowe was invariably at the centre of such wisecracking, his creator had been conscious that he must not make his hero too self-indulgent. When his novels later came to be adapted for radio, Chandler sent the show's producers a letter in which he explained this:

> Don't have Marlowe say things merely to score off the other characters. When he comes out with a smart wise-crack it should be jerked out of him emotionally, so that he is discharging an emotion and not even thinking about laying anyone out with a sharp retort. . . . There should not be any effect of gloating. . . . Too many first person characters give an offensively cocky impression. That's bad. To avoid that you must not always give him the punchline or the exit line. Not even often.[8]

Chandler had applied this well to *The Big Sleep*.[9] Villains in the book, like the mobster Eddie Mars, may be defeated by Marlowe in the end – but they can all hold their own against his taunts:

> 'Just who the hell are you, soldier?'
> 'Marlowe is the name. I'm a sleuth.'
> 'Never heard of you. Who's the girl?'
> 'Client. Geiger was trying to throw a loop on her with some blackmail. We came to talk it over. He wasn't here. The door being open we walked in to wait. Or did I tell you that?'
> 'Convenient,' he said. 'The door being open. When you don't have a key.'
> 'Yes. How come you had a key?'
> 'Is that any of your business, soldier?'
> 'I could make it my business.'

He smiled tightly and pushed his hat back on his grey hair. 'And I could make your business mý business.'

'You wouldn't like it. The pay's too small.'

'All right, bright eyes. I own this house. Geiger is my tenant. Now what do you think of that?'

'You know such lovely people.'

'I take them as they come. They come all sorts.'[10]

Good as Chandler had proved himself to be in *The Big Sleep* with this type of scene, he had really distinguished himself from his pulp contemporaries (including his own earlier fiction) with the novel's linking scenes, in which nothing of note happens. As has been said, his habit of typing on small sheets of paper (which could hold only a dozen or so lines) meant that each scene, regardless of subject, had to contain a 'bit of magic'. In *The Big Sleep*, each scene was self-contained, and of interest in itself. At the cost of overall fluidity, Chandler had placed an almost cinematic emphasis on strong scenes over a strong structure. Whether Marlowe was waiting for a client to show up, or making coffee, Chandler had given these moments in the detective's day as much attention as he gave to the dramatic showdowns:

It was about ten-thirty when the little yellow sashed Mexican orchestra got tired of playing a low-voiced prettied-up rhumba that nobody was dancing to. The gourd player rubbed his finger tips together as if they were sore and got a cigarette into his mouth almost with the same movement. The other four, with a timed simultaneous stoop, reached under their chairs for glasses from which they sipped, smacking their lips together and flashing their eyes. Tequila, their manner said. It was probably mineral water. The pretence was as wasted as the music. Nobody was looking at them.[11]

*

Having received the typescript of *The Big Sleep* from Chandler in the autumn of 1938, Alfred Knopf took the entire front cover of *Publisher's Weekly* in order to advertise his new signing. He was delighted with the book, and convinced that its appeal would go well beyond the tough-crime market. He had, he believed, found the next 'hard-boiled' star. The advertisement appeared on

Christmas Eve, 1938, and was just three lines long:

In 1929 Dashiell Hammett
In 1934 James M. Cain
In 1939 Raymond Chandler

The comparisons with James M. Cain were inevitable. Cain was the author of *The Postman Always Rings Twice*, which Knopf had published with enormous commercial success five years previously. It had been a brutal but well-written story about a Depression grifter called Frank who finds work at a roadhouse outside LA. The place is owned by a friendly Greek immigrant, but Frank is soon committing adultery with the Greek's wife:

> I hauled off and hit her in the eye as hard as I could. She went down. She was right down there at my feet, her eyes shining, her breasts trembling, drawn up in tight points, and pointing right back at me. She was down there and the breath was roaring in the back of my throat like I was some kind of animal, and my tongue was all swelled up in my mouth, and blood pounding in it.
> 'Yes! Yes, Frank, yes!'
> Next thing I knew, I was down there with her, and we were staring in each other's eyes, and locked in each other's arms, and straining to get closer. Hell could have opened up for me then, and it wouldn't have made any difference. I had to have her, if I hung for it.
> I had her.[12]

The couple decide to murder the Greek for his money, and plan to do so in a way that cannot be detected. After an investigation, however, they are arrested and executed.

Cain had not graduated from the *Black Mask* school. Prior to writing *The Postman Always Rings Twice*, he had trained as a professional musician, and had then been a respected industrial journalist in Baltimore. His only other previous publication had been a non-fictional treatise called *Our Government*, which Knopf had published in 1930. *The Postman Always Rings Twice* had made a tremendous impact on the American public. Even critics hostile to hard-boiled writers (which most still were) had been forced to acknowledge the book's publication and concede that parts of it were excellently written. Despite containing all the values associated with the new hard-boiled American style (sex, violence, short sentences, slang), Cain had produced a novel that possessed resonance. Nevertheless, he had been unable to match the success of the book with subsequent efforts, and Knopf now hoped that Chandler could take over. The publisher also believed that *The Big Sleep* was a good enough novel to establish Chandler's name immediately.

In London, Hamish Hamilton agreed with Knopf and bought British Empire rights to the book. It was to be published on each side of the Atlantic in February (America) and March (Britain) of 1939, and expectation in both publishing houses ran high.

*

Once *The Big Sleep* had gone to the critics, however, a major obstacle to the book's success became apparent. Though Cain had portrayed a sordid world, he had not done so quite as lavishly as had Chandler. Apart from murder, blackmail and crooked cops, *The Big Sleep* featured several alcoholics, a drug-taking psychotic nymphomaniac, a pornography racket, multiple adultery, lavishly described corpses and a homosexual assassin. Though Chandler insisted that all these were realistic, given the coverage of actual events in 1930s Los Angeles, no crime writer – including Gardner, Hammett and Cain – had offered such an explicitly sinful backdrop to their stories. Nor had they treated sin with such casual observation. The violence and debauchery of Cain's writing were meant to shock, but Marlowe seemed to treat such things as commonplace, and even darkly amusing. This feature of *The Big Sleep* was to overshadow its other qualities in the minds of reviewers.

Critics in both Britain and America failed to find *The Big Sleep* worthy of serious consideration. Many newspapers did not review it at all, and those that did rejected it on the grounds of its seediness. 'I have only seen four notices,' Chandler told Knopf in the week following the book's American publication:

> [They] seemed more occupied with the depravity and unpleasant-
> ness of the book than with anything else. In fact the notice from the
> New York Times, which a clipping agency sent me as a come-on,

deflated me pretty thoroughly. I do not want to write 'depraved books'.[13]

The Big Sleep's only favourable review was a short piece in the *Los Angeles Times* on 19 February 1939 which was captioned, 'Young Raymond Chandler out-Cains James Cain in his fast, clipped hard-boiled story of Hollywood racketeers.' (Chandler was actually four years older than Cain, but this had been deliberately played down by Knopf since it was not a selling point for a debut novelist to be fifty.) Even this solitary *LA Times* review failed to commend the book except as a potentially good screenplay. Hollywood, however, was as wary of explicit material as anyone in the late 1930s and showed no interest in buying film rights to the story. The book itself sold 18,000 copies – including British sales – which grossed Chandler only $2,000. Compared to Hammett and Cain, this was negligible. The former's 1932 novel *The Thin Man* had sold 20,000 copies in America in its first three weeks, and MGM had bought the film rights for $21,000.

*

Though for the time being he had to continue writing pulp stories to support himself, Chandler was at least now able to move out of Santa Monica. The money he had earned from *The Big Sleep* meant that he and Cissy could leave the cramped apartment they had been in for the last five years. Their departure did not, however, break the spell of their self-containment, and for the next five years, they lived in a series of coastal towns, LA suburbs and budget Californian holiday resorts. They continued to see almost no one except each other. When they left Santa Monica in 1939, Cissy was approaching seventy and had been badly weakened by her bouts of pneumonia. She had 'not particularly liked' *The Big Sleep*, said Chandler. He was still not drinking, and continued to find other people's company unbearable:

A man who has been an alcoholic and has lived his life in the shadow of an alcoholic father (even if he never saw him) so much so that he was glad he could not have children – they might be tainted – can never rid himself of the contempt for his failings which that ensures, and that sometimes, however wrongly, he transfers to others who do not in any way deserve it.[14]

What is remarkable about the couple's life immediately after Santa Monica is not so much that it was nomadic, as the fact that they managed to live in so many places without once settling long enough to meet anyone. They lived out of suitcases while sustaining the intense seclusion of their lives that they had adopted after Chandler's sacking. In March 1939 – one month after the publication of *The Big Sleep* – Chandler and Cissy were in a small house in Riverside, 'a poor man's town' forty miles east of Los Angeles. By August of that year, they were up in the Californian mountains at Big Bear Lake, two hours north-east of LA, where they rented a cabin. The small lakefront town was a holiday resort with gaudy hotels and resident bands: 'In front of the stage there was a small dance floor, and a few fuzzy-eyed couples were shagging around flat-footed with their mouths open and their eyes full of nothing.'[15] Out of the town, however, were a number of remote and cheap lakeside cabins, which Chandler loved after the claustrophobic heat of Santa Monica:

> I could hear a girl with a throaty voice singing 'The Woodpecker Song'. I drove on past and the music faded and the road got rough and stony. A cabin on the shore slid past me. And there was nothing beyond it but pines and junipers and the shine of the water. I stopped the car out near the tip of the point and walked over to a huge tree fallen with its roots twelve feet in the air. I sat down against it on the bone-dry ground and lit a pipe. It was peaceful and quiet and far away from everything.[16]

While embarking on his second novel, Chandler was still having to write pulp stories. He wrote six in the eighteen months following the publication of *The Big Sleep*, five of which were typical hard-boiled numbers – in none of them was the detective called Philip Marlowe.[17] For these stories, Chandler earned an average of $400 each. The sixth was notably different. 'The Bronze Door' was a fantasy story set in post-Victorian London, and was published in November 1939 in a magazine called *Unknown*. It earned Chandler just $100.

Though set far away (in both time and place) from Los Angeles, it is as autobiographical as anything he wrote during this transitional period in his life, not least because the story's protagonist is much closer to Chandler's own age and situation in 1939 than are any of his detectives. If the adventures of Marlowe and the others were helping Chandler to escape from the humiliating scars of his 1930s alcoholism, the character of 'Mr Sutton-Cornish' suggests that those scars were still very much there. There is scarcely a plot to 'The Bronze Door', besides the hero's dejection, and the author's obviously deep nostalgia for London.

The story begins with the alcoholic Sutton-Cornish being found drunk at home one afternoon by his wife. She decides to leave him and walks out of the house:

> Mr Sutton-Cornish stood . . . swaying a little, looking at his long grey face in the wall mirror.
> 'Take a little stroll,' he whispered. 'You and me. Never was anyone else, was there?'[18]

Cornish carries on drinking: 'He was no longer a perfectly sane man. In his dry solitary, poisoned laughter there was the sound of crumbling walls.' He ends up in a bar, in the company of other afternoon alcoholics, including an annoying, talkative man on leave from a tropical outpost of the British Empire. It is easy to see this minor character as a second cameo of Chandler himself. The talkative man has become an alcoholic loner in the tropics: his Englishness is the only form of self-respect he has managed to sustain, and is all that he wants to talk about. He is proudly wearing his old school tie, which he has always kept by his side like a talisman; indeed, he has preserved it in a tin 'so the centipedes wouldn't eat it'. Cornish does not want to talk, and imagines the pathetic man going back to the tropics where he will 'lie awake in the jungle thinking of London'.

Continuing on his binge, Cornish comes across a shop where he buys a bronze door, which possesses the ability to make anyone who walks through it disappear. His wife eventually walks through it, followed by a policeman, followed by Cornish himself.

*

Chandler was not the only man in America to be turning his

thoughts to London in 1939. In the months following the anti-climactic publication of *The Big Sleep*, the attention of most of the world focused on Europe. Adolf Hitler had invaded and annexed Czechoslovakia in March 1939 and was ambitious to expand further. Britain and France responded by offering Poland – Germany's other vulnerable neighbour – a guarantee against further German aggression. A stand-off ensued over the summer of 1939, and expectation of a second major European conflict rose. Britain and France began their own extensive militarization. 'The effort to keep my mind off the war has reduced me to the mental age of seven,' Chandler told Knopf in August. Finally, in September, Hitler invaded Poland and began a war that was to preoccupy Chandler as much as anyone.

He signed up with the Canadian Army – as he had done in 1917 – but was turned down on 27 September 1939 on the grounds of his age: he was fifty-one. He followed events no less closely, and felt initially confident: 'The English troops are at least equal to the Germans,' he wrote to an ex-*Black Mask* colleague in 1940, 'and the British colonials are far better.'

> As for bombing, it will be bad, but it works both ways. If Hitler uses gas on London, Berlin will be bombed. And the English night bombers are better than the Germans, because the British have made a speciality of night bombing for twenty-five years. And on top of this the English civilian population are the least hysterical in the world. They can take an awful pounding and still keep on planting lobelias. The Germans are fundamentally just as decent as we are and the prospect of fighting endless wars on short rations for nothing but the personal aggrandizement of a nasty little man and his gang of Gestapo is going to look sour to them after a while.[19]

*

The lack of attention that *The Big Sleep* had received from the press was not just stunting to Chandler's early reputation; it was also financially damaging. In addition to the prestige of being published in hardback, there had been a strong financial incentive for him to be so. He simply could not write fast enough to make a reasonable living from writing for pulp magazines, or even from writing book-length pulps. (Pulp-book publishers like Pocket Books paid writers only $750 per 100,000 copies sold. The books themselves were priced at 25 cents each.[20] Good hardback sales, on the other hand, such as Cain and Hammett had enjoyed, could afford him the time he needed in which to write. But reviews were crucial to hardback success, if only to inform non-crime readers of Chandler's existence. Dedicated crime readers were too set on buying their fiction in cheap editions, or borrowing it from libraries; they were not used to spending $2.00 on hardbacks. Hammett and Cain had made their money by selling to general readers rather than to mystery fans.[21]

As a result of the lack of notices, just 12,500 hardback copies of The Big Sleep were sold in America. A smart dollar-edition paperback, released twelve months later, sold only 3,500 and earned Chandler just $175. Knopf resisted offers from the pulp-book publishers to buy the rights in The Big Sleep, because he believed that being published in such an edition would further soil Chandler's image among the critics. A crime writer who was published in hardback, but who did not get attention from the press at the start of his career, was in fact locked into a dangerous pattern. He was unlikely to sell well in hardback, so long as his books failed to receive the publicity generated by reviews. Only 25-cent-edition publishers like Pocket Books and Avon could afford to risk the money for advertising and industry promotion needed to offset a lack of reviews. This was less true in Britain, where advertising was easier and cheaper because of the national press. In America, however, it was a problem that fed itself – the more critics ignored a crime writer, the quicker they forced him into the arms of pulp publishers. His work thereby became further associated with cheapness, with quickly written books and garish covers, and consequently even less worthy of serious critical attention in the first place. Erle Stanley Gardner's eventual solution – to print his own books – was too expensive for Chandler even to consider in 1939.

*

Chandler and Cissy had to continue to live cheaply. At the end of the summer of 1939, they moved to the blue-collar suburb of Monrovia in the north of LA, into a small house on West Duarte Street. Chandler was still not drinking. An indication of how he felt at this point in his life comes from another fantasy story, similar in tone to 'The Bronze Door', which he wrote ten years later. 'Professor Bingo's Snuff' was about a fifty-two-year-old man (as Chandler was in 1940) who wakes up one morning in a cheap Los Angeles neighbourhood feeling depressed:

> At ten o'clock in the morning already the dance music. Loud. Boom, boom. Boom, boom, boom. The tone control way down in the bass. It almost made the floor vibrate. Behind the purring of the electric razor which Joe Pettigrew was running up and down his face it vibrated in the floors and walls. The neighbours must love it.
>
> Already at ten o'clock in the morning the ice cubes in the glass, the flushed cheek, the slightly glazed eye, the silly smile, the loud laughter about nothing at all.
>
> He pulled the plug loose and the purring of the razor stopped. As he ran his fingertips along the angle of his jaw his eyes met the eyes in the mirror with a sombre stare. 'Washed up,' he said between his teeth. 'At fifty-two you're senile. I'm surprised you're there at all. I'm surprised I can see you.'[22]

A man comes to Joe Pettigrew's door selling magic snuff that makes people disappear. Pettigrew buys some and takes it. Invisible, he catches his wife with another man, kills them both and takes more snuff to keep away from the police. When he eventually runs out of snuff, however, the police shoot him dead.

Another pointer to Chandler's mood at this time comes from a letter he later sent to his English publisher, Hamish Hamilton, on the occasion of Hamilton's fiftieth birthday:

> Too bad you are such an old, old man of fifty. I have sympathy with you. It is a bad age. A man of fifty is not young, not old, not even middle-aged. His wind has gone and his dignity has not yet arrived. To the young he is old and stodgy. To the really old he is fat and pompous and greedy. He is a mere convenience to bankers and tax collectors. Why not shoot yourself?[23]

*

The rejection of *The Big Sleep* by American and British critics led to the concept of a 'cult' following among those who had now begun to read Chandler. It was word-of-mouth reputation more than any other single factor that was prompting people to read his first novel, and these early admirers included other writers. Chandler received letters of encouragement from John Steinbeck and S. J. Perelman, both of whom had read *The Big Sleep*.

He had been warned by other pulp writers about the critics' particular resistance towards hard-boiled crime fiction, but in *The Big Sleep* he thought that he had produced a book good enough to force 'the intellectual fancy boys' into acknowledging him. When this failed to happen, he was annoyed. He wrote to Erle Stanley Gardner, who had been similarly ignored by the critics for over six years, and asked how he put up with being cold-shouldered when it was 'obvious' that he was a better writer than the intellectual type of writers the critics supported and effectively marketed:

> [Great fiction] is the perfection of control over the movement of a story similar to the control of a great pitcher. That is to me what you have and more than anyone else. Dumas had it, Dickens, allowing for his Victorian muddle, had it; begging your pardon I don't think Edgar Wallace approached it. His stories died all along the way and had to be revived. Yours don't. Every page holds the hook for the next. I call that a kind of genius . . . it must be obvious that if I have half a dozen unread books beside my chair and one of them is a Perry Mason, and I reach for the Perry Mason and let the others wait, that book must have quality.[24]

Chandler believed that the 'smart-aleck' critics had only ever accepted Hammett in a patronizing way, and that though they had been titillated by Cain's first book, they had then ignored him. They were still refusing even to distinguish between the good and the bad writers of hard-boiled fiction. Chandler was determined to break this impasse, and resolved to do so with his second novel. In December 1939, he threw away the entire typescript of *Farewell My Lovely* – having begun it in June – and started the book again. This was not something he could yet afford to do, but without children to support it was a risk he was prepared to take. 'I had to throw my second book away,' he told an old *Black Mask* contemporary, George Harmon Coxe, 'so that leaves me with nothing to show for the last six months and possibly nothing to eat for the next six.'[25]

Chandler and Cissy stayed in Monrovia until shortly before

Christmas of 1939. They spent Christmas itself in the beautiful coastal town of La Jolla, above San Diego and close to the Mexican border. Chandler promised Cissy that they would move there permanently once he could afford it. It was during this Christmas – always his least favourite time of year – that he decided to rewrite his second novel. In the New Year of 1940, he and Cissy moved to a north-eastern suburb of LA called Arcadia, where they lived in a house on Arcadia Avenue.[26] It was as dull as Monrovia and he was never to refer to either place in his writing. It was here, nevertheless, in the spring of 1940, that he managed to finish his second Marlowe novel.

Farewell My Lovely begins with Marlowe being hired by a huge ex-con called 'Moose' Malloy, who has just come out of prison. Malloy wants the detective to find his old showgirl sweetheart, Velma, and not having had a job for weeks, the detective accepts. He starts off by trying to find out who ran the club off Central Avenue in downtown LA where Velma used to perform. The owner has died, and his alcoholic widow says she does not remember anyone called Velma. Marlowe returns to his office, uneasy about how the violent Moose Malloy is going to react to this dead end.

Back in his office, he is offered another job. A rich fop named Marriott hires Marlowe to accompany him out to Purissima Canyon. One of Marriott's girlfriends has had some priceless jade jewellery stolen and the thieves have agreed to sell the pieces back for $8,000. Marlowe doubts Marriott's 'honest broker' story, but again takes the job. The two of them drive up to the remote rendezvous and Marlowe gets out of the car with the money. He is coshed unconscious, Marriott is killed and the money is stolen.

Having already been paid by Marriott, Marlowe decides to try and recover the jewels. He goes to meet the dead man's girlfriend, the beautiful Mrs Lewin Grayle, who is married to a rich old banker and lives in the hills above Santa Monica. She tells Marlowe to forget the matter, but he senses something crooked and decides to go on looking for the jewellery. There ensues a series of incidents involving bent cops, tranquillizers, racketeers, asylum cells and an increasingly violent Moose Malloy. Growing both paranoid and confused, Marlowe suddenly realizes that Velma and Mrs Grayle are one and the same. Knowing this,

Marriott had been blackmailing her for years, threatening to expose Grayle's low-rent past to her husband. Having heard that Marlowe was looking for 'Velma', Marriott had tricked him up to Purissima Canyon in order to have him shot. But by then Marriott's own cronies had caught up with his scam, and killed him instead for not cutting them in on the blackmail racket. The complex story ends with a showdown between Moose Malloy and Velma. Malloy still loves her, but Velma is furious at having her past uncovered and shoots Malloy dead. Marlowe, too exhausted to care, lets her escape before calling the police.

Farewell My Lovely confirmed how far away from the restrictions of *Black Mask* Chandler's fiction was moving. Though he was still using the framework of his old pulp stories, his hero, Marlowe, is even further from being a stock pulp hero than he was in *The Big Sleep* – within the first sixty pages of *Farewell My Lovely* he has lost $8,000, seen his client killed while supposedly under his protection, and forced information out of an alcoholic woman by feeding her whisky. He has none of the infallibility of Gardner's hero Perry Mason. He is knocked out twice, and then drugged when he fails to stop his investigation. When he comes round from being doped, Marlowe finds himself in a cell in a private clinic in Santa Monica:

> I didn't know what was funny about it but I began to laugh. I lay there on the bed and laughed. I didn't like the sound of the laugh. It was the laugh of a nut. . . . The throat felt sore but the fingers feeling it didn't feel anything. They might as well have been a bunch of bananas. I looked at them. They looked like fingers. No good. Mail order fingers. . . . Half an hour of walking and my knees were shaking but my head was clear. I drank more water, a lot of water. I almost cried while I was drinking it.[27]

Marlowe recovers his senses by the end of the book, driven on by his hatred of the book's chief villain, an LA psychiatrist named Jules Amthor. Amthor has been exploiting his position as consultant to the rich by selling details of his clients' wealth, and their secrets, to men like Marriott. There is some indirect evidence that Chandler sought clinical help from such doctors during the alcoholism of his oil days, but in *Farewell My Lovely* Marlowe has only scorn for the type of people who consult Amthor:

> Big strong guys that roared like lions around their offices and were all cold mush under their vests. But mostly it would be women, fat women that panted and thin women that burned, old women that dreamed and young women that thought they might have Electra complexes. . . . No Thursdays at the County Hospitals for Mr Jules Amthor. Cash on the line for him. Rich bitches who had to be dunned for their milk bills would pay him right away.[28]

Marlowe ends the book with Anne Riordan, a girl who is unrelated to the case. Attractive rather than pretty – 'It was a nice face. A face you could get to like' – she and Marlowe get on well, though they do not sleep together. She asks him to explain about the job he has just finished. Marlowe (who has been lied to, framed and beaten up too many times not to feel weary) tells her the plot in crude terms. Anne is fond of Marlowe, but does not like the swear words he uses: 'Do you have to say things like that?' she asks. 'The Shakespearean touch,' replies Marlowe. 'Let's go riding.' (This quip was not accidental: Chandler was increasingly of the opinion that American English was at a similarly exciting point in its development as Anglo-Saxon English had been in Shakespeare's lifetime. It was a vibrant, protean language: played with, reinvented and creatively distorted by those who spoke it every day.)

Farewell My Lovely was published in May 1940, but was again ignored by the critics. Despite an unusually large advertising budget from Knopf, it was not reviewed and sold worse than *The Big Sleep* (11,000 copies in America and 4,000 in Britain). Word of Chandler's writing was continuing to spread beyond his core following, but without publicity he still made only $2,000. Most newspapers in Britain and America failed to register the publication of *Farewell My Lovely* outside their round-ups of newly published mysteries, and not even always there. The most favourable notice the book received came from the Los Angeles press. A critic for the *Hollywood Citizen-News* admired the novel in no uncertain terms: 'I am perfectly willing to stake whatever critical reputation I possess today or may possess tomorrow on the literary future of this author. . . . Lord but it is good to see honesty and pains and fine impulses again.'[29] Knopf agreed, and continued to refuse to sell the book to pulp publishers.

*

In 1940, soon after the publication of *Farewell My Lovely*, Chandler and Cissy moved again, this time back north to Big Bear Lake. Meanwhile, the war was starting to intensify: Russia and Italy had entered a conflict which had spread beyond Europe to the Middle East and Africa. Japan looked ready to extend the theatre further still. As America herself moved towards entering the fray on the side of the Allies, details of the war were being broadcast throughout the States in a way that no other war had been. Photo magazines like *Life,* and cinema newsreels, showed the Germans' aerial bombing Blitz on British cities. Chandler began sending small monthly food parcels to H. F. Hose, his old Classics master at Dulwich, and learnt from him that the Great Hall at Dulwich had already been badly damaged.

A notebook entry that Chandler had made just before the war emphasizes how anxiously he must have followed the escalation of the fighting. Ever since the 1920s he had wanted to take Cissy back to London:

> Since all plans are foolish and those written down are never fulfilled, let us make a plan this 16th day of March 1939, at Riverside California. [Stay in LA] for the rest of 1939, all of 1940, spring of 1941, and then if there is no war and if there is any money, to go to England for material.[30]

It was over the summer of 1940, while in Big Bear Lake, that Chandler wrote what would be his final story for the pulps before starting on his third Marlowe book. In the story, called 'No Crime in the Mountains', a Los Angeles private detective helps crack a German-Japanese propaganda outfit working from a hideaway near Big Bear Lake. The story was more remarkable for its topical villains than anything else. It ends with a shoot-out in a cabin where the two culprits have been printing anti-British literature in an attempt to keep America out of the war:

118

The Jap screamed and streaked out of the door. Barron and I lunged across the table. We got our guns. Blood fell on the back of my hand and then Luders crumpled slowly against the wall.

Barron was already out of the door. When I got out behind him, I saw that the little Jap was running hard down the hill towards a clump of brush.

Barron steadied himself, brought the Colt up, then lowered it again.

'He ain't far enough,' he said. 'I always give a man forty yards.'[31]

*

The Big Sleep was by now available only in libraries, a familiar graveyard for detective novels. Interest in crime fiction was huge – one in every four books lent by American libraries in the 1940s was a mystery story – but so was the number of crime novels that were being published to feed that interest. Since most were of disposable quality, it was very easy for well-written mysteries to become lost in the crowd. Few readers were prepared to buy crime novels in hardback, since the majority of such books were not designed to be kept or reread. Given these factors, combined with the profusion of 25-cent crime books (sold everywhere from remote gas stations to city drugstores), crime fiction was starting to become a victim of its own success. No other form of writing was so widely available in cheap editions or from libraries. The average crime novel in America could expect a hardback sale of only 3,000 copies. Chandler had tripled that with his first two novels, but by the summer of 1940 he was still effectively unknown – and still living in cheap holiday resorts.[32]

After a second summer in Big Bear Lake, the Chandlers spent Christmas of 1940 back at Santa Monica, in a four-room apartment on San Vincente Boulevard. By February 1941, they had moved north along the coast to the town of Pacific Palisades, just south of Malibu, living at an address on Illif Street, which Chandler said had 'a nice garden'. Within two months, they had moved again to Shetland Lane in Brentwood, and by July they were in the desert holiday resort of Idyllwild.[33] October of that year saw them still in the desert, at a cheap resort called Cathedral Springs where they spent the winter. In December, Japanese carrier-borne aircraft bombed the US Naval base at Pearl Harbor in Hawaii, forcing President Roosevelt to bring America into the Second World War.

By Christmas of 1941, the loneliness of life in Cathedral Springs was starting to depress Chandler, as, clearly, was rationing:

> This place bores me. I've just about been talken into sticking out the mountains and deserts for another year [but] after that to hell with the climate, let's meet a few people. We have a one-store town here .... On Thursdays at 10 the inhabitants bring their bronchitis and halitosis into the store and park in front of the meat counter and the numbers are coonshouted. When we, having a very late number, kick our way to the collapsed hunk of hamburger we are greeted with a nervous smile that suggests a deacon caught with his hand in the collection plate, and we leave bearing enough meat for the cat. This happens once a week and that is all that happens in the way of meat.[34]

Chandler had now seen almost every side of Los Angeles. He had lived for eighteen years in central Los Angeles; five years in the satellite town of Santa Monica, and three years in LA's scattered suburbs and holiday towns. He had seen Los Angeles through a boom and through the Depression, while himself experiencing both personal wealth and virtual poverty. He had seen it as a young accountant, as a drunken middle-aged oil executive, and as a sober writer – and he had been there long enough to witness two earthquakes, including a major one at Long Beach in 1933, and the Olympic Games in 1932.

Like others, he was amazed by the colossus which Los Angeles had now become. Already huge in population, LA was starting to exceed its oil-boom wealth and looked destined to become 'the centre of civilization . . . if there is any left'. Much of this resurgence was in line with a national economic improvement following the end of the Depression. But as America began to invest in itself once more, East Coast corporations became particularly attracted to LA's fiercely anti-union tradition. The war was also playing a major part in the region's recovery. As the conflict intensified, the United States had become a major arms manufacturer for both its own military and for its allies. Shortage of raw materials and labour in Britain, as well as the bombing of munitions factories there, had meant an enormous boost for the

American defence industry. In an attempt to offset the particularly heavy scars that the Depression had left on the economy of Los Angeles and its surrounding area, Washington had given priority to the region in its awards of military hardware contracts. This had helped not only the thousands of workers who now found well-paid skilled work there, but also the many service industries which indirectly benefited from this influx of government money. Combined with the almost perfect climate, the standard of living in southern California was starting to become the envy of the nation.

Chandler could not relate to the revitalized Los Angeles. He saw a mass-produced culture emerging around the city; a corporation-sponsored 'culture of the filtered cigarette', where people were turning generic in their tastes and simple in their ambitions. It was all leading, he reckoned, to a 'steakless steak to be broiled on a heatless broiler in a non-existent oven and eaten by a toothless ghost'. He had always imagined moving back to England, but England was being impoverished, perhaps even destroyed, by the same war that was now enriching California.

Chandler's restless movement around LA's suburbs was to continue for a further two years. He did not really enjoy solitude, but each time he looked at Californian society he found it impossible to connect with it unless he was drunk. 'I like people with manners,' he said:

> . . . grace, an education slightly above the Reader's Digest fan, people whose pride of living does not express itself in their kitchen gadgets and their automobiles. . . . I like everything that Americans of the past used to look for in Europe, but at the same time I don't want to be bound by the rule. It all seems a bit too much, now that I've written it.[35]

Cissy had her heart set on settling in La Jolla, the exclusive coastal town 100 miles south of Los Angeles where they had spent the Christmas of 1939, and which they would sometimes visit by car. Chandler was suspicious of the place, insisting that it offered nothing but 'meaningless chi-chi and a climate'. He wanted to be somewhere where he could connect with some sharp-witted company. 'La Jolla is no place to live,' he complained. 'There is no one to talk to, just old people and their parents.' But Cissy had patiently suffered the cramped monotony of their years in Santa Monica, and Chandler resolved to share her dream of a permanent home in La Jolla. 'It has a perfect climate,' he decided:

> . . . the finest coastline of the Pacific side of the country, no bill-boards or concessions or beachfront shacks, an air of cool decency and good manners that is almost startling in California. One may like a free and easy neighbourhood where they smash the empty bottles on the sidewalk. But in practice it's very comfortable.[36]

For the time being, though, La Jolla was well beyond Chandler's means.

Although *Farewell My Lovely* had failed to seriously improve his financial lot, Chandler was now determined to break out of the previous eight years of reclusive living. He was in a brighter mood, and allowing himself to relax the constant regime of self-discipline to which he had stuck since giving up drink in 1932. Wherever he and Cissy were living, he would wake early, work till lunchtime at his typewriter, and then finish for the day. 'The important thing', he decided, 'is that there should be a space of time, say four hours a day at least, when a professional writer doesn't do anything else but write. He doesn't have to write, and if he doesn't feel like it, he shouldn't try. He can look out the window or stand on his head or writhe on the floor, but he is not allowed to do any other positive thing.' The afternoon would be spent dozing, reading magazines and driving Cissy to the stores. The couple listened to the evening classical music programme on the radio (as they always had done), and still took English tea together in the afternoons.

Cissy was now unwell again. Aged seventy-one, she was suffering from fibrosis of the lungs and often had to rely on strong sedatives to kill the pain. Consequently drowsy, she was frequently immobile or asleep. This left Chandler – who still suffered from insomnia – spending more and more time alone. Without drink, he found it difficult to leave the house. His teetotalism had become dependent on avoiding any kind of social life, and however much he now wanted to meet people, he wanted less to be a drunk again. It was drink that had lost him his job in the first place, and forced him and Cissy to live for so long on such humble means.

As a result of this isolation, Chandler started to become a compulsive letter-writer. The letters were addressed to people he had never met or whom he had met only briefly. Publishers and admiring readers who wrote to him began receiving long, funny and semi-personal replies. For a man who had grown so unused to dealing with other people in the flesh, the writing of letters provided a perfect medium for the closer contact he presently seemed unable to enjoy.

The letters would usually begin with some matter of mutual concern or interest and then spin off into friendly chatter. From this distance, Chandler was a warm, entertaining new friend. Early recipients of this correspondence were his publisher, Alfred Knopf, and his wife Blanche. Chandler would always start his letters to them on a matter of business:

> Sorry I haven't any snapshots to send you yet. I don't know how much time there is. My wife will try to take some, a very agonizing process for both of us, since she is very particular and I am very badly behaved. Commercial photos are no good. I am reaching the age where it takes the artistic touch to make anything of me. The fellows who have this want too much money, and I doubt the importance of the cause. While I am compelled by weight of opinion to admit to being one of the handsomest men of my generation I also have to concede that this generation is now a little seedy, and I with it.[37]

He would then go on to write about himself, about what he was reading, how Cissy's health was, where he was living, and how he was feeling. He was also interested to learn about the lives of those he was writing to. He asked Alfred Knopf when Blanche's birthday was, and sent her yellow tulips on the day itself. He would express his own opinions about writing:

> It won't be long before somebody invents a machine to write novels. How often do I pick up a book and say, 'This was written by an individual unlike any other individual.' Practically never.
>
> But don't take me too seriously. I am becoming a pretty sour kind of citizen. Even Hemingway has let me down . . . his eternal

preoccupation with what goes on between the sheets becomes rather nauseating in the end. One reaches a time in life when limericks written on the walls of comfort stations are not just obscene, they are horribly dull. This man has only one subject, and he makes that ridiculous. I suppose the man's epitaph, if he had the choosing of it, would be: Here Lies A Man Who Was Bloody Good In Bed. Too Bad He's Alone Here. But the point is I begin to doubt whether he ever was. You don't have to work so hard at things you are really good at – or do you?[38]

Chandler struck up a similarly friendly correspondence with a Nevada librarian called James Sandoe, who had written to congratulate him on *The Big Sleep*. It was clearly a relief for Chandler to have people, even strangers, to communicate with again. He and Sandoe would eventually exchange more than a hundred letters, swapping crime books they had enjoyed and sharing news of each other's lives. 'Your family sounds wonderful,' Chandler once told him. His own 'family' consisted of Cissy, and their Persian cat Taki. They had taken the animal with them every time they moved house, and Chandler had grown very fond of having it around, as he told Sandoe:

There is nothing worse in nature than seeing a cat trying to provoke a few more hopeless attempts to escape out of a half-dead mouse. My enormous respect for our cat is based on a complete lack in her of this diabolical sadism. When she used to catch mice . . . she brought them alive and undamaged and let me take them out of her mouth. Her attitude seemed to be, 'Well, here's this damn mouse. Had to catch it, but it's really your problem. Remove it at once.' Periodically she goes through all the closets and cupboards on a regular mouse-inspection. Never finds any, but she realizes it's part of her job.[39]

People were now listening to Chandler's thoughts, and he was no longer being regarded, as he had been latterly at Dabney's, as an eccentric nuisance. The critics might ignore him, but that had prompted several admirers to send him letters of encouragement. Another lively correspondence was that between Chandler and the famous East Coast columnist S. J. Perelman: 'I am frankly not interested in your Florida sex hunger,' ran a typical letter to

Perelman. 'Nobody made you go to Florida. And don't tell me you have to earn a living, because your children are certainly old enough and smart enough to support you by now, even if your wife won't work. And I rather gather from your writings that about all she does is put perfume in her hair and loaf around in a mink coat and slacks.'[40] In one letter, Chandler advised Perelman against moving to California if he wanted to have educated children: 'California high schools range from putrid to rotten. . . . I have one relative, fortunately distant, who graduated from the Fairfax high school in Los Angeles while still struggling with the alphabet.' Perelman would reply – the two men never attempted to meet – with gloomily comic sketches of his Florida life. 'I am sitting in an all-plastic motel overlooking another all-plastic motel which in turn overlooks the Gulf Stream, but there is no man in America (or for that matter the world) but yourself who could convey the grisly charm of the place.'[41]

Perelman once sent Chandler a pastiche of detective fiction which he had written for *The New Yorker*. In tribute to Chandler's second novel, he had called it 'Farewell, My Lovely Appetizer':

I came down the sixth-floor corridor of the Arbogast Building, past the World Wide Noodle Corporation, Zwinger & Rumsey, Accountants, and the Ace Secretarial Service, Mimeographing Our Specialty. The legend on the ground-glass panel next door said, 'Atlas Detective Agency, Noonan & Driscoll', but Snapper Driscoll had retired two years before with a .38 slug between the shoulders, donated by a snow-bird in Tacoma, and I owned what good will the firm had. I let myself into the crummy anteroom we kept to impress clients, growled good morning at Birdie Claflin.

'Well, you certainly look like something the cat dragged in,' she said. She had a quick tongue. She also had eyes like dusty lapis lazuli, taffy hair, and a figure that did things to me. I kicked open the bottom drawer of her desk, let two inches of rye tickle down my craw, kissed Birdie square on her lush, red mouth, and set fire to a cigarette.

'I could go for you, sugar,' I said slowly. Her face was veiled, watchful. I stared at her eyes, liking the way they were joined to her head. There was something complete about them; you knew they were there for keeps. When you're a private detective, you want things to stay put.[42]

A third winter spent buying cheap meat in the desert left Chandler feeling jaded. He was still not seeing anyone and, despite his letter-writing, was starting to get bored. This affected his third novel, which he delivered to Knopf in March 1942: 'I'm afraid the book is not going to be any good to you,' he warned. 'No action. No likeable characters, no nothing. The detective does nothing.'

In *The High Window*, Marlowe is hired by a woman in Pasadena to find a precious coin that has been stolen from her safe: 'she was the widow of an old coot with whiskers named Jasper Murdock who had made a lot of money helping out the community', Mrs Murdock suspects her son's estranged wife, a showgirl of whom she has always disapproved. Marlowe tracks the girl down ('From thirty feet away she looked like a lot of class. From ten feet away she looked like something made to be seen from thirty feet away'), but she seems to know nothing. Marlowe goes on and, as usual, finds the case more complicated than he had expected. He is followed, shot at and framed. He finds the coin, but by then he realizes that the coin itself is not what Mrs Murdock is after. She is a scheming woman who clearly has hidden motives in hiring a detective, as well as having some professionally nasty enemies. Mrs Murdock tells Marlowe that she no longer needs him, but he is now determined to find out what is going on and slips back to the house to grill her secretary. He cannot understand why the secretary, from whom he has been trying to prise information from the start, is so petrified of her boss and any discussion of the case:

> She was pale with a sort of natural paleness and she looked healthy enough . . . the whole face had a sort of off-key neurotic charm that only needed some make-up to be striking. . . . She'll always be high on nerves and low on animal emotion. She'll always breathe thin air and smell snow. She'd have made a perfect nun. The religious dream with its narrowness, its stylized emotions and its grim purity, would have made a perfect release for her. As it is she will probably turn out to be one of those acid-faced virgins that sit behind little desks in public libraries and stamp dates in books.[43]

After two attempts, Marlowe finally breaks the girl down. She has been working for the Murdock family since her childhood, at which point in her life she suffered a nervous collapse after being raped by Jasper Murdock. In retaliation for this, Mrs Murdock had killed her husband, by pushing him out of a window. The police at the time presumed that he had fallen out (a procession had been passing the front of the house when he fell), but Mrs Murdock had exploited the girl's subsequent nervous breakdown by convincing her that it was she who had pushed Mr Murdock out the window. In return for her employer's not telling the police, the girl has devotedly subjected herself to emotional and secretarial slavery ever since; even now, she still half-believes herself to be guilty.

Marlowe then discovers the reason for his client's present anxiety. A photographer who had been near the house on the day of the murder – attending the procession – had heard Murdock's cry as he was pushed and snapped a picture. In it, can be seen the murderer's outstretched arms. The photograph has fallen into the hands of blackmailers whose bosses, Mrs Murdock clearly believes, are mobster friends of her showgirl daughter-in-law. She had hired Marlowe on the pretext of retrieving a 'stolen' coin – which she had in fact used as part of a blackmail payment – so as to discover whom she was dealing with. Marlowe smashes the blackmailers, and at the end of the story drives the girl back to her parents' house in the Midwest. Mrs Murdock, who realizes that he knows the truth, does not try to stop him; in return, he destroys the photograph.

(The description of the long drive out to the Midwest at the end of the book may have been based on a trip that Chandler had once made from Los Angeles to visit the Fitts in Nebraska, though there is no firm evidence of when the trip took place. 'I was gone ten days,' says Marlowe. '[Her] parents were vague, kind, patient people, living in an old frame house in a quiet shady street. . . . I had a funny feeling as I saw the house disappear, as though I had written a poem and it was very good and I had lost it and would never remember it again.')

The High Window lacked the verve of Marlowe's previous adventures. It had taken Chandler two years to write, and his lack of enthusiasm shows – Marlowe is bored and frustrated by what he is doing and by the people he meets. A description of one minor character would also suggest that now, in 1942, Chandler was once more starting to yearn for drink, after having been 'dry' so long:

> Breeze looked at me very steadily. Then he sighed. Then he picked the glass up and tasted it and sighed again and shook his head sideways with a half smile; the way a man does when you give him a drink and he needs it very badly and it is just right and the first swallow is like a peak into a cleaner, sunnier, brighter world.[44]

The mystery aspect of *The High Window* does not show Chandler at his most inventive, relying as it does on an accidental and improbable photograph. Instead, the writing's emphasis was becoming more and more centred on Marlowe himself, as he moves cynically and self-deprecatingly through a Los Angeles of liars and killers. He criticizes himself as much as he does the other characters. His frustration hangs over the book: 'I lit my pipe and sat there smoking,' he says at one point. 'Nobody came in, nobody called, nothing happened, nobody cared whether I died or went to El Paso. . . . I drove back to Hollywood, bought a pint of good liquor, checked in at the Plaza and sat on the side of the bed staring at my feet and lapping the whisky out of the bottle. Just like any common bedroom drunk.'[45]

There was a new doubt on top of the lack of energy that marked Marlowe's third adventure. The detective was starting to question even the skills for which people hired him. Disgruntled clients were old news to him, but he was now beginning to make bad procedural mistakes. He calls himself 'cock-eyed', 'careless', 'club-footed' and 'dissipated' in *The High Window*. Neither Chandler nor his hero seem to care enough about the case at hand. 'It's a waste of time talking to you,' one character shouts at Marlowe. 'All you do is wisecrack.'[46]

It was not the book to break the critics' disdain. Only in Britain was there any acknowledgement in the press of Chandler's growing popularity. In a short review, the *Times Literary Supplement* recommended *The High Window* to its readers: '. . . it is not so much the frequent laughter as the jaunty assurance in every line which wins our liking.' It was ironic to receive praise for a book that Chandler had not enjoyed writing. 'Some people liked it better than my other efforts,' he later said. 'Some people liked it much less. But nobody went into screaming fits either way.' The novel sold 10,000 copies in America and 8,500 in Britain. Most copies, Knopf ruefully calculated, went to libraries. For the author, it meant just $3,000 for two years' work.

*

The mood carried into Chandler's fourth novel. Written in Big Bear Lake and Cathedral Springs, and published a year later in 1943, *The Lady in the Lake* continued to show Marlowe's frustration. Nothing makes him happy, all is phoney, and 'everything's for sale in California'. The novel shows Chandler and Marlowe at their most misanthropic.

Death hangs over *The Lady in the Lake* more heavily than in any of Marlowe's previous adventures; from the corpses he keeps stumbling across, to the woman he has been hired to find whose body has been rotting underwater throughout the whole book. The corpses neither surprise nor shock Marlowe any more. The sight of death simply seems to confirm his dejected solitude: 'I sat very still', he says on finding one body in a shower, 'and listened to the evening grow quiet outside the windows. And very slowly I grew quiet with it.' He trusts nobody any more and discounts witnesses out of hand, because he has now decided that what people think and what they say 'don't even have to be on the same map'.

Of all the towns that he and Cissy flitted between, Big Bear Lake was still Chandler's favourite. Despite its tackiness ('overflowing with males in sports clothes and liquor breaths and females in slacks and shorts with blood-red fingernails and dirty knuckles'), he would have liked to live there the year round had Cissy been healthier. Marlowe's own drive up to the mountains in *The Lady in the Lake* provides one of the few upbeat moments in Chandler's otherwise black fourth novel:

San Bernadino baked and shimmered in the afternoon heat. The air was hot enough to blister my tongue. I drove through it gasping, stopped long enough to buy a pint of liquor in case I fainted before I got to the mountains, and started up the long grade to Crestline. In fifteen miles the road climbed five thousand feet, but even then it was far from cool. Thirty miles of mountain driving brought me to the tall pines and a place called Bubbling Springs. It had a clapboard store and a gas pump, but it felt like paradise.[47]

Though not mentioned in the book, the war continued to preoccupy Chandler. In truth, he had little else to occupy him, so few were the distractions in his life now. By 1942, the destruction of London and what Chandler saw as bad tactical mistakes on the part of the Allied commanders began to depress him. The war made worrying about books and publishing, he felt, seem pretty immaterial: 'The things by which we live,' he wrote to Alfred Knopf, 'are the distant flashes of insect wings.' In *The Lady in the Lake*, Marlowe certainly does not feel like a hero any more: 'I brushed my hair and looked at the grey in it. There was getting to be plenty of grey in it. The face under the hair had a sick look. I didn't like the face at all.'

The novel itself begins with Marlowe being hired by Derace Kingsley, the director of a company that makes perfume, who wants his estranged wife found. As he waits outside his client's office before meeting him for the first time, Marlowe looks at a showcase of scent bottles. Perfume was too appropriate a symbol of Californian phoniness for Marlowe to miss it: 'Gillerain Regal, The Champagne of Perfumes. It was definitely the stuff to get. One drop of that in the hollow of your throat and the matched pink pearls started falling on you like summer rain.' The detective is on the defensive from the start. He is sick of Los Angeles and distrusts his client.

The last that Kingsley has heard from his estranged wife, Crystal, was a telegram from El Paso announcing that she was planning to get a Mexican divorce and marry a man named Chris Lavery. Lavery, a high-living gigolo, is well known to Kingsley and his friends. What worries the husband is that Lavery is currently in LA, and swears that he knows nothing about the telegram or Crystal Kingsley's whereabouts.

Marlowe calls on Lavery at his house, dislikes him immediately, but suspects that he is at least partly telling the truth. Crystal Kingsley has last been seen up in the mountains near Big Bear Lake, and Marlowe drives up there to look around the cabin where she stayed. There is nothing there, but in a nearby cabin he finds a local man, Bill Chess, who is drinking himself stupid because his new wife, Muriel, has also disappeared, following an argument with him. She has been gone a month, taking her clothes with her. The local police are uninterested in her disappearance – until, that is, a body is found in the lake and identified as that of Muriel Chess. Her husband is arrested for her murder.

After the usual pulp trail of crooked cops, corpses and blackjacks, Marlowe finds Muriel Chess alive in an LA hotel. Her real name is Mildred Haviland, and she is no stranger, it turns out, to murder investigations. A murderess for the second time, she admits having killed Crystal Kingsley in her cabin, dressing the body in her own clothes and dumping it in the lake. Haviland had figured, correctly, that by the time the body was found, only the clothes would have remained identifiable. She had then sent Mr Kingsley a telegram in Crystal's name from El Paso, so as to give herself enough time to empty the victim's bank accounts. By the end of the book, Haviland has been strangled by a crooked cop called Degarmo, who in turn has killed himself after beating up Marlowe and trying to frame him for Haviland's murder.

The Lady in the Lake was the only novel Chandler wrote that he could never reread in later years. It marked a dangerous low point for him. Marlowe was getting out of control; overshadowing other characters too much, and caring too little. The tension of the first two novels was no longer there because the outcome seems irrelevant to the hero. Moreover, writing the novel had left Chandler feeling as fed up as Marlowe. He no longer cared so much about how little attention the book got in the press, because he no longer thought he deserved it.

Attention was, though, gradually moving in Chandler's direction. Shortly before *The Lady in the Lake* was published in 1943, a 25-cent edition of *The Big Sleep* appeared in America for the first time. Convinced that Chandler was never going to be recognized by the critics, Knopf had finally sold the pulp rights to the first novel to Avon. It immediately sold 300,000 copies, and a further 150,000 copies were sold in a special armed services edition. On the back of this success, Knopf allowed Pocket Books to publish a 25-cent edition of *Farewell My Lovely* four months later. The book sold more than a million copies. As a result of this exposure, more hardback copies of *The Lady in the Lake* were sold in America than any of the other Marlowes, and although

14,000 was still not an enormous number, it earned the author $3,500. The pulp sales that Knopf had always feared would undermine Chandler's hardback status had in fact done quite the opposite.

In Britain, the momentum of Chandler's popularity (predominantly through libraries) meant that *The Lady in the Lake* was the first of his novels to be widely reviewed. The literary editor of the *Sunday Times*, Desmond MacCarthy, devoted his weekly column to the book's publication and to the popularity of American detective fiction in general. 'Of one thing I feel sure,' the review began,

> Mr Raymond Chandler must be a great swell in the detective-fiction line; and in saying that I guess I am giving myself away. Yes, I write this week as an outsider; and whatever interest my comments on The Lady in the Lake may prove to have, they cannot be those of a real connoisseur . . . it is brutally realistic. Here and there I found it ugly. . . . It is most efficiently written; the story travels at an exhilarating speed. It is a brilliant whodunit.[48]

The novel subsequently sold 13,000 hardback copies in Britain, earning royalties of another $4,000. Meanwhile, *The Big Sleep* had been translated into both Danish and Norwegian. It was all slowly starting to happen – paradoxically, just as Chandler was starting to get bored with his writing.

Having finished *The Lady in the Lake* over the spring of 1943, Chandler found himself unsure how to proceed. In May, he received an unexpected but fortuitously timed telephone call at home from a man named Joe Sistrom, a producer at the Paramount studios. Sistrom was looking for someone to adapt for the screen a James Cain novel called *Double Indemnity*, to which Paramount had acquired the rights. He had read *The High Window* and had given his director, Billy Wilder, a copy of the book, suggesting that they try to get Chandler on the project. Wilder had never heard of Chandler, but read the novel and agreed; he would be co-writing the script with whomever they chose. Having tracked Chandler down to an address in Pacific Palisades, they now asked him on the phone whether he would be interested in working in Hollywood. The following day,

Chandler drove to the studio lot on Melrose Avenue and took the job. His years as a nomadic recluse, and a teetollar, were over.

5

Hollywood Days

The picture business can be a little trying at times, but I don't suppose working for General Motors is all sheer delight

(Letter, January 1952)

The call from Paramount Studios could not have been better timed. By the summer of 1943, Chandler was mentally finished both with writing books and with town-hopping. Working at Hollywood would temporarily postpone having to think about either of these issues. 1943 was to prove an ideal year in another way. Just as he had done with the oil business in the 1920s, Chandler was about to enter a booming American industry at the optimum moment. The post-Depression, pre-television 1940s would turn out to be one of Hollywood's greatest (and richest) decades. This had much to do with the continuing war, which was providing the American movie industry with a captive market, both at home and abroad. 'The truth is that all films were doing well,' the producer John Houseman explained. 'With transport drastically limited by rationing, there seemed to be no way to spend money except at the movies.'[1]

If he could manage to translate some of his fictional verve on to the screen, Chandler was well placed to make both a private fortune and a public reputation. He and Cissy moved into a small house at 1040 Havenhurst Drive, off Sunset Boulevard in West Hollywood. It was just five minutes from the Paramount lot.

*

Chandler had long been intrigued by Hollywood. Without it, he said, modern Los Angeles would have become even more faceless than it was: 'a mail order town. Everything in the catalogue you could get better somewhere else.'[2] As a writer, he also felt some empathy for the movie studios, given the criticism that was regularly levelled at them by intellectuals. He disliked the way East Coast and British critics were patronizing about cinema. They treated it too similarly to the way in which they treated crime fiction for him not to side with the industry:

> Hollywood is easy to hate, easy to sneer at, easy to lampoon. Some of the best lampooning has been done by people who have never walked through a studio gate, some of the best sneering by egocentric geniuses who departed huffily – not forgetting to collect their last pay check – leaving behind them nothing but the exquisite aroma of their personalities and a botched job for the tired hacks to clear up.[3]

There were other reasons why Chandler's immersion in the movie industry would prove less troublesome for him than it had been for other novelists. Geographically, he never had to 'go to Hollywood'. He was already living within an easy drive of the studios, and he had in fact been in LA longer than most people who worked in Hollywood. Nor was his decision to accept movie work complicated by the sort of vocational priorities that troubled other writers – at fifty-five, and a veteran of career changes, Chandler was jeopardizing little by agreeing to work in the movie world. Equally, as a former pulp writer, he was less likely to feel artistically insulted by the quality of the plots he would be asked to work with. Making something memorable out of a cheap plot had in fact become his vocation. As an ex-accountant, he also appreciated the fact that Hollywood was an industry like any other. He would think it a badly run one at times, but he was never shocked by the fact that studios wanted to make money first and films second.

Nor was Chandler's enthusiasm for Hollywood dampened by the low opinion in which many other novelists-turned-screenwriters held cinema as a medium. Cissy, a failed screen actress herself, had always been interested in films and had turned her husband into a semi-regular cinema goer. He was already an admirer of Orson Welles (*Citizen Kane* had been released in 1941), and he had seen enough films with Cissy by 1943 to understand that a bad film did not mean that the medium was itself bad.

The circumstances of Chandler's break into Hollywood in May 1943 were just as fortunate as had been his fast promotion within the Dabney Oil Syndicate in the early 1920s. He was, it turned out, a last-ditch choice as screenwriter for Sistrom and Wilder. The studio had an option on James Cain's murder novel *Double Indemnity*, which had been published in 1936 but which, despite Cain's popularity following the publication of *The Postman Always Rings Twice*, had never been adapted for the cinema. The studio's first choice as screenwriter, Cain himself, was unavailable to work on the project because he was already contracted to Twentieth-Century Fox. Wilder's other choice, the senior screenwriter Charles Brackett, refused to work on a film that looked so obviously destined for censorship trouble. (*The Postman Always Rings Twice* had yet to be adapted for the same reason.) At the root of this fear was Catholic censorship. The American Catholic Church, which had kept a wary eye on Hollywood from the earliest days of film-making there, had originally given the studios an advisory Code of Recommendation. But after one suggestive Mae West film too many – the 1933 movie *I'm No Angel*, in which she starred, was denounced by one of the Code's authors as having 'no more pretence of romance than a stud farm' – the Church had decided to take tougher action.

It threatened effectively to ban all American Catholics from cinema going unless the studios agreed to present scripts to a censorship board prior to production. Also to be submitted were 'wardrobe photos', showing the length of actresses' costumes, and which would have to be included with a proposed script. In effect, the Church subsequently took over the role of Hollywood's self-regulatory body, the Hays Office, setting up a full-time office of ethical censorship in Hollywood called 'The Production Code Administration'. The Code was in force by 1934, and by the late 1930s it was having a visible effect on the type of films being made. Comedies, musicals and big budget romances like *Gone with the Wind* (1939) and *Rebecca* (1940) were the order of the day.[4]

Chandler already knew about the effects that the Production Code was having on the industry. Ever since the publication of *The Big Sleep* in 1939, his New York agent, Sydney Sanders, had been trying to sell Marlowe to Hollywood. It had proved an impossible task: the Marlowe novels depicted a world – and language – in complete opposition to what the censors would accept. The Production Code was more than ethical policing – it imagined a cinema which could play a positive role in disseminating acceptable notions of good behaviour. The Code's original wording had drawn producers' attentions to

> the magnificent possibilities of the screen for character develop-ment, the building of right ideas, the inculcation in story form of right principles. If motion pictures consistently held up high types of character, presented stories that would affect lives for the better, they could become the greatest natural force for the improvement of mankind.[5]

Within these precepts, it was the Code's priority that evil in movies – even when it was condemned and punished – should never be presented in an alluring way. Indeed, the Code would not allow such films to be made. The market for hard-boiled scripts had subsequently been negligible in Hollywood during the early 1940s, and the only studio money Sydney Sanders had been able to find for Chandler's novels had come from selling their story-lines. In 1941, he had sold the rights in *Farewell My Lovely* to RKO Pictures for $2,000, and those in *The High Window* to Twentieth-Century Fox for $3,500. In Hollywood terms these were pittances: studios regularly paid over $50,000 for screen rights. The resulting films bore no similarity to Chandler's books, whether in terms of title, dialogue or characters, and in neither adaptation was the detective called Marlowe. RKO had turned *Farewell My Lovely* into *The Falcon Takes Over* in 1942 as part of the studio's 'Falcon' adventure series, which was itself a rip-off of *The Saint*. Twentieth-Century Fox had similarly used the plot of *The High Window* as part of their 'Michael Shayne' series, filming it under the title *Time to Kill* (1942).

Production Code intimidation had left both films even more unrecognizable, when compared to the Chandler originals, than had been intended. Film scripts often had to pass through the Code's offices three or four times before clearance was given to shoot. Objections to the third rewrite of *The Falcon Takes Over* in 1942 requested the following phrases and words to be cut: 'Sorry, I live with my mother'; 'It ain't that kind of place'; 'tramps'; 'joint'; 'can'; 'lousy'; and 'dope'. The studio was also reminded of a permanent list of forbidden words, which included 'broad'. The same refusal objected to the implications of effeminacy in one of the screenplay's male characters – 'We assume that there will be nothing even remotely suggestive of a "pansy" about Marriott'- and to the excessive drinking of a female character. On top of this, the whole script was deemed to be still 'too violent':

> If you will examine the script carefully, you will find that almost every character in the story possesses a gun and seems to show a willingness to use it on the slightest provocation. Any such suggestion is completely unacceptable.[6]

It was hardly possible to convey Marlowe's Los Angeles when such staple Chandler props blackjacks, whisky and loose talk were all but cut. Where most other movies provoked only specific objections from the Code Office, *The Falcon Takes Over* had brought sweeping complaints. The Code also demanded that the 'imitable' way in which the Marlowe character (now called Gay Lawrence) broke into a house be cut, as well as such lines as 'curled up with a highball and a good blonde'. In short, Production Code officials held hard-boiled fiction to be everything they were protecting America against. It was not surprising that when *The Falcon Takes Over* was eventually made in 1942, starring George Sanders, it looked limp. Chandler had ignored its release, as he did that of the even weaker *Time To Kill*.

*

It was in this atmosphere of censorship and caution that Raymond Chandler was asked to work on *Double Indemnity*, a story which not only contained Cain's trademark sexual frankness – publication of *The Postman Always Rings Twice* in 1934 had already made Cain an object of suspicion to the Church – but which encouraged sympathy for two homicidal adulterers. This last fact alone had been enough to scare off most of Paramount's luminaries from becoming involved with the project. Since all scripts had to be submitted to the Code Office before shooting could begin, there was often a laborious process of pre-production revisions to be negotiated. Too many hold-ups had occurred with projects far more innocuous than *Double Indemnity* not to make the latter look a potentially exhausting prospect. As James Cain later recalled, an initial proposal to Production Code officials for adaptation of *Double Indemnity* had resulted in 'one of those things that begin UNDER NO CIRCUMSTANCES and wind up WAY, SHAPE OR FORM'.[7] Paramount's chief screenwriter, Charles Brackett, had not been the only person scared off the project; none of the studio's leading male actors were willing to risk their images by playing a murderer.

As a result of this suspicion, *Double Indemnity* was delegated to less established hands at Paramount: Billy Wilder, who had directed only one Hollywood film before (*The Major and the Minor*), and first-time screenwriter Raymond Chandler. Like many people, Wilder had never heard of Chandler in 1943, but on reading a copy of *The High Window* he had immediately been impressed: 'How often do you read a description of a character that says he had hair growing out of his ear long enough to catch a moth?' he said. 'Not many people write like that.'[8] Having rung Chandler at his house in Pacific Palisades, both Wilder and his producer, Joe Sistrom, had anticipated meeting a man in his thirties.

Chandler arrived on the lot, Wilder recalled, dressed in tweeds and chain smoking his pipe. He was two months short of his fifty-fifth birthday. Wilder said Chandler, when he came to Sistrom's office, looked like an accountant, spoke slowly and had a habit of frowning. He was given Cain's story and told to read it. Having done so, Chandler agreed to work on the project and asked to see a copy of a typical screenplay. 'He had no idea how these things were done,' recalled Wilder.

> I remember well what he said: 'I would be interested if you think I'm the right man; but this is already Tuesday; I cannot promise you the script until next Monday.' And we looked at him as though he was a maniac. He didn't know he was going to work with me. Then he

said: 'I want a thousand dollars.' We just looked at each other.[9]

It was explained to Chandler that he would be getting $750 a week, that he would be working with Wilder, and that the job was expected to take about fourteen weeks. They would be based in the Writers' Building, a white, cloistered courtyard on the Paramount lot containing identically furnished rooms: office table and chairs, and a telephone. Wilder, an ebullient Austrian-born thirty-seven-year-old who carried a Malacca cane everywhere he went and would swing it in the air continuously, had directed his first film in Paris ten years earlier, and had previously worked as a crime correspondent in Vienna in the 1920s. Shorter, younger and more excitable than Chandler, Wilder could be just as stubborn.

Once work began, the relationship between the two men soured. The collaboration had brought Chandler into close daily contact with another human, apart from Cissy, for the first time since Dabney's. Wilder, for his part, initially found Chandler 'peculiar, a sort of rather acid man'. His second impression was that the writer hated him. Working in the same room as Wilder, Chandler became increasingly annoyed by him. One morning, four weeks into the script, he failed to show up at the studio. Wilder went to his producer's office to find Joe Sistrom holding a letter from Chandler:

> It was a letter of complaint against me: he couldn't work with me anymore because I was rude; I was drinking; I was fucking; I was on the phone with four broads, with one I was on the phone – he clocked me – for twelve and a half minutes; I had asked him to pull down the Venetian blinds without saying 'please'. A whole list of complaints. So we got him in, and said, 'Come on, cut out this shit, come on for Christ's sake, we don't have court manners here.' And I apologized: I will never talk, I will never drink in your presence, and so on. And we finished the script.[10]

Chandler started drinking again. 'He was a reformed alcoholic,' said Wilder. 'Then he fell off the wagon.' Wilder's next movie, *The Lost Weekend*, was to be a study in alcoholism, and he spotted his co-writer's relapse immediately; even though Chandler continued to claim to be teetotal. Wilder's biographer recorded what his subject had known was happening:

> Every time Wilder went to the toilet, Chandler went to his briefcase. He took out a pint of whisky. He always carried his briefcase. It was a capacious brown briefcase with three compartments. Inside was a small writing board and sheets of cut up yellow paper – and some liquor. Chandler was wont to wander around the city and sit at bars looking around.[11]

Despite the antipathy, Wilder quickly recognized Chandler's ability as a screenwriter: 'We would start scene by scene, and we started with the dialogue, and then with transition. And he was very good at that, just very, very good.' (Years after the project, Wilder would describe Chandler as 'one of the greatest creative minds I've ever encountered', as well as 'a naive, sweet, warm man'. He also said that the crime writer gave him 'more trouble than any other writer I ever worked with'.)[12] Notwithstanding their differences, the two men were forced into a form of solidarity against the Production Code, whose officials were watching the script with special wariness. Joseph Breen, who ran the censor board at this time, had made three preliminary objections to the film: firstly, that both the hero and the heroine were murderers; secondly, that they were also adulterers, and thirdly, that there were too many 'imitable details of crime' in the story. The last point was one that the Production Code officials took very seriously, as they pointed out on returning Wilder and Chandler's script for the second time in July 1943. It was felt that there were far too many felonious tips that might be used by criminals. One line, for instance, was to be cut 'in line with the Association's regular policy re. fingerprints', because it featured the use of gloves. Also to be cut was 'reference to specific poisons'. Negotiations between Joseph Breen and Paramount producer Joe Sistrom continued until late November of 1943. 'You go in with dreams,' said Chandler, 'and you come out with the Parent-Teachers' Association.'

This battle against the Production Code was complicated for Chandler by the fact that he himself also objected to Cain's use of sex in his novels. He had never had a problem with violence, and indeed had written some of the most explicitly violent scenes ever to appear in *Black Mask*, but he thought explicit sex was both boring and insidious:

> Synthetic stallions like James Cain have made a fetish of pure orgasms, which the middle classes seem to regard as a semi-respectable adjunct to raising a family. The literary glorification of lust leads to emotional impotence, because the love story has little or nothing to do with lust. It cannot exist against a background of cheese cakes and multiple marriages.

By shifting the censorable aspects of Cain's story away from the details of sin into a less censorable atmosphere of sin, Wilder and Chandler eventually finished a script Breen accepted.

The co-authorship of *Double Indemnity*'s script makes it difficult to distinguish which parts Chandler had a greater hand in writing, but there are some scenes that clearly bear his trademarks. The film's wit is much less conceptual than Wilder's later films like *Some Like It Hot* and *Sunset Boulevard,* and most critics, as well as Wilder, now attribute that to his co-writer. The filmmaker Woody Allen once described *Double Indemnity* as Wilder's best movie, and 'practically anybody's best movie'. As director and co-screenwriter, it was understandably Wilder who received most attention at the time of the film's release. Few critics recognized or mentioned Raymond Chandler's name on the credits. Few film critics had heard of him.

One typical Chandler scene in *Double Indemnity* is the moment when Fred MacMurray (a comedy actor whose career consequently turned around after accepting a lead role that all of Paramount's male stars had been wary of accepting) meets Barbara Stanwyck, as Phyllis Dietrichson, for the first time. The carnality of Cain's novel had been shifted into double-entendre banter. MacMurray plays Walter Neff, an insurance salesman who drives to the LA house of a Mr Dietrichson in order to renew the latter's car insurance. He is not at home, but his beautiful wife is. She flirts knowingly with Neff, who responds in kind. Eventually he pushes it too far and Mrs Dietrichson playfully puts her foot down:

Dietrichson: There's a speed limit in this state – 45 miles an hour.

Neff: How fast was I going, Officer?
Dietrichson: I'd say about 90.
Neff: Suppose you get down off that motorcycle and give me a ticket.
Dietrichson: Suppose I give you a warning instead.
Neff: Suppose it doesn't take.

As Neff leaves, she tells him to come back the next afternoon to speak to her husband about the insurance:

Neff: Will you be here too?
Dietrichson: I guess so. I usually am.
Neff: Same chair, same perfume, same anklet?
Dietrichson: I wonder if I know what you mean.
Neff: I wonder if you wonder.

The couple soon consummate their flirtations, and hatch a plot to kill Dietrichson in a way that will be undetectable and which will reap the highest insurance payoff. At the other end of the plot, Neff and Mrs Dietrichson (who has by then betrayed him) have their final encounter. Neff approaches her with a gun, and she makes a final effort to seduce him again. The scene, which does not read as powerfully as it films, illustrates Chandler's later belief that the best scenes in films are the ones with the fewest words.[13] 'Sorry, baby,' says Neff, with his gun still pointed at her, 'I'm not buying.' 'I'm not asking you to buy,' she begs, 'just hold me.' He holds her, the camera focusing on her eyes, which widen in terror. 'Goodbye, baby,' says Neff, with the camera still frozen on Dietrichson's eyes. Then comes the sound of the gun firing. As with the double-entendre banter of their first meeting, which managed to be sexual without being explicit, the final scene between them showed how Wilder and Chandler had managed to achieve terror without gore. It was this clever displacement by the co-writers that forced the Production Code into finally allowing the film to be made.

In the character of Keyes, played by Edward G. Robinson, Chandler also had a Marlowe-type figure to play with. Keyes is Neff's colleague, and nemesis, at the insurance company, where he is the company's chief claims investigator. In Cain's novel, he was a minor character of authority, but in the screenplay he is a fully sketched and cynical bachelor. He is fond of Neff and has an innate suspicion of all women which, in the case of Mrs Dietrichson, proves justified. At the start of the film he tries to persuade Neff to change departments and work under him as an investigator. It is a promotion, but Neff turns it down because he likes selling. Keyes isn't impressed: 'I thought you were a shade less dumb than the rest of the outfit. Guess I was wrong. You're not smarter, just taller.' Like Chandler, Keyes is a suspicious eccentric in his mid fifties and, like Chandler, he smokes throughout the film. It has been suggested by one critic that the screenplay version of the Neff–Keyes relationship became a subconscious commentary by Wilder and Chandler on their own working relationship: antipathy tempered by grudging respect.[14]

Chandler claimed he never enjoyed working on his first film. It had been a superhuman test of patience for him, both in having to work at such close quarters with another person, and in having to accept the compromises forced on a studio writer by censors and producers. He did not want to be a prima donna screenwriter, he said, but it was

> an agonizing experience and probably shortened my life; but I learned as much about screenwriting as I am capable of learning, which is not very much. . . . The wise screenwriter is he who wears his second-best suit, artistically speaking, and doesn't take things too much to heart. He should have a touch of cynicism, but only a touch. The complete cynic is as useless to Hollywood as he is to himself.[15]

It was usual for a screenwriter, particularly a debutant, to be taken off salary once the last revision to his script had been made, but at Wilder's request Chandler was kept on throughout the ten-week shooting of *Double Indemnity*, and no change was made on set without his approval. There continued to be bad blood between the two writers, however. After the first preview of the film in Westwood Village, an ecstatic James Cain waited in the lobby to embrace the pair, but Chandler had already reached his car by way of a fire exit. He claimed that he was not invited to the full première of the film. Wilder said he was invited, but did not make the première because he was 'under a table drunk at Lucey's', the same restaurant where, at about this time, Humphrey Bogart was beginning many of his own drinking binges.

With *Double Indemnity* still in post-production over the winter of 1943, Paramount signed Chandler on contract – he was to be paid $1,250 a week as an in-house screenwriter. And in confirmation of the studio's excitement over *Double Indemnity*, the film was an immediate success on its release in 1944. There had not been a movie as blackly comic and 'contemporary' since the pre-Production Code days of the 1930s, and *Double Indemnity* attracted as many plaudits as it did outbursts of moral indignation. Chandler was impressed by how alert the movie press was to the quality of *Double Indemnity,* in a way that book reviewers had never been to his Marlowe books. The *New York Herald Tribune* described it as a 'superb' film of 'such eloquence, fluency and suspense that it is something more than a fascinating thriller'. *Variety* echoed this, saying that the film set a new standard for crime films and that, 'as a piece of screen craftsmanship', it was masterful, both in writing and direction.

Because *Double Indemnity* created such a box-office and critical sensation, it prompted almost all the other studios in Hollywood to start dropping their excessive caution towards the Production Code. The seeds of hard-boiled cinema had been sown in Hollywood long before, but *Double Indemnity* made the making of such films look both feasible and bankable. On 6 December 1945, nearly twelve months after the film's release, the *Daily News* underlined the effect that the film had had on Hollywood:

> Since Paramount's Double Indemnity became one of Hollywood's box office smash hits last year, all the studios have gone in for making pictures based on realistic murder stories. The tougher and gorier the better it seems. . . . This may go down in film history as the year in which Hollywood hoisted the crime picture from its long accepted and slightly deprecated status as the old reliable of the B and lesser brackets.

Double Indemnity was nominated for two Oscars – Best Movie and Best Screenplay – awards it was deprived of by an Academy still unsure how to react to such a film in front of the Catholic censors. Both Oscars went to another Paramount film, *Going My Way*, a musical comedy starring Bing Crosby as a priest. Word at the studio was that the Academy had told Paramount bosses it felt unable to be seen condoning *Double Indemnity* in front of the Production Code officials, and so had made the awards in question to the other Paramount production.

If *Double Indemnity* had been almost too appropriate a film for Chandler to make his debut with in 1944, the next two tasks that Paramount put him to were far from hard-boiled. The studio now saw Chandler as a 'dialogue doctor' first and a hard-boiled writer second, and so put him to work on salvaging weak scripts. The first was *And Now Tomorrow*, an Alan Ladd and Loretta Young vehicle which was released later in 1944. It was a leafy New England love story about a beautiful deaf heiress and a young local doctor named Vance who cures her and falls in love: less dark a setting or more narrow a space for wisecracks could not be imagined. Even when the script was funny, it was a shadow of anything Chandler had done in his books:

Vance: Coffee
Counter Man: How do you like it?
Vance: Hot, strong, and made this year.
Counter Man: You won't like ours.
Vance: Got a match?

The acting was worse. 'A very stupid little movie,' said the *New York Times* on its release; 'whatever it was this actress never had, she still hasn't got.' The film was still a success, however, largely because Alan Ladd was one of the biggest box-office draws of the day.

Chandler started to enjoy the weekdays he spent at his Paramount office. *Double Indemnity* had been a gruelling experience, but it had been an unusually intense collaboration. Chandler's work as a dialogue doctor was far less claustrophobic. Once reaccustomed to being with other people, he enjoyed the company. 'The screenwriter meets clever and interesting people and may even make lasting friendships. . . . I heard some of the best wit I've ever heard in my life,' he said. 'Some of the boys are at their best when not writing.' Others on the lot began to warm to Chandler, including the studio's publicity director, Teet Carle: 'He was incredibly friendly. I often sneaked up from my office to get close enough to speak to him.' Another Paramount contemporary, Robert Presnell, confirms Chandler's good spirits:

> He took time from his own work to talk to me practically any time I popped into his office looking forlorn. He said he loved interruptions more than anything – because things you do when you're supposed to be doing something else are always more fun. Digression is the spice of life. He told me to write whatever I wanted to because no one in the front office could read anyway.[16]

Chandler and Cissy had now moved to Drexel Avenue, further to the south of Hollywood, off La Cienega. Though it was as cheap a residential area as that in which they had been previously living, their house, number 6320, was on a broad and leafy stretch of Drexel Avenue and was set back from the road, as well as having its own garden. Chandler had also bought a huge, grey-green vintage Packard convertible in which he and Cissy would drive up the coast at weekends.

After *And Now Tomorrow,* he was asked to salvage *The Unseen*, a melodramatic 'horror' movie which had been three-quarters written and then abandoned. The story was again set in East Coast America, in a sleepy, civilized town where unexplained things go on in a large house containing two nasty children, their pompous father, his dubious friend, and the children's frightened new governess. *The Unseen* was intended primarily as a sequel to a slightly better Paramount film called *The Uninvited,* but it was irredeemably clichéd. 'You're pretty,' the new governess is told menacingly when she arrives at the house. 'Last one was pretty too.' As if to emphasize the film's slightness, the script failed to provoke even one objection from the Production Code when it was submitted in 1944. Chandler's touch is invisible, and the only redeeming aspect of the project was that he met and liked the film's young English producer, John Houseman, whose first film this was. Houseman admitted later that the only reason the film was distributed was because, by the 1940s, every film Hollywood put out was making money. The war in Europe had both enriched America and left it with gasoline rationing. There was little else for Americans to do but go to a local cinema, and since Hollywood studios also owned the nation's cinemas, people were watching whatever the studios gave them.

Chandler was now a popular figure among Paramount writers. 'It was a club,' said Robert Presnell, 'and Chandler presided.' There would always be champagne in the fourth-floor fridge, and if a group of writers started drinking in the morning they would often sit about talking until lunch. Hollywood's wealth at this time had relaxed everyone's deadlines. 'Studios were pretty easygoing places then,' said Presnell. 'We'd take six or eight months to write a screenplay.' The writers would sit together at lunch in the studio canteen, Chandler often being encouraged to launch into a spiel: 'He was so vivid, so right-on, so aware of the Human Comedy.' With his pipe and tweeds and incongruously modern banter, he was a source of both entertainment and amusement to those around him. As an industry, Hollywood also attracted enough eccentrics to give Chandler's own character leeway. 'The only employer I ever had that I got along with was in Hollywood at Paramount Studios', he later wrote, 'and there as a matter of course one began each day by telling everybody to go to hell. At least I did. They even seemed to like that.'[17]

In 1944, Chandler had an affair with one of the secretaries at Paramount. Like his affair at Dabney's, it was very brief, and known now only through the recollection of his colleagues. Cissy's reaction, either to the affair or to the fact that her husband had started drinking again, is unrecorded. As an old woman with three husbands to her credit, and who in younger years had been an opium-taking nude model, it is possible that she forgave, overlooked, or was becoming too ill to care about Chandler's behaviour. And most evenings, he would return home rather than go out with people from Paramount. As he had been at Dabney's, he was a lively man in the office, but for the most part extremely private outside it; moreover, he had now begun to plan a new Marlowe novel. 'In Hollywood,' recalled John Houseman, 'where the selection of wives was frequently confused with casting, Cissy was something of a phenomenon. Ray's life had been hard; he looked ten years older than his age. His wife looked twenty years older than he did and dressed thirty years younger.' Houseman was one of very few Hollywood colleagues to be invited by the Chandlers on one of their Sunday drives along the coast.

After eleven years of penny-pinching self-discipline, Chandler enjoyed being overpaid and underemployed at Paramount. He disliked the vanity that surrounded such things as screen-credit pecking orders ('the constant fear of losing all this fairy gold and becoming the nothing they have really never ceased to be'), but he accepted it as part of the entertainment business. He was more appalled, however, by the massive waste and inefficiency of Hollywood, which he saw as a messily run industry, whose profits were ensured only by the monopoly it enjoyed. This commercial aspect of Hollywood's stranglehold fascinated him. In the Marlowe novel on which Chandler had started to work at weekends, Philip Marlowe comes across a studio boss called Oppenheimer, whose only real affection is for his dogs:

> I must have been wearing my stupid expression again. He waved a hand around the patio. 'Fifteen hundred theatres is all you need. The motion picture business is the only business in the world in which you can make all the mistakes in the world and still make money.'
>
> 'Must be the only business in the world where you can have three dogs pee up against your office desk,' I said.
>
> 'You have to have the fifteen hundred theatres.'
>
> 'That makes it a little harder to get a start,' I said.[18]

There were other aspects of boom-time Hollywood that Chandler distrusted. 'Actors used to enter by the back door,' he said after his first film, 'and most of them still should.' His exceptions to this rule were Cary Grant – another Anglo-American, whom Chandler always said was his first choice to play Marlowe – and Humphrey Bogart. Producers, Chandler found, were generally 'low-grade individuals with the morals of a goat and the artistic integrity of a slot machine', though there were enough 'able and humane' ones to give hope. The same proportion of integrity applied, Chandler decided, to the world of agents, directors and publicists: there were abundant bad ones to make Hollywood stink, but always enough decent, friendly and amusing ones to make working there enjoyable. Had that not been the case, he insisted, the money alone would not have been enough to keep him there:

> Money buys pathetically little in Hollywood beyond the pleasure of

living in an unreal world, associating with a narrow group of people who think, talk and drink nothing but pictures, most of them bad, and the doubtful pleasure of watching famous actors and actresses guzzle in some of the rudest restaurants in the world.[19]

*

The success of *Double Indemnity* indirectly raised Philip Marlowe's stock in Hollywood as much as it had Chandler's. The film was groundbreaking enough, in censorship terms, to make the possibility of a more faithful Marlowe adaptation now appear feasible, and it also raised the industry's curiosity about what fiction Chandler had written before starting at Paramount. Even before *Double Indemnity* had gone on general release in 1944, Warner Brothers bought the rights to *The Big Sleep* for $10,000, and had begun to make plans for a major production. RKO, realizing what it had missed with its earlier adaptation of *Farewell My Lovely* (but still owning film rights to the book) now made a second adaptation, with the actor Dick Powell playing the first-ever screen Philip Marlowe.[20] Contracted as he was to Paramount, Chandler had nothing to do with the making of the film, but it was a considerable improvement on RKO's previous effort. The project encountered the same initial problems as had *Double Indemnity*. No established actor on the RKO lot was willing to jeopardize his reputation in a murder film, and in the end the movie relaunched the career of Powell, another comic actor:

It ended my ten-year effort to escape musicals. . . . Offers for hard-boiled roles poured in after the picture was released and a new career was opened for me.[21]

Though still robbed of much of its spine by the censors, who had not failed to notice the flurry of activity around Chandler, the movie was well made, and had a major 'A' budget. Lacking Wilder and Chandler's ability to subvert the Production Code, the script was more that of a crisp mystery movie than anything truly hard-boiled, but it still portrayed a fairly convincing Marlowe. By using a voice-over, it also used passages of Chandler's original narrative:

1. Chandler as a boy on an early summer holiday in Ireland, c. 1896.

2. House photo at Dulwich College, c. 1902, with Chandler circled.

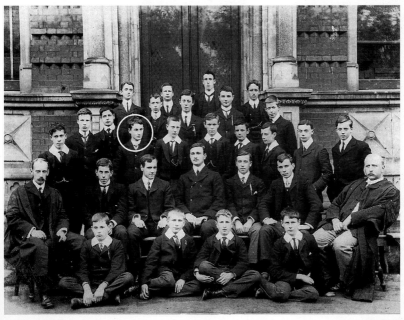

C·CLARE
Hofphotograph

FREIBURG ½B
Holzmarktplatz 10.

3. Chandler on his 'grand tour', in southern Germany, 1907.

4. The First World War: Chandler in the Canadian Gordon Highlanders, 1917.

5. Florence Chandler, Raymond's mother, after her arrival in Los Angeles.

6. Chandler back in California after the war.

7. Cissy Pascal (née Pearl Eugenie Hurlburt) before her marriage to Chandler.

8. A long way from Dulwich: Chandler on a California beach in the 1920s.

9. With colleagues at the Dabney oil fields: Chandler circled, left; Joseph Dabney, centre front with hat.

10. Chandler with his mother outside Los Angeles, shortly before her death.

11. Chandler, circled, at an oil industry annual banquet, 1927.

Facing page:

12. (*Top*) Barbara Stanwyck, Fred MacMurray and Edward G. Robinson in *Double Indemnity*, 1946, Chandler's first Hollywood screenplay, written with Billy Wilder.

13. (*Bottom*) Humphrey Bogart and Lauren Bacall in the classic film version of Chandler's *The Big Sleep*, 1946.

14. (*Right*) Cissy, Chandler's wife for over thirty years.

15. (*Below*) Chandler at La Jolla, with Taki, the cat.

16. Dinner with his agent, Helga Greene, in the 1950s (Chandler wearing white gloves to cover a skin condition).

17. Chandler, shortly before his death in 1959.

'Okay Marlowe,' I said to myself. 'You're a tough guy. You've been sapped twice, choked, beaten silly with a gun, shot in the arm until you're crazy as a couple of waltzing mice. Now let's see you do something really tough – like putting your pants on.'

Released in 1944 as *Murder My Sweet* – the title was changed at the last minute after it was found that people thought *Farewell My Lovely* sounded like a musical – the movie impressed Chandler, though it did nothing to reduce his suspicion of the censors. It was for him a suspicion exacerbated by the long-held distrust of the Catholic Church which he had inherited as an Anglo-Irish child in Waterford:

> My belief is, Hollywood will never find itself until it has the guts to tell the Catholics to go to hell. I hope I am not being offensive, but I believe (and I believe they know it) that the political power of the Catholic Church is an evil thing, that it is used without scruple or fairness for only one purpose – to maintain that power.[22]

*

To add to what he was now earning in Hollywood, Chandler was continuously receiving reprint royalties – and, increasingly, advances for foreign-language rights – for his first four Marlowe books. Both recognition and reputation were slowly beginning to surround his writing. In 1945, he was briefly profiled in *Newsweek*. The following year a journal published by the University of Toronto described him as a 'genius'.

After so long in self-imposed exile, Chandler was now 'connecting' with people again. In Hollywood, he was surrounded by sharp and funny minds of a similarly cynical bent to his own. He enjoyed spending time with screenwriters, since he found that the industry had generally eroded whatever East Coast pretensions they might once have had. 'Writers as a class', he said, 'I have found to be oversensitive and spiritually undernourished. They have the egotism of actors and rarely the good looks or charm. . . . That's one thing I like about Hollywood. The writer is there revealed in his ultimate corruption. He asks no praise, because the praise comes to him in the form of a salary check. In Hollywood the average writer is not young, not honest, not brave, and a bit overdressed. But he is darn good company.'[23] And although Chandler may have resisted the temptation to overdress, he was certainly earning the money: in 1946 he paid $50,000 worth of income tax. Despite this wealth, he and Cissy had not moved out of the house on Drexel Avenue. 'No swimming pools,' he said, 'no stone marten coats for a floozie in an apartment, no charge accounts at Romanoff's, no parties, no ranch with riding horses . . . fewer friends but a lot more money.'

The Unseen marked the end of Chandler's first contract at Paramount. The release of *Murder My Sweet* had meanwhile prompted another surge in sales of the Pocket Book editions of his novels, which were now approaching 2 million copies. He was too big a name to hide in the screen credits and in H. N. Swanson he had a Hollywood agent who was too sharp to let that fact go unrewarded. Getting on to Swanson's books so quickly was almost enough in itself to cement Chandler's reputation in Hollywood. 'Swanie' was a notorious power-broker, and had represented both F. Scott Fitzgerald and William Faulkner. He would later represent the crime writer Elmore Leonard, who recalls visiting Swanson for the first time:

> Everyone in the motion picture business and the publishing field knows him as Swanie. They say 'Sure. Swanie, a very dear friend of mine, known him for years.' Then they smile and shake their heads with a faraway look in their eyes remembering the time they went a few negotiating rounds with him. . . . [When I first went to meet him] I climbed the stairs of the Swanson Building to Swanie's second-floor office of dark wood, wall scenes, venetian blinds, and a thousand books. A silver-haired gentleman in a double-breasted, pin-striped suit, a carnation in the buttonhole, said, 'Well, kiddo, welcome to Hollywood.'

Chandler liked Swanson. 'It is remarkable to me,' he said, 'that Swanie has been able to operate in Hollywood all these years without degenerating into a petty chiseller or large-scale racketeer.'[24] Swanson was famous in Hollywood for his Savile Row panache and his hard dealing, both of which Chandler enjoyed watching. The two men would often lunch together at Lucey's, and held a considerable, if ironic, respect for each other. Chandler said he always knew where he stood with Swanson.

When Swanson sent him a Sherlock Holmes tie one Christmas, Chandler wrote a thank-you note, adding that 'A guy who worked his way up to a wrist watch, and then slid back down to a tie knows exactly what his rating is.'

Swanson was an imaginative agent, and he had big plans for Chandler. The diverse projects he began pitching around Hollywood for his new client included a Joan Crawford vehicle, an A-movie western, a racing thriller set in France, and a British film contract. There were also plans for a Chandler adaptation of *The Great Gatsby*, a book both men admired. Swanson knew how to deal with the occasionally irascible and frequently suspicious Chandler: a balance of ignoring a lot of what Chandler said, he decided, and of paying careful attention to the rest.

Having served as agent to such infamous alcoholics as Fitzgerald and Faulkner, Swanson understood Chandler's own temperament well. 'Some of the best writers I have known,' said Swanson in 1989, 'seemed to do their best work when they were drying out after a drinking bout. Perhaps the urgency of lost time and uncompleted work spurred them on.' He included Chandler in this. He had the kind of common-sense attitude to life that Chandler appreciated. Whenever asked what kind of writing was the most profitable, Swanson would reply, 'ransom notes'.

Swanson now negotiated an agreement with Paramount whereby Chandler would begin work at the studio on an original screenplay. He would have a room on the lot and no undue time pressures. Paramount would pay him a weekly rate of $1,000 and have first refusal on buying the rights to whatever he produced. Chandler was delighted with the deal and had begun working on story ideas by the end of 1944. In January 1945, however, Alan Ladd was recalled to fight in the war and Paramount was thrown into panic. Ladd was arguably the leading male star of his day, and the studio was paying a fortune to keep him on their books. News that he had been called up for a second time by the US Army, and had only twelve weeks left in America, sparked a blizzard of memos from head office insisting that a Ladd vehicle be rushed through.

According to John Houseman, when news of the Alan Ladd situation got out, Chandler offered to turn his half-finished story into a script. Houseman read the typescript, bought it for $25,000, and pre-production began immediately. The story, filmed as *The*

Blue Dahlia, involved a soldier returning from war with two friends only to find that his wife has been playing around in his absence with booze, gangsters and parties. On the night of her husband's return she is murdered, and the soldier (played by Alan Ladd) is immediately suspected. His only chance of proving his innocence is to avoid the police, who are seeking to arrest him, and find the real murderer himself. He eventually does so with the help of the wife of his wife's lover (Veronica Lake), and the movie ends with the two of them falling in love.

By the time a director, cast and set had been arranged, Chandler was well into the adaptation and shooting began. As the round-the-clock shooting schedule started to catch up with him, however, he began to get bad writer's block. Paramount bosses offered him a $5,000 bonus if he finished on time, which made him even more tense, and then, to cap his panic, the US Navy insisted that he change the story's ending. The original murderer was to have been 'Buzz', one of the two friends with whom the hero has returned from the war. Buzz has committed the murder while suffering a blackout, the result of shell-shock, and is now helping the hero find his wife's murderer, unaware that he himself is the killer. Wartime military censors in Hollywood, however, were not prepared for a big Hollywood film to have a serviceman portrayed as a murderer, and Chandler was told by Paramount to change it quickly.

On top of this problem, the shooting that had already taken place was proving Veronica Lake ('Moronica Lake', Chandler called her) and Alan Ladd to be so unconvincing as tough desperadoes that several of the love scenes between them had to be rewritten. This tipped it for Chandler. Two weeks into the shoot, he left his fourth-floor office and went to see Houseman, explaining that he could not think of a new ending and that he was going home. Which he then did. The following morning he reappeared in Houseman's panic-stricken office and announced that he had been up all night and had come to a decision: he had, as he believed Houseman knew, previously been an alcoholic. Because he felt that he could not let down a fellow English public schoolboy – Houseman had been educated at Clifton College, near Bristol – he was prepared to break his writer's block by relapsing completely. He said that this was the only way he could finish the script and that it would probably damage him irreparably. He had, however, to be allowed to work at home rather than at the studio. Houseman agreed, and Chandler then presented a list of further requirements that he had written up the night before. Houseman recounted the list in his memoirs:

A.
Two Cadillac limousines, to stand day and night outside the house with drivers available for:
1. Fetching the doctor (Ray's or Cissy's or both).
2. Taking script pages to and from the studio.
3. Driving the maid to market.
4. Contingencies and emergencies.
B.
Six secretaries – in three relays of two – to be in constant attendance and readiness, available at all times for dictation and other possible emergencies.
C.
A direct line open at all times to my office by day and the studio switchboard at night.

Houseman agreed to all the conditions:

Ray now became extremely cheerful. It was almost noon, and he suggested, as proof of my faith in him, that we drive to the most expensive restaurant in Los Angeles and tie one on together. We left the studio and drove to Perino's, where I watched him down three double martinis before eating a large and carefully selected lunch, followed by three double stingers. We then drove back to his house, where the two Cadillacs were already in position and the first relay of secretaries at their posts. . . .

I went over there from time to time and he would extend a white and trembling hand and acknowledge my expressions of gratitude with the modest smile of a gravely wounded war hero who has shown courage well beyond the call of duty.[25]

Chandler finished the script at the house on Drexel Avenue. *The Blue Dahlia*, which in all had taken only forty-two days to make, was a flawed triumph. The 'kick-'em-in-the-teeth hit', as the *Hollywood Reporter* called it, was widely praised and several reviews singled out the contribution of 'Raymond Chandler'.

Paramount were delighted, and offered their reluctant saviour $4,000 a week to stay with them, to which Chandler – suffering the familiar effects of extreme alcohol abuse – agreed.

Although parts of the acting in *The Blue Dahlia* had not been convincing, some good Chandler lines had been delivered: 'Just don't get too complicated Eddie,' a nightclub owner is warned at one point by his accountant. 'When a guy gets too complicated he's unhappy. And when he's unhappy, his luck runs out.' Despite their weaknesses, Lake (whose character name was Joyce Harwood) and Ladd (Johnny Morrison) had also managed to carry some strong scenes:

> *Joyce:* I suppose you've seen me before.
> *Morrison:* Have I?
> *Joyce:* Probably, I used to work in a dance hall down on Main Street.
> *Morrison:* Yes, I've seen you before alright. But not in any dance hall and not on any main street.
> *Joyce:* Where then?
> *Morrison:* Every guy's seen you before somewhere. The trick is to find you. And when he does, it's usually too late.

Chandler had also added some autobiographical touches to the character of the shell-shocked Buzz. In the screen notes, he described Buzz as having a father, 'who was found drunk if he was found at all. Buzz doesn't want any part of him. He's going to get a job and bring his mother out to live with him in Los Angeles. . . . He wanted to get his own mother out here and make a home for her. He wanted a lot of things.' As Chandler had in the days when he drank heavily, Buzz also suffers from blackouts, something the author went on to explain in the screen notes: 'He gets headaches and loud noises bother him, and once in a while after excitement, he blacks out. He can't remember what happened. Some people do this from drinking too much.'[26]

While Chandler's self-sacrifice in making *The Blue Dahlia* is something of a Hollywood legend (it has even been the subject of a BBC radio play), there is another version of events which is less epic and melodramatic than Houseman's account. In 1978, in a magazine article subtitled 'How Raymond Chandler Screwed

Hollywood', Billy Wilder's biographer, Maurice Zolotow, claimed that Chandler's *Blue Dahlia* 'sacrifice' was in fact a scam 'of such daring and brilliance that rich old screenwriters still tell the story with awe as they sip their martinis in the late afternoon on Brentwood patios'. He claims that after having sold the rights of *The Blue Dahlia* to Paramount for $25,000 while still in its half-finished prose form, Chandler started having problems keeping up the pace because he was already drinking heavily again. Zolotow says that well before Chandler announced his offer in Houseman's office, he was drinking so heavily that he was having trouble making it on to the Paramount lot in the mornings. He may have been looking tense and haggard when he went to see Houseman, Zolotow continues, but 'wouldn't anyone who had been drinking around the clock?'

Chandler, again according to Zolotow, simply wanted to work at home, which was strictly against studio policy, and so 'concocted this terrific story that he had been sober for years, and if he went back to heavy drinking he was likely to die'. In short, with the limos, secretaries and doctors on call, Chandler had managed to secure for himself an alcoholic's dream job description: 'He swilled his bourbon. He passed out. He awakened. He took a shot. He dictated a few speeches. He passed out again.'[27]

The Blue Dahlia was certainly written under the extreme influence of drink: an influence betrayed in the very text of the script. The Production Code's first refusal of the script contained thirteen separate warnings against the excessive mention of alcohol. 'Please hold to a minimum the emphasis of the general drinking by the guests at the party,' ran an early objection. Another insisted that the phrase 'double Scotch' be removed from the script. Despite this purge, the movie both starts in a bar and ends on the way to another. At the end, the three heroes leave an Los Angeles police station with Veronica Lake. 'Uh, let's find some place where we can get a drink, huh?' asks Buzz. 'We gotta wait for Johnny,' says his friend, pointing to Veronica Lake and Alan Ladd, who are kissing. 'We gotta wait for Johnny?' says Buzz, in the script's very last line, 'Whatya think I am, a camel?'

What Zolotow possibly overlooks was Chandler's ability to

believe his own fantasies. Wilder's biographer presumes deviousness, when more often Chandler's lies were a form of self-delusion. The fact was that Chandler frequently resorted to fantasy when making excuses for his alcoholism, or for other truths he wanted to forget. Later in his life, he would sometimes claim that he had been mugged as an excuse for arriving late and dishevelled; moreover, he was often already drunk when he made up such stories. He had certainly started binge drinking before *The Blue Dahlia*, but his refusal to admit this may have been for reasons more complicated than a simple ploy to enable him to work from home. Chandler was hard to fathom, confirmed Swanson, but it was only really reductive people who would interpret his baffling privacy as scheming self-interest:

> Ray Chandler was a strange man, and he liked making up stories to amuse himself. . . . Ray loved his cat. He had a cat he would talk to for hours. That cat knew more about him than anybody else. He was a loner. He was a shy man and he struck some people as cold and rude. He was good to his cat and his wife, who was sick and dying. Took care of her himself, he did. Wouldn't let a nurse touch her. Once bought her a large car. She was too sick to drive it. But he wanted her to know that she had it in case she ever got better.[28]

*

It was after *The Blue Dahlia* that Chandler decided that he wanted to return to his novels. He also wanted to get Cissy out of Los Angeles, as he had been promising to do for ten years. He took her up to Big Bear Lake for three months, but on his return, in July 1945, MGM hired him to adapt his fourth Marlowe novel, *The Lady in the Lake*. Chandler found the project so tedious, however, that he began making up scenes that were not in his own book. Eventually he gave up, after three months' work at $1,000 a week.

> I worked at MGM once in that cold storage plant they call the Thalberg Building. . . . About that time some potato-head, probably Mannix [Edgar Mannix, deputy boss at MGM], had decided that writers would do more work if they had no couches to lie on. So there was no couch in my office. . . . I got a steamer rug out of the car, spread it on the floor and lay down on that. . . . I said I would

work at home. They said Mannix had issued orders no writers to be allowed to work at home. I said a man as big as Mannix ought to be allowed the privilege of changing his mind. So I worked at home, and only went over there three or four times.[29]

The screenplay, rights to which had cost MGM $35,000, was finished by the screenwriter Steve Fisher, and the film was directed by Robert Montgomery, who also played Marlowe. He used a 'camera-eye' technique whereby the camera is Marlowe, whom the audience only sees if he is in front of a mirror. 'Old stuff,' said Chandler. 'Let's make the camera a character; it's been said at every lunch table in Hollywood one time or another.' He refused screen credits for the film.

Instead, he took Cissy back up to Big Bear Lake: 'We go out to the woods and I chop knots out of fallen trees and break up a few stumps of ironwood or mountain mahogany, a very hard reddish wood that burns like coal.' He was still officially under contract to Paramount, but he now simply refused to turn up at the lot. The studio told Swanson that Chandler could direct or produce his own films if he came back, but this too failed to bring him in. Eventually, in January 1946, he was suspended for what Paramount termed his 'failure, neglect and unwillingness to report to the studio'. In May, Paramount tried again, offering him $1,500 a week to adapt any book he chose. He began on a novel by Elizabeth Sanxay Holding, called *The Innocent Mrs Duff*, but once more he grew bored and the film was never made. The write-off cost Paramount $53,000, of which $18,000 had been paid to Chandler for seventy-two days' work. Samuel Goldwyn then met with Chandler in an attempt to persuade him to work for MGM again. Chandler was amused ('I suppose everyone ought to meet Samuel Goldwyn this side of paradise,' he said), but resolved to pull out of Los Angeles altogether. Apart from anything else, his body needed a rest.

He bought a house near San Diego, in the town in which he and Cissy had so long planned to live – La Jolla. Ten miles north of the Mexican border, the house was brand-new and luxurious, and looked out on the Pacific. He and Cissy would live there for the next nine years. Before he left LA, though, Chandler issued a parting critique of his erstwhile employers, in an essay for the magazine *Atlantic Monthly*, entitled 'Hollywood and the Screen-writer', which appeared in November 1945:

> What Hollywood seems to want is a writer who is ready to commit suicide in every story conference. What it actually gets is the fellow who screams like a stallion in heat and then cuts his throat with a banana. The scream demonstrates the artistic purity of his soul and he can eat the banana while somebody is answering a telephone call about some other picture.[30]

Although even this article betrayed Chandler's exhaustion, it provoked an aggressive reaction from Hollywood. 'Have been blackballed at all the best bistros and cat-houses,' he beamed to a correspondent shortly after its publication. *Atlantic Monthly* liked the article, however, and asked Chandler to cover the Oscar ceremony for them. What, he asked of the ceremony, was everyone celebrating? With cinema, America was squandering its greatest cultural opportunity:

> In painting, music and architecture we are not even second-rate by comparison with the best work of the past. In sculpture we are just funny. In prose literature we not only lack style but we lack the educational and historical background to know what style is. . . . Our novels are transient propaganda when they are called 'significant', and bedtime reading when they are not. But in the motion picture we possess an art medium whose glories are not behind us.

It was Hollywood's constant failure to realize the medium's real potential that made the 'annual tribal dance' of the Oscars offensive to Chandler. He used a pastiche of Kipling's poem 'If' to make his point:

> If you can go past those awful faces on the bleachers outside the theater without a sense of the collapse of the human intelligence; if you can stand the hailstorm of flash bulbs popping at the poor patient actors who, like kings and queens, have never the right to look bored; if you can glance out over this gathered assemblage of what is supposed to be the elite of Hollywood and say to yourself without a sinking feeling, 'In these hands lie the destinies of the only

original art the modern world had conceived'; if you can laugh, and you probably will, at the cast-off jokes from the comedians on stage, stuff that wasn't good enough to use on their radio shows; if you can stand the fake sentimentality and the platitudes of the officials and the mincing elocution of the glamor queens (you ought to hear them with four martinis down the hatch); if you can do all these things with grace and pleasure; and not have a wild and forsaken horror at the thought that most of these people actually take this shoddy performance seriously; and if you can then go out into the night to see half the police force of Los Angeles gathered to protect the golden ones from the mob in the free seats but not from that awful moaning sound they give out, like destiny whistling through a hollow shell; if you can do all these things and still feel next morning that the picture business is worth the attention of one single intelligent, artistic mind, then in the picture business you certainly belong.[31]

These attacks prompted Charles Brackett, the man whom Chandler had replaced as Billy Wilder's co-writer on *Double Indemnity*, to tell Swanson that he did not think Chandler's books were good enough, nor his screenplays bad enough, to justify his criticism of Hollywood. To which Chandler replied that 'had my books been any worse I would not have been invited to Hollywood and if they had been any better I would not have come'.

The year that Chandler left Hollywood was, paradoxically, capped by his greatest triumph of all. The release of *The Big Sleep* in 1946, starring Humphrey Bogart and directed by Howard Hawks, propelled both Chandler and Marlowe into the realms of international stardom. Though much of the script departed from the novel once it had been submitted to the Production Code, it was a film in which large chunks of the novel's original text had gone unamended into the screenplay. Chandler attended a couple of shoots and told Hawks and Bogart that he was impressed; Bogart, he said, was 'the genuine article'.

The screenplay was an adaptation by William Faulkner and a young woman crime writer named Leigh Brackett. As Wilder and Chandler had done with *Double Indemnity*, Faulkner and Brackett ran the Production Code gauntlet, and largely survived it, by conveying the censorable elements of the original novel through the non-censorable means of atmosphere: 'When and if you see

The Big Sleep,' as Chandler told Hamish Hamilton in London, 'you will realize what can be done with this sort of story by a director with the gift of atmosphere and the requisite touch of hidden sadism.' Although mention of drugs, nymphomania, and pornography were dropped, the eroticism was instead re-created through double-entendre banter between Bogart and Lauren Bacall. These scenes proved so popular when a preview of the movie was shown to American servicemen overseas, that a further one was added before *The Big Sleep* was put on national release in 1946:

> *Bogart:* I like you. I've told you that before.
> *Bacall:* I like hearing you say it. You didn't do much about it.
> *Bogart:* Well neither did you.
> *Bacall:* Well speaking of horses, I like to play them myself. But I like to see them work out a little first, see if they're front runners or come from behind, find out what their whole kind is, what makes them run.
> *Bogart:* Find out mine?
> *Bacall:* I'd say you don't like to be rated, you like to get out in front, open up a lead, take a little breather in the back stretch and then come home free.
> *Bogart:* You don't like to be rated yourself.
> *Bacall:* I haven't met anyone yet who could do it. Any suggestions?
> *Bogart:* Well, I can't tell till I've seen you over a stretch of ground. You've got a touch of class but I don't know how far you can go.
> *Bacall:* A lot depends on who's in the saddle. Go ahead Marlowe, I like the way you move. In case you don't know it, you're doing alright.

Chandler thought Bogart was ideal for the role of Philip Marlowe. 'Bogart can be tough without a gun,' he said. 'Also he has a sense of humour that contains that grating undertone of contempt. Ladd is hard, bitter and occasionally charming, but he is after all a small boy's idea of a tough guy.' Bogart had agreed to the film on the basis of having already read Chandler's novel. As the actor's biographers have emphasized, Marlowe was a part that was perfect for him:

Bogart felt a bond with this character who, having little time for food, managed to exist through lunchless dinners and dinnerless days with the aid of a bottle of bourbon. 'Why doesn't he go overboard for a girl?' he asked Chandler. 'Marlowe would lose something by being promiscuous,' said Chandler. 'I know he can't go on forever saying no the way he does – the guy's human – he'll have to break sometime but I've never wanted the sex bit to dominate either him or the story.'

Of Bogart's interpretation of Marlowe, Chandler commented: 'Bogart is always superb as Bogart.' But by the time *The Big Sleep* had been completed, Bogart had acquired something of Marlowe. He never lost it.[32]

Apart from being able to identify with Marlowe's mentality, and his drinking, there was another reason why Bogart was so credible as Chandler's detective during the filming of *The Big Sleep*. He and Bacall had fallen in love with each other, and were married soon after the film's release: 'After we made *The Big Sleep* together,' said Bogart later, 'I said "That's my Baby". I called her Baby ever after.'

Howard Hawks, who would later direct *Rio Bravo*, was also influenced by the making of *The Big Sleep*. Though Chandler was contractually forbidden by Paramount from any serious involvement with the Warner Brothers project, he and Hawks got on well, and had met up on a number of occasions. Hawks once cabled Chandler during the shoot to ask who was supposed to have killed General Sternwood's chauffeur in the original story. Chandler sent a wire back saying 'NO IDEA'. Plot twists had never been what he concentrated on, and the death of Sternwood's chauffeur in *The Big Sleep* (before even appearing in the story) was typically serpentine. It was the characters, the style and the atmosphere that were engaging about Chandler's writing, and Hawks eventually understood that. 'I never figured out what was going on,' the director said afterwards, 'but I thought that the basic thing had great scenes and it was good entertainment. After that I said "I'm never going to worry about being logical again."'

Chandler said that he and Hawks once planned an alternative ending to the film which was eventually pulled by the Production Code. In it, Marlowe finds himself trapped in a house with the girl he now knows to be a murderess. There are gunmen outside waiting to shoot whoever walks out of the house first, and Marlowe cannot decide what to do:

> So he put it up to God by tossing a coin. He wanted that decision made by the authority who allowed this mess to happen. If the coin came down heads he would let the girl go. He tossed the coin and it came down heads. The girl thought this was some kind of game to hold her there for the police. She started to leave. At the last moment, as she had her hand on the doorknob, Marlowe weakened and started for her to stop her. She laughed in his face and pulled a gun on him – you could see that she was going to shoot and was delighted with the situation. At that moment a burst of machine gun fire walked across the panel of the door and tore her to pieces.[33]

Despite its success in otherwise side-stepping the Production Code, *The Big Sleep* was still held up by censors in Ireland, Sweden, Denmark and Finland. The Irish censor rejected the film in no uncertain terms:

> This is a thoroughly immoral film in the widest sense of the word. Blackmail and murders are mere incidents in it. The entire atmosphere is sordid, and there are many suggestive situations and not a little double meaning dialogue. Altogether an unsavoury picture for which a certificate cannot be granted.[34]

The United Kingdom granted the film a certificate, although its Board of Censors asked for the colloquialism 'punk' to be cut from British reels.

Nor was the film shown intact throughout America. Once a movie had cleared the Production Code, it was the practice of each American and Canadian metropolitan area to impose their own levels of pre-release censorship. Several Midwestern and Canadian states used this power of veto on *The Big Sleep*. Cinema goers in Ontario, for instance, would not have seen the 'view of Bogart securing revolver from secured compartment under the dashboard of his automobile' because the province demanded that the studio cut that scene from their reels. Most of these regional censor boards were run under the auspices of local police departments – making the portrayal of bad cops a rarity in American cinemas up until the 1960s – and Marlowe's line 'I stink of cops' was removed from most reels of *The Big Sleep*.[37]

Though *The Big Sleep's* release in September of 1946 was hugely successful, it proved too hard-boiled for many critics. The *New York Times* deplored its 'emphasis on toughness and malevolence' and reminded its readers that 'it was such films that predominated on the German screen between the wars'.[36] Despite this type of criticism from the highbrow press, however (and despite receiving no Oscars), the film was the most unexpected box-office draw of the decade, both in America and abroad – everyone, everywhere seemed to have seen it. On 12 October 1946, Warner Brothers issued the following press release:

> A royal request for a showing of *The Big Sleep* at Balmoral Castle has been made by King George and Queen Elizabeth of England. The showing is planned for the entire royal family in the castle near Edinburgh, Scotland [sic].

*

Once he had actually left Hollywood, Chandler's reputation as a screenwriter soared all the more. An article assessing his influence appeared in a movie journal called *Sequence* three years after his departure:

> Just as Chandler has many literary imitators, so has his work exercised a considerable influence on the treatment of crime and violence in the cinema. . . . He helped to bring back to the cinema some of the healthy realism lost so carelessly in the early Thirties to the demands of a minority censorship. What is certain, at any rate, is that since 1944 his work has done much to form the basis of a school of film making as indigenously American as the Western, the social comedy, the musical, and the gangster film.[37]

Chandler would remain grudgingly fascinated by Hollywood even after he had left Los Angeles. He would often take Cissy to see movies. Of *A Place in the Sun*, starring Montgomery Clift and Elizabeth Taylor, he wrote: '. . . the portrayal of how the upper classes live is about as ridiculous as could be imagined. They ought to have called it Speedboats For Breakfast.' Nothing was ever so irksome to him, however, as films that tried to use big or topical issues as a way of giving themselves fashionable kudos; 'hipped on significance', as he described them. 'I wish to God that Hollywood would stop trying to be significant,' he said, 'because when art is significant, it is always a by-product and more or less unintentional on the part of the creator.' Chandler could not understand why the studios made so many bad films, given the resources open to them, the money available, and a captive market. Even financially, he said, it made no sense: 'If Hollywood makes money out of poor pictures, it could make more money out of good ones.' All in all, he had decided, it was a badly run industry squandering a massive opportunity. Before leaving Los Angeles in the late summer of 1946, he wrote to Alfred Knopf to tell him that he was through with Hollywood and was returning to his novels:

> It is like one of those South American palace revolutions conducted by officers in comic opera uniforms – only when the thing is over the ragged men lie in rows against the wall, and you suddenly know that this is not funny, this is the Roman Circus, and damn near the end of civilization.[38]

Chandler rang the La Jolla police station to say that he was going to shoot himself. He had been drinking heavily since breakfast. His former secretary, Juanita Messick, was in the house keeping an eye on him, as she had done on and off since Cissy's death. When the police arrived at 3.50, Messick left Chandler and went to apologize to the patrol: the writer was a popular figure among the La Jolla police and three cars had responded to the call. On re-entering the house, Messick could not find him. She then heard a shot come from a bathroom, followed by what sounded like a second. She ran back on to the street to stop the police. They found Chandler slumped, drunk, on the stone shower floor, trying to put a .38 calibre revolver in his mouth. The first shot, it turned out, had gone off by accident, when he fell getting into the shower. 'The charge seemed to me to be very weak,' he said later: 'This was borne out when the second shot (the business) didn't fire at all. The cartridges were about five years old and in this climate I guess the charge had decomposed.' The second 'shot' that Messick heard had in fact been the sound of the accidentally fired bullet ricocheting around the stone walls of the shower (and miraculously missing Chandler in the process). The first policeman to reach Chandler asked him to hand over the gun, and he did so. The police then drove him to the psychiatric ward of the San Diego County Hospital, where he was put in a solitary cell overnight.

Chandler had blacked out from drink by the time he got into the shower, and 'hadn't the slightest recollection' of the police arriving. Blackouts when he drank heavily were something he had often experienced, especially while at Dabney's. The all-important detail as to whether he intended the second shot to be 'the business' is blurred now, because it is almost certain that Chandler himself did not know his intentions before, during or after his failed suicide attempt. The La Jolla police refused to release their full report of the incident at the time.[27] When, later, it was released, it revealed that the call on 22 February had not been Chandler's first suicide threat since Cissy's death: 'Chandler dramatized his wife's death pretty severely,' the report read, 'and his active imagination had something to do with the motivation.' The first sergeant to arrive on the scene had 'talked him out' of suicide attempts before. 'I have no idea whether I meant to go through with it,' said Chandler.

He had clearly thought about suicide ever since he realized Cissy was going to die, and in *The Long Goodbye* he had made several references to it. Both Terry Lennox and Roger Wade write suicide notes. Lennox addresses his to Marlowe: 'When it happens to you, when all you have is the gun in your pocket . . . believe me pal, there is nothing elevating or dramatic about it. It is just plain nasty and sordid and grey and grim.'[28] In Roger Wade, Chandler had depicted a man with the intention, but without the nerve, to commit suicide. 'No one hurt,' says Wade meekly to Marlowe after letting off a gun. 'Just a wild shot at the ceiling.' Marlowe has no time for that: 'You were swimming in a sea of self-pity . . . you fired a shot not meant to hit anything.'

On 23 February, the morning after the incident, Neil Morgan read about Chandler's 'suicide attempt' in the *San Diego Union*. The paper carried a photo of the author, captioned 'Raymond Chandler . . . two shots rang out', and a brief account of what had happened. Morgan drove to the County Hospital, where he persuaded the doctors to let him take Chandler to the Chula Vista Sanatorium, a private clinic close to the Mexican border:

> The superintendent waved me into his office, and I explained that I knew Chandler. He flipped through the night's admission sheets and whistled. He knew who Chandler was; he read. He got up and unlocked the white iron door and nodded to me to follow. It was an old hospital . . . it smelled of puke, and the eyes behind the heavy wire mesh were like those of caged animals.
>
> Chandler stood among them like a wet puppy that had been bad.[29]

It was the private sanatorium, perversely, which brought Chandler to his senses for the first time since Cissy's death. Such places, and the assumed premise of their authority, had always offended him. His incarceration in Chula Vista managed to provoke just enough irreverence and wit to keep him interested in life. Californian-style psychiatry was an old enemy, which he regarded as 'fifty per cent fraud, forty per cent parrot talk and the remaining ten per cent just fancy lingo for the common sense we have had for hundreds and perhaps thousands of years':

I stuck it for six days and then I got a feeling I was being strung along with half-promises. At that point I announced that I was going to discharge myself. Upheaval. This simply was not done. All right, I said, Tell me the law that keeps me here. There wasn't any and he knew it. So finally he consented that I could leave any time I wished, but would I come to his office and talk to him. I said I would, not because I expected any good from it, but because it would make his case record look better, and in addition, if he was perfectly frank with me, I might be able to help him.[30]

When Morgan came to pick him up from the sanatorium, Chandler had a nurse on either arm and announced that if he was sane enough to charm two pretty ladies he was 'better than he had been for a long time'. The journalist drove Chandler home to La Jolla. When they reached the house, Chandler asked Morgan to come in with him. He made two drinks and then rang a property agency, telling them to sell the house to the first bidder. 'He told me I had done something only a real friend would do,' said Morgan: 'I just felt strange. He did not seem embarrassed at all at what had happened.'

Having sold the house for $75,000 within a fortnight of his release from Chula Vista, Chandler had, with royalties from his books, enough cash to live on for the rest of his life. Spread among accounts with the Bank of America and the Bank of Canada, and in government bonds and uncollected European royalties, he had approximately $300,000. He moved into the nearby Hotel Del Charro. He abandoned his writing, released his secretary and decided to leave as soon as he could for London. There was a rootlessness to him which exceeded the nomadism of the years before he had met Cissy. He had no idea how long he would be away, or whether he would return to La Jolla. Apart from his publishers, he knew almost no one in London. The furniture from the house on Camino de la Costa was stored or given away, for he had decided that if he ever found somewhere permanent to live, he would take only the linen sheets with him.

Chandler's self-control continued to fall away in the loneliness into which he had plunged after Cissy's death. He made desperate midnight phone calls to people he had only ever known by letter. He was drinking constantly: 'I met him occasionally,' said

Morgan, 'and rather terrifyingly he would drive home in his Oldsmobile after a dinner that was mostly alcohol.' Whether Chandler had meant to kill himself or not, the incident had been picked up as a suicide attempt by newspapers and radio stations throughout the world. He received letters about it from the public, including one, he said, from a Tokyo private detective. Another came from a fan in San Francisco called Louise Loughner:

> Dear Raymond Chandler: You have helped me – you and Philip Marlowe – through many white nights and troubled hours. May I intrude into your life just long enough to hope that things are better for you today?
>
> Peace is an unattainable word. But I could wish that some of the beautiful compassion which shines through every word you have written about tired, dirty old men and bad girls and tough boys, might be spared for yourself, by yourself, for a while.[31]

As someone who had always taken nourishment from the correspondence of people he had never met, letters like this lifted his spirits. Days before departing from La Jolla, he replied in resilient tones to a crime writer who had sent him one of 'a hundred kind letters from all parts of the world':

> I thought I was extremely lucky to get as far as I did in our field, and believe me when I say lucky I am not talking to the birds. Talent is never enough. The history of literature is strewn with the corpses of writers who through no fault of their own missed out on the timing or were just a little too far ahead of their generation. The world never hears of its greatest men; the men it calls great are just ahead enough of the average to stand out, but not far enough ahead to be remote. Don't ever write anything you don't like yourself and if you do like it, don't take anyone's advice about changing it. They just don't know.[32]

In the first week of April 1955, Chandler took a train out of Los Angeles for New York, there to connect with the *Mauretania*, bound for Southampton. Travelling alone, and with very little luggage, he sailed from New York on 12 April. He had booked himself a room at the Connaught in London. 'He was like a child,' said Morgan, 'with no firm ideas about anything.' It was an ominous frame of mind for someone travelling by himself, with no fixed abode, and with almost a third of a million dollars to his name.

8

London License

I have lived my whole life on the edge of nothing.
                                                    (Letter, June 1957)

Travelling first-class to England on board the *Mauretania* over the
third week of April 1955, Chandler met a Manhattan banker
called Jessica Tyndale. A senior executive at Guinness Mahon
Bank in her forties, Jessica was independent and cynical. Roger
Machell had planned to meet Chandler at Southampton, but
received a mid-Atlantic telegram from him saying: 'Don't meet.
Have woman with much luggage.'

Chandler's return to full-scale drinking both emboldened and
confused him in his search for someone to replace Cissy. He needed
to be around women. He was exceptionally chivalrous: no woman
was allowed to sit herself down at a table, take off her own coat or
light a cigarette, so long as he was around and sober enough to help
her. He was as chivalrous as he was forward to those women he
liked. He wanted a graceful but modern female audience: 'If I sound
a little as if I had been smoking reefers', he wrote to Jessica after she
had returned to New York, 'I had a tooth out this morning and am
still a little on the goofy side . . . Have you read *Bhowani Junction*
[by John Masters]? I think you should, it's a damn good job and
there are several effing scenes in it that I should have been proud to
write, but God knows much prouder to have lived them.'[1]

Alcohol always had a stirring effect on Chandler's libido. The two office affairs that he had had during his marriage had both started while he was heavily drinking; the first while at Dabney's and the second at Paramount. There was another side to the coin, however. Hard drinking may 'provoke the desire', as the porter says in *Macbeth*, 'but it takes away the performance'. Long-term drinking, according to medical consensus, accelerates the loss of 'performance' which happens with age. On his arrival in London in 1955, Chandler was not only a hard drinker, and a long-term drinker, but he was also sixty-six years old. It would seem more than likely (both logically and from later evidence) that he had drunk himself to a point of impotence.

*

Landing at Southampton on 19 April, Raymond Chandler was immediately caught in the limelight. Following the publication of *The Long Goodbye*, his fame in Britain was on a par with that of a film star. He was interviewed everywhere – something he was still unused to – and his photograph appeared so often in the press that he began to be recognized in hotels and restaurants. His bright ties and white gloves, combined with what the *Observer* described as the 'manic glint' in his eyes, all made him immediately recognizable. 'I am not happy,' he wrote to his American publisher five days after arriving. 'The racket here is just too intense.'

Formal invitations (made initially through Hamish Hamilton) arrived constantly during Chandler's first few days at the Connaught. Hamilton hosted a lunch for him; there was a dinner party at the house of the poet Stephen Spender and his wife Natasha; and a lunch party thrown by staff writers on the *Sunday Times*. Here Chandler was introduced to Ian Fleming, who later recalled the meeting:

> He was very nice to me and said that he liked my first book, *Casino Royale*, but he didn't really want to talk about anything much except the loss of his wife, about which he expressed himself with a nakedness that embarrassed me while endearing him to me. He showed me a photograph of her – a good-looking woman sitting in the sun somewhere.[2]

Fleming invited the American to a lunch at his own house near Victoria station. Chandler turned up late and confused. He seemed, Fleming said, intensely uncomfortable, and gave the impression of 'a senator broken by an inquiry into some oil scandal'. He spoke to almost no one.

When drunk enough, though, Chandler could rise to the occasion of his celebrity among what he called the 'St John's Wood–Chelsea hyperthyroid set'. Two weeks after arriving in London, he wrote to Hamish Hamilton from his hotel to say that he had been at a dinner party the previous night where George Orwell's wife had told him that he was 'the darling of the British intellectuals and all the poets raved about me and that Edith Sitwell sat up in bed and read my stuff with passion. . . . Well anyhow it was a lot of fun.'[3] There were soon stories of Chandler holding court at West End restaurants, and keeping not only his own table enthralled by his performance, but all the neighbouring tables as well. Chandler's London solicitor, Michael Gilbert, once lunched with him at Le Jardin des Gourmets in Soho. The subject of violence arose, and with the aid of wineglasses and saltcellars, Chandler proceeded to illustrate in detail how Marlowe would fight off two assailants. By the end of the demonstration, according to Gilbert, every waiter in the restaurant was around their table.

Even emotional solace seemed available in London. Everyone he met presumed that Chandler's flash depressions and excessive drinking were a direct result of his wife's recent death. They were unaware that Cissy's death had also been a catalyst for the return of demons that had haunted him before; most obviously his alcoholism. Some of the people Chandler now met took it upon themselves to try to cheer him up on a day-to-day basis. This began after one of the first parties he attended in London. Natasha Spender recalled the occasion:

It was an amusing evening: he seemed delighted by compliments. . . .
Yet in spite of all our gaiety, and his sudden flights of glorious nonsense, his great brooding silences and the shadow of his desperation had hung in the air. Later, one of the guests, Jocelyn Rickards, talked to me of the alarm we both felt concerning his survival. She believed that his gentlemanly good manners would never permit him to implement his evidently strong suicidal

impulses if he had an imminent social engagement with a lady. So in turn we each invited ourselves to a meal with him, or him to one with us, other friends joined in, and so began the 'shuttle service' by which our group tried to ensure that he was never out of sight of an impending gentle and undemanding social engagement, and that he could at bad times telephone one of us at any time in the twenty-four hours.[4]

Consequently, there were soon four or five women in London – mostly in their thirties – whom Chandler could telephone whenever he wanted to.[5] In return for their attentiveness, he entertained these 'minders' with stories, bought them jewellery and took them to restaurants. Alien in his despondency one minute, Chandler could suddenly switch to being funny and attentive company.

The problem with the arrangement was that Chandler began to fall in love with each member of the 'shuttle service', and also with almost every other woman he now met. He was chiefly attracted to women he considered vulnerable, unappreciated or ill-treated. The idea that he could help them became as important to him as it was confusing to those trying to coax him through his bereavement. Sometimes the gifts he sent his new friends were so expensive that the women returned them straight to Asprey's, the Bond Street jewellers where Chandler had opened an account:

> In his despairing times, his anxiety rose as he talked of his wife's death, and it then seemed strange to us that after a traumatic loss a person could seem anxious rather than sad, almost as if still in anticipation of the shock. His reminiscences of her were adoring, irresistibly lyrical and full of delight at Cissy's exploits which showed her spirit and charm. He wished to deliver us from the 'hardships' of our lives, and thought of rescuing all of us because 'there was nobody around so I had to'. . . . His sympathy was genuine and abundant. To [one woman, Alison Hooper] he even offered to arrange to have somebody in America bumped off for having mistreated her – 'It'll cost a thousand bucks!' he said, with a swagger, suggesting that he had only to lift a finger for the Mafia to act.[6]

Chandler fell in love with women without even meeting them.

Soon after arriving in London, he became fixated with Ruth Ellis, who was then awaiting execution for murder and whose publicized plight awoke all his chivalrous instincts. Ellis was a London nightclub hostess who had repeatedly shot her estranged racing-driver lover, David Blakely, outside a Hampstead pub in April 1955, the month of Chandler's arrival in Britain. Blakely had been trying to extricate himself from what was an apparently violent and tempestuous relationship. Ellis was the perfect love-object for Chandler for, like Cissy, she was going to die unless he did something to help her. He wrote to the London *Evening Standard* about the matter, saying that he could not understand how a civilized nation could 'put a rope around the neck of Ruth Ellis and drop her through a trap and break her neck'. The paper published his letter, in which Chandler pleaded for a reconsideration of the case:

> I could understand perhaps the hanging of a woman for a bestial crime like a multiple poisoning, and axe murder (à la Lizzie Borden) or a baby-farm operator killing her charges, but this was a crime of passion committed under considerable provocation. No other country in the world would hang this woman. . . .
>
> This thing haunts me and, so far as I may say it, disgusts me as something obscene. I am not referring to the trial, of course, but to the medieval savagery of the law.[7]

Chandler's appeal had no effect. One of the few entries in his 1955 pocket diary is for 13 July, which reads, 'Ruth Ellis hanged.' 'The basis for my fury over the Ruth Ellis case,' he said later, was that 'I have never for a moment failed to realize that they [women] face hazards in life which a man does not face.'

*

Chandler continued drinking heavily in London. He also began to spin fantastic stories in order to conceal his alcoholism, as he had done in Hollywood. Now that he was not working, these stories became a new kind of fiction for him: as has been said, on more than one occasion, having arrived late and dishevelled at an engagement, he would claim to have been attacked on the way. He was so adamant about the fight, says Natasha Spender, 'that you couldn't dissuade him. When he was like that, he was like a small child.' He created his own imaginary characters, and would regale incredulous and confused friends with these invented figures:

> For instance, there was the 'posh doctor' [who] was always eclipsing Raymond in worldliness, success with women, money, and suavity of manners . . . but in these various fantasy encounters Raymond always got the best of it with some brilliantly delivered insult, after which he would leave the 'posh doctor' with sagging jaw, and go on his way laughing . . . or there was his heroic, victorious punch-up by which he foiled the attempt by two hoodlums to snatch his wallet.[8]

Chandler now began to write short autobiographical sketches, which he sent indiscriminately to people he had met in London. It was impossible for the recipients to know, however, to what extent the sketches were exaggerated. Within a month of his arrival, he was evicted by the management of the Connaught for being intolerably drunk. He wrote a sketch about the episode which, he claimed, had led to his eviction, entitled 'Do You Terribly Mind Being Seduced?' Though long and fantastic in detail, it is also – given the circumstances of its writing – both funny and knowingly tragic; a combination of attitudes with which Chandler had always been familiar. It would also seem frankly to confirm both of the effects that drink was having on his libido. The sketch was written on 20 May 1955, five days after his eviction from the Connaught:

> Lately, my thoughts seemed to have a rather limited range so when this lithe, fine-drawn blonde looked at me twice at the porter's desk late at night in the Connaught, I looked at her three times. She looked away. I forget what the porter was doing, but nothing I cared about. I looked away. I turned my head quickly. She wasn't quick enough, so she giggled.
>
> I said to the porter, 'Would you mind keeping this charming and adorable woman either a little farther away from me or else a damn sight closer?'
>
> It confused him, and while he was confused I found myself in the lift with her. The lift boy asked which floor she desired.
>
> She murmured: 'I'm not sure.'
>
> I said, 'Third please.'

She said, 'Thankyou.'

The lift boy turned his head halfway around, but decided to keep his job. 'Third floor, thankyou sir,' he said, bursting the doors open. 'Thankyou, madam.'

We thanked him back and went along the red carpet and around the corner and I had my key in my hand, but I was shaking so hard that I had a hell of a time getting it into the lock. However, I accomplished it eventually.

'Not much of a room,' she said. 'Mine is much better.'

'You'll take this and like it. A little Scotch?'

'Not too little.'

I ordered ice. I needed it. She sat down and crossed her legs carelessly, which is the way I like them crossed. She produced a cigarette. I produced a lighter. That produced a silence. It's curious, but one is always embarrassed at these moments.

'Lovely rings you are wearing,' I said.

'I've been married six times,' she said.

'And now?'

'I'm resting,' she said.

The ice came. I fixed her a Scotch and soda that would have floored a dinosaur. It had no more effect on her than a spray of violets.

'I'll take them off,' she said. 'So scratchy.' She proceeded to cover the coffee table with diamonds, emeralds, rubies and more diamonds.

'You don't mind?'

'I was looking forward to it.'

She smiled faintly and held out her glass. I fixed her another that would have floored a megatherium. I was a little worried for fear she might pass out. Silly me.

'Anything else you would care me to take off?' she enquired, after downing the second drink in a lump.

'I've always thought one should do one's own homework. Without assistance, I mean.'

'A point,' she said. 'But it does slow things down. Why not just turn your back for five seconds and turn the light down a little?'

She needed only four. She looked very nice in bed. I gathered that she had spent a lot of time there. She bit me.

'Look,' I said, trying to staunch the blood, 'let's keep this civilized.'

'I can't imagine why,' she said, and bit me again. I screamed.

'Bastard,' she sighed. She relaxed. It was about time. Another two minutes and I'd have been a hospital case.

'Another Scotch,' she said, 'and put a little whisky in this time, would you?'

I gave her a drink that would have floored two megatheria. (Once a classical scholar, always a classical scholar.)

She downed it in a gulp and gathered me into a fast clutch.

'Now take it easy,' I said. 'I'm not Casanova.'

'Shut up!'

She bit my lip. I could see myself being taken away in a sack. She relaxed momentarily, for the usual reasons.

'Make me a decent Scotch,' she said, toying with a tendril of my hair. I thought I was lucky to have any left, and I certainly hoped she wouldn't start pulling it out in handfuls.

I managed to elude her enough to mix her a Scotch that was really explosive.

She knocked it back and sighed and I jumped backwards just fast enough.

'What on earth is the matter?' she asked coldly.

'You told me earlier that you were resting – between marriages as it were.'

'So I am. Then?'

'How about me resting a little?'

'Oh, I see. A quitter.' She arose with a little movement and pulled on a couple of hundred thousand dollars' worth of jewellery.

'Turn your back, you jerk,' she said.

I refused. Better to be a cad than a corpse. She dressed with enormous skill.

'Make me a decent Scotch,' she said when she had attired herself immaculately, combed her hair, retouched her face and done all the things women do in such situations.

I handed her a full bottle and opened the door. I watched her carefully. She strolled past me on the way out.

'Do you terribly mind being seduced?' she said languidly.

'If that's what you call it. . . .'

With a polite sneer she shut the door in my face. I was rather worried about the lift boy.

I was justified as it happened. No one ever saw him again.[9]

Despite the growing awareness of his physical failings, Chandler was becoming fascinated by sex. When an American schoolmaster sent him a list of questions about his writing, he replied with a long letter which included an irrelevant discussion of an *Esquire* magazine article he had read, called 'Latins Are Lousy Lovers'. 'It gave great offence,' he assured the schoolmaster, 'and the issue was even banned in Cuba. But I happen to know that she [the author of the article] was absolutely right. Latins talk a great game.'[10] His chivalry was still central to him, none the less, and because of their generosity to him, the women that made up the 'Chandler patrol' were chiefly objects for love rather than lust. 'Damn you,' he wrote to Jessica Tyndale, 'I don't stay with "my women". I do have some rather intimate women friends . . . but I don't park in their boudoirs.' 'For all his jolly talk,' confirms Natasha Spender, 'he didn't ever make the slightest advance on me or any of my friends.' Despite the free flow of hormones that the drinking brought, Chandler's perfect woman remained one he believed he could help. Looks were less important than grace. Another woman who met him in London, Helga Greene (a friend of Jessica Tyndale's), realized this:

> He would always bat for the underdog. If at a party there was someone in a corner or a bit neglected he would try to see that woman had a good time whether she was beautiful or not. Voices were important to him, in both men and women.[11]

Chandler's simultaneous fascination with the women he met and with sex itself was, like his tall stories about being mugged, also the product of a sudden childishness. On one occasion, when he implied that he had enjoyed an illicit afternoon with a friend of Natasha Spender's, it emerged that he had met the woman in question for lunch and had been in so bad a state that she had marched him off to see her doctor.

*

Despite having hosted a disastrous lunch for him, Ian Fleming kept in close touch with Chandler over the spring and summer of 1955. A prominent figure at the *Sunday Times*, Fleming was at a low point in his embryonic fictional career, feeling that he had taken James Bond as far as he could in 1953 with his debut novel *Casino Royale*. Sales of the book (and of its sequel, *Live and Let Die*) had been weak, and there was as yet no interest being shown in either by film producers. Chandler went out of his way to encourage

Fleming, writing a foreword for the US and British editions of his third novel *Moonraker*. According to Fleming's biographer, it provided Bond's creator with an enormous boost to his confidence:

> The interest and support of Raymond Chandler had come at a crucial time for Ian Fleming, and the friendship between them in May and June [1955], even before the testimonial was written, had an electric effect on the attitude of Fleming to his writing and his hero. It was undoubtedly Raymond Chandler's interest which restored Fleming's interest for both.[12]

Chandler's admiration for Fleming was based predominantly on Bond's first adventure, *Casino Royale*. Published in the same year as *The Long Goodbye*, it was a violent and hard-boiled book in which the hero falls in love with a woman whom he subsequently discovers to be a traitor. Bond is badly tortured at one point in the book, and occasionally shows himself in *Casino Royale* to be as vulnerable as Marlowe. He discovers his lover's betrayal only at the end: 'Suddenly, he banged his temples with his fists and stood up. For a moment he looked out towards the quiet sea, then he cursed aloud, one harsh obscenity. His eyes were wet when he dried them.' Like Marlowe, Bond has to force himself not to care, and relegates his pain 'to the boxroom of his mind'. The novel ends with the line: 'The bitch is dead now.'

Through the summer of 1955, the two writers began to meet for lunch when they could, as well as corresponding. 'Could you lend me Solitaire for a week?' Chandler wrote, adding in the same letter that he counted Fleming among the 'few friends I know well enough to care about'.[13] Like S. J. Perelman and Somerset Maugham, Fleming was a writer on Chandler's wavelength – an intelligent but also commercial writer, without intellectual snobbery or bitterness towards the material world. They were on the same literary team, and they shared an impatience with those who considered them (in Fleming's words) 'slacking Shakespeares'. Fleming was used to 'having my head ragged off' about James Bond and had stopped taking his books seriously. Chandler was no stranger to being chaffed about his novels, and told the other man not to drop Bond, but instead to make him more three-dimensional: 'If I wasn't hard I wouldn't be alive,' as

Philip Marlowe had once put it; 'If I couldn't ever be gentle, I wouldn't deserve to be alive.'[14] Fleming replied that he would always consider his books to be of the 'bang-bang, kiss-kiss variety', but would start to see if he could 'put more feeling into my typewriter'.[15]

The English writer once addressed a letter 'Dear Field Marshal Chandler', signing it 'Private Fleming'. Inspired by Chandler, he wrote to Jonathan Cape, his London publisher:

> By the way and sucks to you, I had a drink with Raymond Chandler last night and he said that the best bit of *Live and Let Die* was the conversation between the two Negroes in Harlem, which he said was dead accurate. Perhaps you remember that you nearly sneered me into cutting it out on the grounds that 'Negroes don't talk like that'.[16]

After having been kicked out of the Connaught, Chandler had moved into the Ritz on Piccadilly, still spending as little time as possible either sober or alone. He continued to visit the warehousemen at Hamish Hamilton and play darts with them. They presented him with a pornographic dartboard which he hung up behind his hotel room door, playing from time to time with other guests or bellboys. His address book from this period records the names of virtually every fine restaurant in London. He opened an account at Harrods and with the wine-merchants Justerini & Brooks, and he became a member of the Garrick Club, having been proposed by the English mystery writer Eric Ambler. Chandler said that he had three rules: no one was allowed to buy a drink at his table in any bar; he would not sign a cheque in front of a guest, and if he was taking a lady out, he would arrange for her menu to be handwritten. 'I suppose this may all sound a bit chi-chi,' he said, 'but dammit I'm entitled to a few tricks.'

Chandler could often be absurd. Helga Greene recalled sending him a postcard from the Continent when she was on a driving tour with friends. She mentioned to him that they were having a few problems with the car. The next Greene heard, Chandler was ringing her friends in London to find out exactly where she was, 'so he could wire £1,000 to save the situation'. On another occasion that summer, Natasha Spender, who was an accomplished concert pianist, went down from London to Bournemouth to perform with the local orchestra. After the recital, she attended a large formal dinner. Towards midnight, Chandler, dressed in black tie, arrived out of the blue from London in a hired Rolls-Royce to escort her back home. Natasha asked the orchestra conductor to come with them. The car was full of flowers and champagne which everyone – including the driver – was made to drink during a stop in the middle of the New Forest. Chandler fell asleep before the car reached London:

> Waking as we neared London, Raymond said very quietly and very soberly: 'I know what you are all doing for me, and I thank you, but the truth is I really want to die.' It sounded simple, undramatic, and the natural inspiriting reply seemed suddenly impossible to utter.[17]

Chandler was losing control over his finances. His generosity was also often followed by paranoia – having showered excessive presents and hospitality on his new friends, he would then worry that people were taking advantage of him. He was, perhaps, haunted by traces of Quaker guilt towards such extravagance. There was no rhythm to his mood swings any more. He took a female fan (who had written to him) to lunch at Boulestin, and at the end of the meal wrote her a cheque, only to cancel it that evening. A furious letter reached him two days later, accusing him of 'double-crossing':

> I do feel extremely sorry for you. Nothing can be more pathetically true than the way they call you Raymond (The Big Sleep) Chandler. I must insist that you will apologize to me for your action, so that I can show your letter to my bank manager. You see, I built there a very respected position for myself ever since I started a tiny fashion shop in Kingston-on-Thames with a capital of five pounds. I am not going to allow you to ruin my name there by your childish behaviour.[18]

Chandler's reaction to this letter is unknown, but such episodes can only have exacerbated his confusion as to what extent he had ever really helped any woman.

He began a correspondence from London with Louise Loughner, the fan in San Francisco who had written one of the most comforting letters he had received after his suicide attempt:

> At the darkest and most desperate moment of my life, when I had
> nothing left to fight with and hardly cared to fight, there came to me
> out of the unknown a spray of flowers and a letter. And suddenly I
> had all the fight in the world. I out-talked them and out-thought
> them, so that in the end they sent me home in a limousine, merely
> because they were dazzled by the display of wit and courage I put
> on. But why? Solely and entirely because of you.[19]

Chandler would sometimes include erotic poems with the letters
he sent to Loughner over the summer of 1955: 'On a night of velvet
mist fondling the trees . . . I also fondled you'. He suggested to her
that on his return to California she should meet him because he
was a 'very handsome and elegant person'. With this letter, he
enclosed another poem, which ended with the verse: 'Therefore I
claim you know, and in/ The lambent flame between your thighs/
I die the only death I know/ A death of prayer.' He also tried to
describe London life accurately to her; 'I think you overrate the
English in some ways', he warned:

> There is a great deal of mad telephoning back and forth, searching
> for some trifle of fact, hopefully scandalous, on which to build a
> cobweb of intrigue. During the war there was an immense amount
> of courage and endurance. It may be that when people are uncertain
> of ever meeting again they feel they must say everything in one
> breath and that breeds a certain hysteria of talk that survives long
> afterwards.[20]

*

The London press sustained its interest in Chandler. This was
partly because he was a celebrity guaranteed to speak his mind, or
get drunk, or, as in the case of one *Daily Express* interview, start
weeping over Cissy.[21] His colourful past and way of talking
offered a strong antidote to the well-mannered ghost of
Bloomsbury that still haunted Britain's own literary celebrities. A
novice at interviews, Chandler did not have pat answers. 'He
wanted,' wrote the *Sunday Times*, 'to explain everything the way
it had happened.'

The interviews varied extravagantly in the way they portrayed him, depending on his own mood and on who was interviewing him. He was, being simultaneously championed by both the quality and the popular press. An interview in the *Daily Mirror* was titled ' *"Money Is For Taking Out Beautiful Women" Says Ace Mystery Writer*'. The three underlined copy breaks read 'Luxury', 'Beautiful' and 'Whisky':

> Raymond Chandler, who . . . is one of the world's highest paid crime writers, is 'too much of a gentleman' to admit that women chase him.
>
> 'But, I will say this' he told me. 'English women are the loveliest in the world.'
>
> 'They are fragile and hard-to-get, and completely unmercenary. They don't care how many thousands of dollars you're making – they're even offended if you offer them their cab fare home.'
>
> Chandler, an American, is reputed to make £35,000 a year as the creator of fiction's toughest private detective, Philip Marlowe.
>
> 'But' he says 'the only luxury that matters is the money to dine beautiful women.'
>
> 'I've never made a pass at a woman unless I was sure she wanted me to.'[22]

When asked by the *Mirror* whether he would ever marry again, he replied that he would never settle for a woman out of her thirties. He said that a doctor had just told him he would live for another three decades. Chandler drank whisky throughout the interview at the Ritz, readers were told, and was constantly being interrupted by autograph hunters. 'I don't suppose they've ever read my books,' he joked, 'they probably only want my signature to help towards a Liberace swap.' He was asked whether he would have liked to have had children: 'I never missed them,' he said. 'I was completely happy with Cissy. But I suppose now I should have been glad.'

For the *News Chronicle*, he appeared in bow tie and 'professor' tweeds. The *Chronicle*'s reporter again mentioned the presence of whisky. This time, Chandler held forth on the ways in which the McClellan Committee, recently set up in Washington by Robert Kennedy, should try to achieve its objective of eliminating organized crime in America:

The only people who could break it are the members of the American Bar Association. The gangsters operate entirely behind a screen put up by their lawyers. Break that down and the gangs will lose their power in six months.[23]

In a *Daily Express* interview, he was asked which character he would back if James Bond and Philip Marlowe were to go head to head: 'He reflected for a moment. "I'd back Marlowe, I think. More subtle." '[24]

The photographs of Chandler that accompanied these articles showed the obvious effects of his drinking. He was shocked to see pictures of himself looking like 'a dope smuggler' or 'Grandma Moses'. One interviewer called him 'small':

What is his standard. I have hardly ever weighed less than twelve stone – is that small for England? I have often weighed almost 13 stone. Attired for the street I am an inch short of six foot. My nose is not sharp, but blunt, the result of trying to tackle a man while he was kicking a ball. For an English nose it would hardly be called prominent. Wispy hair like steel wool? Nuts. Walks with a forward-leaning lope, huh. . . . No wonder this man thinks me 'observant'. By his standards anyone who noticed how many walls the room had would be observant.[25]

Chandler had not lost all his claws in London. His outspoken and public criticism of the Ruth Ellis hanging, so soon after his arrival, had provoked some resentment among those impatient with foreigners who criticized post-war Britain. When he read an attack on modern America by a *Daily Express* columnist, he likewise demanded the right to reply on behalf of his country. For years, Chandler had privately held forth to correspondents on every subject imaginable. Now he was being given a national platform from which he could declaim about whatever happened to grab his interest, including political history:

We [America] became too rich and too powerful through a sort of genius of production technique, and as a result I think we placed ourselves in a position to dominate the world before we had any knowledge of how to do it or any real desire to do it. We were just stuck in the No. 1 spot.

For 100 years, as you may remember, England dominated the world and was rather cordially detested by everyone else. That seems to be the price of power, however unwanted or undesired. The position we find ourselves in is almost impossible to maintain either gracefully or cleverly.[26]

While he was in London, Chandler showed little interest in music, art or theatre, though he told those who asked about his future plans that he intended to write a play for the West End. This was proving a useful excuse for his lack of output, since he said he was going to set the play in England: it would take him two years, he explained, to grasp the way British characters would speak. Whatever his plans, however, it was clear that, for the time being at least, he intended to stay in London. He moved out of the Ritz into a rented Belgravia apartment at 116 Eaton Square, the most handsome of all Georgian addresses in London. In a letter, he told Louise Loughner how he had secured the lease:

> The interview was very formal and by appointment. I was so bloody polite that I began to sicken myself. So I suddenly said to the man: 'I'm naturally a very polite person, but I do think I'm overdoing it a little at the moment.' He laughed and stood up and held his hand out and thanked me for coming in. I said 'What about the lease?' He said 'Well, usually we do like some sort of document, but in practise we rather tend to overlook the necessity.' That's the way they work over here. And that's why for generations they were the bankers of the world.[27]

Chandler rarely left London, though weekend invitations to the country were often extended by those whom he met in the capital. The countryside made him restless, and he found that he needed the city. Cloudy weekends, he said of the country, spent 'waiting for tea – as if it were a revolution'. When he read books, they were almost always mysteries now. His favourite (and one he kept trying to get people to read) was called *Mr Bowling Buys a Newspaper*, by Donald Henderson.

As his drinking continued, however, so his behaviour became more erratic. To William Townend, the old Dulwich friend whom he had last seen in San Francisco in 1913, Chandler confessed that he 'had not drawn a sober breath since arriving in Britain'. No longer the novelty he had been at the start of the summer, fewer people in London were willing to continue humouring him. His loneliness was made worse by the fact that he was no longer amidst the bustle of a hotel. His minders began to despair of his recovery, and started to drop away. With time proving to exacerbate, rather than heal, Chandler's mood swings, the task of looking after him grew hopelessly exhausting.

The most resilient of the London minders was Natasha Spender. It became a matter of personal (and 'agnostic Christian') resolve for her to persevere with Chandler when the others gave up. Her life had been more similar to his than any of the others. Like Chandler, she had grown up feeling protective towards a husband-less mother. As had been Chandler's to Cissy, her marriage to Stephen Spender was a deeply affectionate one but – because of Spender's previous homosexuality – it was also one both misunderstood and ridiculed by others. She was driven (in a way like Chandler) by a strong sense of moral imperative in helping those who needed help. Dark-haired, and then in her late thirties, and with a broad, bright smile, she was very beautiful. Raymond Chandler was by no means the only person Natasha Spender was trying to cheer up within her London circle, but he was by far the most dependent on her now.

By the end of the summer of 1955, Chandler's drinking was entirely out of hand – 'I have a blood count on the edge of nothing,' he warned his solicitor. He had initially refused to accept that it was drink that was making him ill, and tried to find a doctor who would believe him. Having consulted different specialists in Kensington, Mayfair and Harley Street (all of whom told him to stop drinking), the need to dry out became urgent. He did so at the flat in Eaton Square, with a snap and sustained determination which surprised everyone. The drastic cure seemed to work, and Chandler emerged in early September teetotal.

His metabolism and brain had become so dependent on drink, however, that his rehabilitation had left him shattered. 'My mind seems to lack a little or a lot of its exuberance,' he admitted to Roger Machell. 'I don't miss it physically at all, but I do miss it mentally and spiritually.' By now, he was, in fact, incredibly frail. It was decided by what remained of the 'shuttle service' that he should be got out of London for a while, and Natasha Spender offered to take him to Italy. The two of them flew to Lake Garda in September, where for a fortnight they stayed at a hotel the Spenders knew well, and where they had a family doctor on hand. The one condition of the trip was that Chandler would maintain his abstinence. There were car trips to Verona and Venice, where he sat unhappily in cafés drinking iced coffee, physically and mentally uninterested in sightseeing ('I simply refused to look,' he said later). It was the first time he had been on the Continent since the Great War, but without the impulse of drink, the natural curiosity that had once been his life-force was waning. 'The toughest thing about trying to cure an alcoholic or a user of dope,' he had written before Cissy's death, 'is that you have absolutely nothing to offer him in the long run . . . your alcoholic cured or your former dope addict looks around him, and what has he achieved? A flat landscape in which there is no road more interesting than another.'[28] It was as if he was sleepwalking, said Natasha. She and Chandler returned to London in October.

*

Chandler's British visa had now expired, and he decided to return to America. He sailed in October on the *Queen Elizabeth* to New York, and was miserable:

> The voyage was hell. Still practising to be a non-drinker (and it's going to take a damn sight more practice than I have time for). I sat alone in the corner and refused to talk or to have anything to do with other passengers, which did not seem to cause them any grief.[29]

Before going back to La Jolla, Chandler went to the town of Old Chatham in upstate New York to stay with his friend from the oil days, Ralph 'Red' Barrow. Barrow had been a lawyer in Los Angeles before moving to New England with his wife. He and Chandler had been good friends in the 1920s, and had kept in touch by letter after Barrow had moved to the East Coast. 'I wish you weren't so damn far away,' Chandler had written to him in 1949, 'I miss you.'

The New England countryside, however, bored Chandler. 'I

don't know how long I will last,' he wrote to Neil Morgan in La Jolla. He was in no mood for the wholesomeness of other people's family lives, particularly since he was trying not to drink. You couldn't go out in a car with Jane Barrow (Red's wife), he complained, 'without having every bloody tree pointed out to you and hearing the history of every damned house between Old Chatham and Bennington'.

> Yesterday we went into Chatham . . . to get the laundry from the Laundromat. The man carried it to the car, seeing that I was somewhat old and feeble and said, 'Thankyou Mr Barrow.' I said (always too fast with the answer): 'Oh, I'm not Mr Barrow. I'm just her lover.' He didn't turn a hair, but wait until the local postmistress gets the lowdown.[30]

After two weeks with the Barrows, Chandler returned to La Jolla, and to the room he had taken at the Hotel Del Charro there.

While he resolved where he wanted to live, it was important that he did not revisit Britain for twelve months; otherwise he would have to pay British as well as American taxes for 1955. But having been in America for just four weeks, Chandler began plotting his return to London. His decision was given added urgency by the news that Natasha – whose welfare Chandler now considered entirely his responsibility – was to have surgery. The date for the operation had been set for 12 December, which, unknown to anyone he knew in London, was the date Cissy had died. On hearing the news in November, Chandler flew immediately from San Diego to London, with a sleepless night's stopover in Copenhagen. He insisted that he take Natasha away from the English winter so that she could prepare for what was in fact a routine operation. More hesitantly this time, she agreed. They decided to go to Spain and Tunisia, where Natasha had friends.

It proved an entirely different trip from the one they had made in September. Chandler had started drinking again. He alternated between inertia and hyperactivity; sometimes he would shut himself in his hotel room for hours at a time and fail to turn up for meals. This was harrowing for his travelling companion who, apart from having to deal with Chandler's overdramatization of her operation, now realized that she was travelling alone with a full-blown alcoholic who was in the midst of some kind of major breakdown:

> He spoke almost incessantly of Cissy, but his previous moods of lyricism and resignation had given way to far more complex emotions concerning his whole past life, and he would be submerged in retrospective anger and active despair . . . it amazed me afterwards to learn from friends that he had given only a happy account of the trip, particularly of a gloriously sunny day in Chauen, when in fact he was shadowed in silent grumpiness punctuated by descriptions of Cissy's hatred of snow and their sojourns at Big Bear Lake.[31]

The trip was not altogether without interest for Chandler. Now that he was drinking, his curiosity in his surroundings returned. Apparently oblivious as to how unsettling he could be to those around him, he decided that he liked Toledo and hated Madrid:

> My vigour and enterprise are on a high level, but my brains do seem to be a bit addled. In Tangier, I found myself talking in several languages at once. . . . The Spanish are stupid and unwilling to learn. French gets you anywhere, English and Italian mostly just draw blank looks. German they never heard of. The Arabs are far brainier than the Spaniards, but you get tired of them, there are so damn many.[32]

In Tangier, Natasha and Chandler stayed at the fashionable El Mirizah Hotel. The town, he told an American correspondent, was full of 'the taxless younger sons of peers who can no longer live in England without degrading themselves by work'. Despite his natural scepticism, however, he was fascinated by English aristocrats. He had been entertained in London by some members of the nobility, both at their homes and at clubs like Boodle's and the Athenaeum. He believed, as he told Hamish Hamilton, that the thoroughbred Englishman was 'the most unpretentious animal in the world', and he found the Hon. David Herbert (a younger son of the Earl of Pembroke and friend of the Spenders, whom he met in Tangier), 'a damn nice fellow and very witty'. He reckoned that 'like all really well bred people', Herbert did not have good manners so much as no concept of manners at all. It was all natural.

For her part, Natasha Spender was growing more and more disturbed by Chandler's instability. She too now began to despair of him, not least because the situation was made more intense by his complete reliance on her. It was clear that, in the increasingly 'addled' mind of Chandler, Natasha was starting to appear as Cissy reincarnated: she was beautiful, she played the piano, and she seemed to understand him.

If Natasha Spender and her family were still reasonably unworried about her operation, Chandler was an anxious wreck when they returned to London in the first week of December. Stephen Spender took over personal care of him while Natasha was in hospital, often having to stay up with the American through the night, trying to calm his mind. It was Spender's name and address that Chandler now carried in his wallet for notification 'In the event of an accident'. The drinking had again got out of hand, and he had himself admitted to hospital shortly before Christmas of 1955 and there stopped drinking. Natasha's operation, meanwhile, had gone without a hitch.

Chandler was collected from the clinic by Jocelyn Rickards, another of the old Chandler patrol, who took him back to the Ritz, only to watch him pour 'the largest Ballantynes' she had ever seen. He was, temporarily at least, in good spirits. He told anyone who inquired after his hospitalization that he had caught malaria in Tunisia, still unprepared to admit that he was an alcoholic.

In January 1956, the Spenders decided to move Chandler into a flat on Carlton Hill – a quieter area of London near their own house in St John's Wood. Without daily supervision, it was now clear that he would otherwise have to be institutionalized. It was not a particularly beautiful flat; indeed, he could not afford expensive quarters if he was going to continue spending money at the rate he had been, while producing no new work. Chandler grew miserable and troublesome. Living by himself through an English winter was worse than living alone in the Californian sun. To make matters worse, he started telling people that he was principally unhappy because he and Natasha wanted to get married but could not, because of her two young children. Natasha was angry when she found out, and grew more impatient with Chandler's delirium:

The overriding reason for bad times at Carlton Hill was drink, I believe, to drown the fiercely conflicting images of his past life; and any other reason he projected to certain selected friends of his was a self-deception similar to reasons he had invented in earlier crises to explain, for instance, the abrupt end of his oil-tycoon career. But there were also good times when his wit and originality sprang into life again and he would improvise more serial tales of adventure. An expedition to meet Frances Cornford [a Cambridge poet and granddaughter of Darwin] amused him. Having asked him what his favourite expression in the American vernacular was, she was visibly startled when he replied vigorously: 'Aw, turn blue'.[33]

There were times when Chandler seemed soberly aware of what was happening to him. 'I am one of those people,' he conceded, 'who has to be known exactly the right amount to be liked.' Natasha recalled one lunchtime conversation about psycho-analysis, during which someone suggested that people's neuroses mostly originated in childhood. 'Oh I don't know,' sighed Chandler, 'I pick mine up as I go along.' He started writing poetry again while at Carlton Hill:

> I have become a pilgrim in the rain,
> To some abandoned shrine too far away,
> Or lover of the saccharine refrain
> That lilts of longing for a golden day
> That will not come again.[34]

'I am apt to get up at around 4 am,' he told Louise Loughner in San Francisco, 'take a mild drink of Scotch and water and start hammering at this lovely Olivetti 44 which is far superior to anything we turn out in America. It is a heavy portable and put together like an Italian racing car, and you mustn't judge it from my typing.'[35]

He got on well with the Spenders' children, Matthew and Elizabeth, and was moved by the family's kindness to him. 'I rather feel,' he wrote to Stephen, 'that the Spender family is my family. And I need the Spender family far more than the Spender family need me. Insofar as it is possible I shall always consider myself one of the Spender family.'

Having been so open in interviews about his suicide attempt and his loss of Cissy, Chandler began to receive several letters from those who had suffered similar unhappiness. Some of the people who wrote to him were subsequently invited to tea at Carlton Hill. A compulsive letter-writer himself, Chandler never thought it unusual that people he did not know should pour out their emotions in letters to him. The idea that writers of fan letters were 'psychopathic', he had once said, was judging the general by the exceptional:

> If I get a letter (I haven't lately) from a lady in Seattle who says she likes music and sex and practically invites me to move in . . . it is safe not to answer it. But intelligent people write intelligent letters – he may be just lonely, just generous, or just someone who finds pleasure in letter writing.[36]

The most intelligent fan mail, he added, came from the Scandinavian countries.

*

Chandler was now in deep trouble with the British tax authorities, unaware – or simply unwilling to make himself aware – that it was not enough to say that he had stayed in Britain beyond the allowed six months in order to look after Natasha. For the time being he still refused to pay anything, but it was clear that he was not helping his situation by remaining in Britain. In a lucid moment in May 1956, a year after his original arrival in London, he resolved to return once more to America. He left almost immediately, flying first to New York, where he stayed for a week at the Grovesnor Hotel on Fifth Avenue, seeing Jessica Tyndale daily and drinking moderately. He planned to meet Louise Loughner in San Francisco, and sent her a note saying: 'Please make a reservation for a suite at the Cliff Hotel, seven days from 3rd June.' A follow-up letter from New York gave Loughner his flight details; he intended to fly straight to her in San Francisco rather than go to La Jolla first, and he asked her to bring 'a bottle of Scotch' to the airport.

First, though, Chandler went to New England, for what was to be another two-week stay with the Barrows. But there his body buckled under a tidal wave of whisky. After less than a week with the Barrows, he fell down the stairs and was taken by ambulance to a New York hospital, where he was given a blood transfusion. He sent Loughner a telegram from his bed, asking her to cancel his hotel booking: 'EXTREMELY SORRY BUT REQUIRED MEDICAL TREATMENT HERE MAKES IT NECESSARY POSTPONE TRIP. WILL WRITE SOONEST. PLEASE CANCEL AT CLIFF. YOURS RAYMOND CHANDLER.'[37] Jessica Tyndale, who took over responsibility for Chandler, was now seeing a side to him that she had only heard about from her London friends. 'He seems,' she wrote, 'to have a singular capacity to involve others intensely in his own life – and as one so involved I am beginning to despair completely.'[38]

Despite this catalogue of humiliations, Chandler was still managing to send off upbeat letters. 'I rather liked New York this time,' he told Ian Fleming while recuperating, 'having hereto loathed its harshness and rudeness. . . . I haven't got a damn thing to do but potter about a bit or just go for a walk through the Village.' He wrote another sketch while resting at the Grovesnor Hotel, which he titled 'How To Ruin Doctor'. It showed that one thing at least had changed – Chandler had given up trying to deny the nature of his sickness:

He came in with his white medical coat and his beaming and terribly expensive smile. I stood up. He sat down at his desk and prepared to take notes on my condition, if any. He asked my age, which I lied about as usual, and then rather suddenly:
   – May I ask why you are wearing dark glasses?
   – Of course? My eyes are bloodshot from boozing.
   – Oh really? How much do you drink in an average day?
   – Not a terribly large amount, really. A bottle of scotch, eight or nine cocktails (doubles of course) and various wines at luncheon and dinner.
   He studied me with little pleasure.
   – Have you always been an excessive drinker Mr Chandler?
   – Don't be silly, I said, I can still get my shoes on.
   – I should regard you as verging on alcoholism, he said in an annoyed voice.
   – Well, it's a nice little verge, I said.[39]

Back in La Jolla by the middle of June, Chandler stayed for a time at the Hotel Del Charro, and then moved into a small two-bedroomed beach apartment at 6925 Neptune Place:

> This place is an unfurnished apartment on the ocean front. That is, it was unfurnished. It now has so damn much furniture in it that only a steeple-chaser would feel at home in it. But in spite of having all this lovely (and to me now detestable) furniture, a fine electric stove, a Frigidaire and some curtains, in spite of being full of nice yellow cartons which keep me from putting my shirts and underclothes away, in spite of having a small private patio and a large private storeroom, all I have to eat off of is one cup, one saucer, one plate, all borrowed. But a full set of sterling silver, oh my yes.[40]

Within two weeks of this return, he felt well enough to make the trip north to see Louise Loughner in San Francisco. It was the first time they had met and he stayed there for a month, living at the Cliff Hotel – he also started drinking again and told his London solicitor, Michael Gilbert, that he planned to marry Loughner. By the start of August, however, Chandler had collapsed again and was admitted to the Las Encinas Sanitarium in Pasadena, Los Angeles. The brief relationship was over: 'I'm very sorry,' he wrote to Loughner, 'and very lonely.'

There was now a respite. Chandler found the Pasadena clinic 'a very wonderful place', and his health and spirits picked up. He was able, he told Jessica Tyndale, finally to put his behaviour of the last twelve months in perspective. He was no longer refusing psychological treatment:

> They have a psychiatrist there that an intelligent man can really respect. They treat all kinds of people (with money, natch), incurable alcoholics, guys on benders . . . a few psychotics who have to be kept in a special locked bungalow, depressed people etc. . . . I said that I had been married so long and so happily that after the slow torture of my wife's death it seemed at first treason to look at another woman and then suddenly I seemed to be in love with all women. . . . They gave me tests, apperception tests, Rorschach tests, wood block tests. I haven't had the lowdown on them yet, but I think I was pretty brilliant except on the drawing. . . . Finally the head guy said 'You think you are depressed, but you are quite wrong. . . . All that's the matter with you is loneliness. You simply

cannot and must not live alone'. . . . I hadn't expected anything so penetrating.[41]

Chandler returned by himself to La Jolla where, for the first time since Cissy's death, he began doing some writing. He decided to resurrect *Playback,* the unused screenplay that he had written for Universal in 1947, and turn it into a Marlowe book. Following his Pasadena treatment, it was now clear to him (as it had always been to those who received letters from him) that he was far more stable when he was writing.

This return to his senses during the last months of 1956 was shattered, however, when he discovered that Natasha Spender had embarked on an American concert tour. Persuaded by Chandler that he had recovered both mentally and physically since he had last seen her, she agreed to meet up with him for Christmas. Chandler subsequently took a driver to Arizona to pick her up in the week before Christmas, quietly implying to Jessica Tyndale that he and Natasha were planning to have an affair.[42] He was drunk when he turned up alone to meet Natasha, who immediately realized that his recovery was illusory and that it had been a mistake to see him. 'He drove first of all straight into a fence, and then weaving across and even off the road.' Chandler next had his driver take him and Natasha to the town of Chandler, Arizona, and the Grand Canyon, before going on to Palm Springs, where they spent Christmas Day.

No longer feeling comfortable with the man she had tried so hard to help, Natasha left him in Palm Springs and drove by herself to Los Angeles, to spend New Year with friends there, the Hookers. Evelyn Hooker was a pioneer of gay studies in America and a friend of the English writer Christopher Isherwood, a sometime tenant at the house she and her husband owned in Brentwood. When Chandler telephoned the Hookers' house soon after Natasha's arrival, to announce that he, too, was coming to Los Angeles, on 6 January, they invited him to dinner. He sat moodily through the meal and refused to speak: 'Topics ranged widely,' recalled Natasha, 'mescalin, Chinese jades, the piano music of Schubert, Tolkien, and the private life of Dr Swift, all of which Raymond found very boring.'

As a trained psychologist, Evelyn Hooker could immediately

detect how close Chandler had become to insanity, and tried to dissuade Natasha from returning with him to Palm Springs. Evelyn was convinced that he needed professional help. Conscious that she would, in any case, soon have to abandon Chandler to resume her tour, Natasha none the less went with him, but the two had no sooner returned to the desert resort than, quite unexpectedly, Evelyn Hooker's husband died from a heart attack. Natasha wanted to return to Los Angeles immediately, but Evelyn urged her now to stay put for Chandler's sake. The latter was deeply moved by the gesture and insisted that Evelyn, Isherwood, and Isherwood's lover, Don Bachardy, come to Palm Springs at his expense after the funeral. They accepted, and Natasha drove back to Brentwood to pick Evelyn up.

'I think he is the only queer I have ever felt entirely at ease with,' said Chandler of Isherwood. 'I do think that homosexuals (not bi-sexuals, that is a matter of time and custom), however artistic and full of taste they may seem to be, always lack any deep emotional feeling. Their physical bravery was proved in the war, but they are still essentially the dilettante type.'

The friendship of Terry Lomax and Philip Marlowe in *The Long Goodbye* had been taken by one American critic to be a latently homosexual one. 'You can certainly dismiss the remarks of Mr G. Legman,' Chandler had replied, adding that to him the critic belonged to a class of American neurotics 'which cannot conceive of a close friendship between a couple of men as other than homosexual'. By examining only the detective writing of Chandler, Legman had also pointedly failed to make allowances for the genre within which Chandler wrote. Like westerns, hard-boiled detective stories had always held up strong, handsome and honest men for heroes. That these men were invariably bachelors, and invariably got on best with other bachelors, was a part of the tough genre. Because of Chandler's appeal to intellectuals, however, his books had become prone to being analysed out of the context of their *Black Mask* roots. Seeing this, Chandler had actually tried to pre-empt various 'clever-clever' analyses – including the charge of homosexuality – from within the text of *The Long Goodbye*:

'I had a male secretary once' [Roger Wade tells Marlowe towards the end of the novel]. 'Used to dictate to him. Let him go. He bothered me sitting there waiting for me to create. Mistake. Ought to have kept him. Word might have got around I was a homo. The clever boys that write book reviews because they can't write anything else would have caught on and started giving me the build-up. Have to take care of their own, you know. They're all queers, every damn one of them. The queer is the artistic arbiter of the age, chum. The pervert is the top guy now.'

Having met the Hon. David Herbert, Stephen Spender and other homosexuals in London, however, Chandler had become more tolerant by the time he met Isherwood. He had decided to read the infamous cross-examination of Oscar Wilde by Edward Carson, from Wilde's unsuccessful libel case against the Marquess of Queensberry, and concluded that it read like 'two people shouting across oceans of misunderstanding. . . . They [homosexuals] threaten us because our own normal vices fill us at times with the same sort of revulsion.'

Some posthumous criticism of Chandler has none the less suggested that Philip Marlowe was a fantasy figure inspired (as was his homophobia) by Chandler's deeply repressed homosexuality. This is obviously speculative, since it can be neither proved nor disproved. Such speculation generally revolves around Marlowe's physical description of certain male characters he comes across. In *Lady in the Lake*, for instance, he meets an honest old country sheriff:

He had large ears and friendly eyes and his jaws munched slowly and he looked as dangerous as a squirrel and much less nervous. I liked everything about him.

In *Farewell My Lovely* there is a similar character, whose description by Marlowe (because the character is younger than the sheriff) might typically be used by those who detect the homoerotic in Chandler. Initially seeing him as a 'big red-headed roughneck in dirty sneakers', Marlowe thinks the man is about to attack him. On a closer look, his fear subsides. Chandler's detective always uses the way a character looks to denote his integrity; and this character is clearly no villain:

He smiled a slow tired smile. His voice was soft, dreamy, so delicate for a big man that it was startling. . . . I looked at him again. He had the eyes you never see, that you only read about. Violet eyes. Almost purple. Eyes like a girl, a lovely girl. . . . But except for the eyes he had a plain farmer face, with no stagy kind of handsomeness.

A correlation between the way a character looks and the way they think (common in most melodrama) is just as true of good female characters in Chandler's books. In *Farewell My Lovely* there is such a character called Anne Riordan:

She was about twenty-eight years old. She had a rather narrow forehead of more height than is considered elegant. Her nose was small and inquisitive, her upper lip a shade too long and her mouth more than a shade too wide. Her eyes were grey-blue with flecks of gold in them. She had a nice smile. She looked as if she had slept well. It was a nice face, a face you could get to like. Pretty, but not so pretty that you would have to wear brass knuckles every time you took it out.

In a California of phoney beauty, where every burger restaurant claimed to be a palace and every woman looked a princess from a distance, Marlowe relies on eyes, skin and voices to tell him what he needs to know. Clothes and furnishings mean almost nothing to him. In the same story that he meets Riordan, Marlowe encounters the story's glamorous femme fatale. He has little to go on initially, so mannered and predictable is her demeanour: 'I didn't pay much attention to her clothes. They were what the guy designed for her and she would go to the right man.' It takes longer before he can finally break the girl's motives down in his mind.

Marlowe was always on the lookout for such details that might betray a character's real intentions, whether they were male or female. In *The Long Goodbye*, however, the focus of attention had shifted. Natasha Spender believes that in Lennox, Wade and Marlowe, Chandler was creating three versions of himself. No longer living in Los Angeles, she believes he turned his attention from the streets and into his own mind. There are several details in each of the three characters' lives, she explains, that corresponded to different aspects of Chandler's own personality. The three represent, together, everything that Chandler both wanted to be and was afraid he was. By this definition, Terry Lennox becomes less a love-object for Marlowe or Chandler, than an alter ego:

All three characters were drinkers, like Raymond himself, two of them disintegrating and despairing. . . . As with aspects of Raymond's own character, their dominance veered with his mood. Roger Wade his 'bad self', Philip Marlowe his 'good self' and Terry Lennox his anxious one. These three, often in conflict, were in good times subordinated to a fourth, the genial, generous and benevolently paternal friend.[43]

*

Edward Hooker's heart attack had unsettled Chandler, and he could not stop talking about death while in Palm Springs. He kept repeating the phrase 'Cissy is gone for ever'. To Natasha's horror, he explained to the so recently bereaved Evelyn Hooker that one of the reasons he had been so devastated by Cissy's death was that he did not believe in an afterlife. The situation was saved only by Evelyn's tolerance, and by the fact that Isherwood and Chandler got on well. A fragment of the holiday was recorded on film, in colour, though without sound, by Don Bachardy, the only footage of Chandler known to exist. It shows him monkeying around on a diving board and looking suspiciously lively. According to Evelyn Hooker, who minded Chandler's tactlessness and drinking far less than Natasha now did, Chandler kept asking her and Natasha to give him marks out of ten for his dives.

It was all too much for Natasha Spender, who in any case now had to resume her concert tour. During an elaborate 'farewell dinner' that Chandler insisted they should have after the departure of Evelyn and Isherwood, she made it clear that she was no longer prepared to be caught up in his flights of fantasy about their own relationship, or about his own stability. In reply, Chandler made one of the chivalric gestures of which he was so fond. He wrote her a formal letter, acknowledging her decision to end their friendship, and sent it to her via his solicitor in London:

> I was rather stupid all along. You were so kind and tender to me in my troubles that I believed it was to me, not merely to someone in trouble. I know now that I was wrong, that you would have done the same for anyone in deep trouble.[44]

Three days after Natasha Spender's departure, Chandler's driver arrived in Palm Springs to take him back to La Jolla.

9
Playing It Back

*What did it matter where you lay once you were dead?
In a dirty sump or in a marble tower on top of a hill?
You were dead, you were sleeping the big sleep, you
were not bothered by things like that*
(*The Big Sleep*, 1939)

In the New Year of 1957, Chandler moved back into his apartment
on Neptune Place in La Jolla, put himself on a course of vitamin
injections, and attempted to get back into a routine of self-discipline.

He placed an advertisement for a new secretary in the *San Diego
Tribune*. The woman who answered, Jean Fracasse, was a striking-
looking Australian, formerly an actress and newsreader. Born in
Sydney and educated in Paris and London, Jean had originally
moved to California with her husband, a successful doctor. Now
with two young children, she was in the middle of expensive
divorce proceedings and in need of work. She was more than
qualified for the post of Chandler's secretary, having worked for a
time in advertising, gained a doctorate in music, and been 'one of
the first three women ever employed by a network TV company'.
Like Cissy, and Natasha Spender, she was an accomplished
pianist.

Having taken her on as his secretary in January 1957, Chandler
soon became deeply involved in Jean Fracasse's divorce; he also
gave her money. He went to the lengths of personally tracking
down witnesses for Fracasse's attorney ('Of course, I could have
served subpoenas, but I wanted willing witnesses'), and decided

that Dr Fracasse was a villain and a fraud, as well as 'a dangerous manic depressive and paranoiac'. Unimpressed by what he had learnt from his involvement, he resolved to write a book about divorce lawyers once he had finished his new Marlowe story: 'I have found out the way the divorce racket works in California,' he told his American publishers. 'I have investigated other cases. [The book] will be about the typical divorce lawyer and believe me, he ought to be under a rock.'

These efforts to help the situation immediately backfired, however, since Dr Fracasse's lawyer began suggesting that Jean had found a new means of support in Chandler. Such deviousness only strengthened his resolve to protect her. As 1957 went on, he encouraged her to bring her two small children to his apartment on the days when she worked for him. Chandler enjoyed playing with the children, a boy and a girl, and they would often watch television with him. He took all three of them on holiday to Palm Springs and started telling friends in England that he planned to marry Jean Fracasse. She was a blithe and elegant woman who took no nonsense from him, something that served only to deepen his love for her. She had no interest in remarrying yet, and certainly no interest in sleeping with Chandler. He wrote her a limerick:

A lovely young lady named Jean,
Is dainty and tender and clean.
Though her legs I adored,
I always deplored,
That I never could get in between.[1]

While working on what would be his seventh novel, Chandler also fell in love with his new agent. Helga Greene, whom Chandler had taken on as his worldwide representative before leaving London, was the former wife of Hugh Carleton Greene, Director-General of the BBC. As an heiress to part of the Guinness fortune and a friend of Jessica Tyndale, Helga already knew many of the people Chandler had met in London. In November 1957, she made a flying visit to La Jolla to see how he was progressing with the new book, since no one in London, including Hamish Hamilton, believed that he was capable of finishing another novel. She spent a week in La Jolla, and was then Chandler's guest for a week in

Palm Springs. He found her company a tonic: 'Somehow, just by the way she talks and acts, by her simplicity, her lack of pettiness, the keenness of her mind, she inspires me.'[2] As Helga recalled, Chandler began working with some resolve on the novel:

> He would go to bed early, around 10.00, and would wake up bright as anything – never the trace of a headache – any time after 4.00 am. . . . He usually worked till lunchtime on his own or with a secretary. After lunch I have never known him do a stroke of work though sometimes he dictated letters lying on his back like a great porpoise.[3]

Helga's stay in California was short because she ran a full-time literary agency in London and had various other clients to attend to, including (for a time) Roald Dahl. Like others before her, though, she was quickly drawn into Chandler's life. She liked him, and liked his irreverence: 'He was able to make me laugh,' she wrote after his death, 'which is unusual. He was so unexpected, such a mixture of naiveté and brilliance. The occasional drinking was a bore, because he then became repetitive, but he was the best company in the world, and he got the best out of you . . . he was stimulating, and he had himself such an immense amount of charm – not only for his friends, but also for the shopkeepers, the charwoman, the waiters.'[4] Chandler wrote Helga a limerick, as he had done for Jean Fracasse:

> A beautiful charmer named Greene,
> Is never ill-bred or obscene,
> So I never can say,
> Even in a nice way,
> The things that I really mean.[5]

Playback,[6] the book which Chandler now completed, is arguably the funniest of all his novels. The tones of depression in *The Long Goodbye* are replaced by a sense of resigned absurdity. Marlowe's fate is no better, nor his self-respect stronger, but he seems to see his situation as comical rather than tragic. In more than one scene the detective, who is now in his mid-forties, finds himself giggling. There is no murder until near the end of the story, and the detective sleeps with both of the book's main female characters.[7]

The story begins with a phone call which wakes Marlowe in his LA apartment at dawn. He fumbles with the receiver, clumsier and slower than he used to be. 'I'm not a young man,' he moans to his caller, 'I'm old, tired and full of no coffee.' The voice on the line is impatient: 'Did you hear me! I said I was Clyde Umney, the lawyer.' Marlowe stares at the phone, and then replies: 'Clyde Umney the lawyer. I thought we had several of them.' Later that morning, while he waits outside Umney's office for further instructions, Marlowe gets into an argument with the lawyer's glamorous and snooty assistant, whom he keeps calling 'sister'. 'Don't call me sister,' she warns him:

> 'Then don't call me buster, you very expensive secretary. What are you doing tonight? And don't tell me you're going out with four sailors again.'[8]

Umney wants Marlowe to follow a girl called Eleanor King from the train station in Los Angeles to wherever she is going. He is told that he will receive further instructions from Umney's client later. The girl, it turns out, is heading for a hotel in a coastal town outside San Diego called Esmeralda. Marlowe books himself into the same hotel. When he is coshed unconscious in his room by another private detective, he begins to suspect that he is not the only person following the girl. He discovers that King has come to California from the East Coast under an assumed name, after having been found not guilty, albeit narrowly, of causing her alcoholic husband's death. As in the screenplay version of the story, the reader does not know whether King actually killed her husband or not. What Marlowe does learn is that King's powerful father-in-law, who is convinced of her guilt, has sworn to make her life a misery. It is he who has ordered Umney to have her trailed.

Having now changed her name to 'Betty Mayfield', the girl is degenerating into a paranoid and suicidal wreck. Too tired to move on again, even though she knows she has been followed, she starts drinking in local bars. She immediately attracts the attention of two local hoods. One is Larry Mitchell, who on discovering her reason for running, starts hassling her for money. The other is Clark Brandon, a former Kansas mobster who has retired to

Esmeralda where he operates legitimate businesses, including the hotel in which King is staying. Brandon falls for King, as does Marlowe, who decides to change sides and protect her instead of following her.

There was one criticism which Chandler chose to redress in the pages of *Playback*. There had been a slur of anti-Semitism sticking to him since his depiction of a coin dealer called Elisha Morningstar in *The High Window*. 'There's a bit of an anti-Semite in all of us,' he had once admitted to Hamish Hamilton; 'Jews and Gentiles alike.' The Shylock-like character of Morningstar had certainly fitted most of the traditional anti-Semitic stereotypes. Initially, Chandler had defended the portrait against letters of complaint by pointing out that most of his characters were exaggerated types. His nightclub girls were not just skimpily dressed; you could hide what they were wearing 'behind a matchstick'. His hoods (like Moose Molloy in *Farewell My Lovely*) were not just big; they were giants. His tycoons (like Potter in *The Long Goodbye*) were billionaires rather than millionaires. His bad cops were not just bent; they were evil. His starlets, similarly, were psychotic rather than just neurotic.

Everyone was over the top, because that was what Chandler believed melodrama – in the tradition of Shakespeare and Dickens – to be. Even Philip Marlowe, he said, was meant to be 'the most honourable, wittiest, brave and resourceful man imaginable'. The witch-hunting sniffers-out of anti-Semitism, Chandler replied to one aggrieved letter, 'should look for their enemies not among those who . . . put Jewish characters in their books because there are many Jews in their lives and all interesting and all different and some rather nasty – like other people – but let them look for their enemies among the brutes (who they can easily recognize) and among the snobs who do not speak of Jews at all.'

Chandler did not consider himself a racist, and indeed had always refused to join the La Jolla tennis club because it did not allow Jewish members. In *Playback*, none the less, he chose to qualify his stereotyping. The qualification is made by a grizzled motel owner called Fred Pope:

> Of course we got Jews here now, but let me tell you something. A
> Jew is supposed to give you a sharp deal and steal your nose, if you

ain't careful. That's all bunk. A Jew enjoys trading; he likes business, but he's only tough on the surface. Underneath, a Jewish businessman is usually really nice to deal with. He's human. If you want cold-blood skinning, we got a bunch of people in this town will cut you down to the bone and add a service charge. They'll take your last dollar from between your teeth and look at you like you stole it from them.[9]

*

The strange ending to *Playback* betrays Chandler's weariness in 1957: King finds Larry Mitchell dead in her hotel room and panics. She tells Marlowe that if the police find the body, they will suspect her. She promises him that she did not kill Mitchell, but insists that she cannot face another trial. Marlowe almost suspects her himself, but since he is now in love with her, he agrees to help. But when they go up to the girl's room to see the body, it has gone. This further traumatizes King, who by now is on the point of nervous breakdown. Marlowe decides that the only way the body could have been removed is through the basement car park, and goes to see the night parking attendant at his home. He finds him dead, too, hanging from the ceiling. Meanwhile, Goble, the private detective who coshed Marlowe at the start of the book, is also found badly beaten up. The local police now begin to circle ominously around Eleanor King, of whose past they have now been informed by King's father-in-law. Mitchell's body is not found, but the police know that he has disappeared.

Marlowe finally realizes what has been going on and confronts Clark Brandon. It was he, not Eleanor King, whom Mitchell and Goble were blackmailing. Goble was from Kansas, and had come to Esmeralda to threaten Brandon with exposure of his mobster past: he had only coshed Marlowe because he thought that he was on to Brandon as well. Goble had let Larry Mitchell in on his scam, because he wanted Mitchell to approach Brandon for the money. But rather than agreeing to a payoff, Brandon had thrown Mitchell off the top floor of his hotel. Mitchell had landed on the lower balcony of King's room (the most tenuous part of the story) where she had found him dead. The police can prove nothing: Mitchell's body has been disposed of by Brandon; Goble has run back to Kansas; and the parking attendant's hanging appears to be suicide.

Eleanor King, who thinks it has all been done for her sake, falls in love with Clark Brandon. Dejected and lonely, Marlowe drives back to LA.

In his other books, Chandler had made a point of not always giving Marlowe the best punchlines, lest he seem to readers too confident. This is not true in *Playback,* however, in which the detective is older and different. He is no longer a hero so much as a man who has realized that, despite his honesty, he has 'failed' at life. On the point of retirement, he has only his ego and his wit left. His persistent wisecracking is similar in tone to the triumphant, and not wholly truthful, letter that Chandler had written after his release from the Chula Vista Sanitarium, following his unsuccessful suicide attempt. 'I out-talked them and out-thought them,' he had written to Louise Loughner, 'so that in the end they sent me home in a limousine, merely because they were dazzled by the display of wit and courage I put on.'

It is this type of doomsday bravado that Marlowe displays in *Playback*. He relishes the small, verbal victories that he used to score without thinking. When one hood tells him that he is going to cut him down so small he'll need a stepladder to tie his shoe-laces, Marlowe responds only to the phrasing of the threat: 'Somebody did a lot of work on that one,' he says, 'but hard work's no substitute for talent.' Nothing is taken seriously any more:

> Oh guns. . . . Don't scare me with guns. I've lived with them all my life. . . . Guns never settle anything. . . . They are just a fast curtain to a bad second act.[10]

Even pain is now just a wry joke to Chandler's detective. He no longer has the physical reflexes to deal with villains, but he has also gone beyond the self-pity of *The Long Goodbye* to a state of absurdist complacency:

> Somebody who loved me very much had put ice cubes on the back of my head. Somebody who loved me less had bashed in the back of my brain. It could have been the same person. People have moods.[11]

Marlowe is like a once-great matador urging the bull to gore him rather than let him go further to seed. Chandler's hero had always stood his ground against hoods, but in a way that in the end made them grudgingly respect him. Now he is merely provocative. 'Don't get funny with me buster,' one gunman warns him in *Playback*, 'I get annoyed rather easy':

> 'Fine. Let's watch you get annoyed. What do you do – bite your moustache?'
> 'I ain't got no moustache, stupid.'
> 'You could grow one. I can wait.'[12]

Perhaps influenced by Hitchcock – who took a walk-on role in the films he made – Chandler allowed himself a cameo self-portrait in *Playback*. Henry Clarendon IV is rich, lonely and old, and is living out his life in expensive hotels. He is an over-intelligent and undernourished man letting his mind go to waste on hotel gossip, aimless global itineraries and hopeless infatuations with middle-aged women. He is conscious of being both very wise and very stupid. 'I'm egocentric,' he tells Marlowe, 'and absurd, and I prattle like a schoolgirl.' Like Chandler, Clarendon wears white gloves and, again like Chandler, he is both cynical and romantic:

> Very few things amuse a man of my age. A humming bird, the extraordinary way a strelitzia bloom opens. Why at a certain point in its growth does the bud turn at right angles? . . . Why will a mother rabbit trapped in a burrow by a ferret put her babies behind her and allow her throat to be torn out? Why? In two weeks more she would not even recognize them.[13]

Chandler was sixty-nine when he wrote *Playback* and had been out of Los Angeles for so long that he was reluctant to write about the city any more. That had been one of the exhausting aspects of writing *The Long Goodbye* – he had had to describe LA from memory rather than from observation. His solution in *Playback* was to bring the action away from the city to a place he knew better: the suburbs of San Diego. Modern Los Angeles was starting to leave Marlowe behind, as the detective admits in *Playback*. How long, he wonders, before cars there are equipped with 'radar, sound-recording equipment, a bar, and an anti-aircraft battery'. Marlowe's enemies had always accused him of being a ridiculous figure (he had been called 'Tarzan on a big red scooter' in *The Long Goodbye*), and now he seemed to agree with them. Fleming's James Bond was embracing a world of modern deceit and technology in order to win his battles. Marlowe was still just a lone operator wasting his talents to help out ungrateful clients. 'Isn't it about time you stopped following me around?' the heroine asks him in *Playback*:

> 'You're my client. I'm trying to protect you. Maybe on my seventieth birthday someone will tell me why.'[14]

Alcohol looms large in the book, as it did once more in Chandler's life. Despite his long history of drinking, however, *Playback* was the only one of his books that he wrote drunk. It would seem, too, that he was also dabbling with prescription drugs; in one letter he reports having had a throat infection and it being 'fun' because 'it gave me the chance to be shot full of penicillin, a very wonderful thing that makes you feel that God is on the side of the right people'.[15] Despite Cissy's dabbling with opium as a young woman in New York, there is no evidence that Chandler used illegal drugs himself, though in *Playback* he shows a knowledge of 'the honeyed reek of well-cured marijuana', as well as some of its effects: 'The guy was out of circulation, he was in the valley of peace, where time is allowed to stand still, where the world is all colour and music.'

The last chapter of *Playback* is a poignant summary of Chandler's own circumstances as he finished the book. At the end of the story, Marlowe returns to a home similar to the faceless La Jolla apartment in which his creator was now living:

> I opened a couple of windows and mixed a drink in the kitchen. I sat down on the couch and stared at the wall. Wherever I went, whatever I did, this was what I would come back to. A blank wall in a meaningless room in a meaningless house. I put the drink down on the side table without touching it. Alcohol was no cure for this. Nothing was any cure for this but the hard inner heart that asked for nothing from no one.[16]

Happily for Marlowe, Chandler provides his hero with the same sort of fantasy escape from the doldrums that he had been using himself since Cissy's death. If it had seemed that the writer was only capable of optimism when he was entertaining entirely unrealistic hopes, then in his fiction at least these fantasies could be made to happen. Sitting on his couch with nothing to live for, Marlowe gets a phone call out of the blue from the beautiful heiress he had met in *The Long Goodbye*. Linda Loring is calling from Paris to declare her love for Marlowe and to tell him that she wants to marry him: 'Hold me in your arms,' she tells him. 'Hold me close in your arms. I don't want to own you. Nobody ever will. I just want to love you.'

Stranded in California, Chandler himself had taken to making countless transatlantic phone calls of his own while writing *Playback,* and had been running up massive phone bills as a consequence. He would ring friends like Helga Greene in London without giving a thought to time differences or cost. Letters had once been the reclusive Chandler's chosen lifeline to the outside world, but from Cissy's death onwards the telephone started to become just as important to him. Following Loring's call from Paris, Chandler's detective, who had just been on the point of abject depression, puts the phone down in a happy daze. The book ends more cheerfully than any of Marlowe's other adventures:

> I reached for my drink. I looked around the empty room – which was no longer empty. There was a voice in it, and a tall, slim, lovely woman. There was that soft, gentle perfume of a woman who presses herself tight against you. Whose lips are soft and yielding, whose eyes are half blind.[17]

*

After finishing *Playback* over Christmas 1957, Chandler told Helga Greene that he was planning to accompany Jean Fracasse and her children back to Australia, where he was going to live for a while. He was also growing increasingly interested in military history. 'I'd like to tell the wonderful story of how the wharflies beat MacArthur when he tried to act like royalty. I never could stand the man myself. Neither could the American navy . . . his advance from Seoul to the Yalu [during the Korean War of 1950–3] was one of the worst military mistakes ever made. The hell with him.'

Chandler said he planned to travel to Australia via London, so as to say goodbye to his friends there and introduce them to Jean. He had put his Oldsmobile in Jean's name after crashing it in October 1957, and he now had it shipped to Sydney.

Chandler flew ahead to London by himself in February of 1958, took a room at the Ritz and wired Jean three tickets for her and the children to join him, which they did in March. The prospect of staying in London with Helga, however, suddenly seemed, to him at least, as attractive a prospect as going to Australia. During March 1958, with Jean and her children waiting in London, he tried to make up his mind. Meanwhile, the British press continued to interview him, though they found him more subdued:

> Heavy bifocals fail to disguise Chandler's own restlessly observant contemplation of general human frailty, ready to catch the outward lineaments of character and setting and file them for future use. 'You must always look at life as if from the inside of a prison cell,' he declared. His voice is so quiet that many of the sardonic comments which make Marlowe's talk so engaging are lost by the unwary. His writing and his conversation are scarcely distinguishable. He talks as he writes, out of an inward world that is part fantasy, part hard business sense. Marlowe, like most of the other characters, is a cynic, but he has a soft centre and Kipling ideals.[18]

As Chandler attempted to resolve the confusion in which he found himself with Jean Fracasse, even the option of Australia was complicated for him by his intimacy with yet another woman. Deirdre Gartrell was an unhappy Australian undergraduate who had written a letter to Chandler in 1956 telling him how much his books had meant to her in times of depression. She was at university in Armidale, a town in New South Wales between Brisbane and Sydney, and a correspondence had begun which ran through the course of 1957, in which Chandler tried to comfort the young woman:

> You pay me a great compliment in feeling sure and happy when you put your thoughts and feelings in my hands, but you are quite right. I do have a strange sort of instinct for understanding people, especially women.[19]

The correspondence grew quite intense, with Deirdre confessing emotional crises and Chandler sending her poems similar to those he had sent Louise Loughner. 'In some strange way', he told her in July 1957, 'you have become a part of me, so that I wake in the night and wonder what is Deirdre thinking or doing. The older you get, the less you know.'[20] Chandler was now addicted to this type of intimacy, and his letters to Deirdre were often full of Cissy:

> I always opened the car door for her and helped her in. I never let her bring me anything. I always brought things to her. I never went out of a door or into before her. I never went into her bedroom without knocking. I suppose these are small things – like constantly sending her flowers, and always having seven presents for her birthday, and always having champagne on our anniversaries. They are small in a way, but women have to be treated with great tenderness and consideration – because they are women.[21]

In his correspondence with Deirdre Gartrell, Chandler's mood swings were transparent. Just when he seemed to be exploiting the girl's hero worship, he would start to talk about Cissy. And just when the talk about Cissy appeared to be becoming mawkish, Chandler had come up with common-sense advice for Deirdre, who wanted to be a writer:

> You have never described your room, your university, the buildings, the place, the atmosphere, the climate, what sort of place Armidale is. . . . I am interested in Australia, in everything about it, what it looks like, what its houses are like, how many rooms they have and what sort, what flowers grow there, what animals and birds are there, what the seasons are, what the ordinary life of your sort consists of. You tell me a great deal about your thoughts, but nothing about the life around you. Do you suppose that I became one of the most successful mystery writers of any age by thinking about me – about my personal torments and triumphs, about an unending analysis of my personal torments. I did not.[22]

But Deirdre Gartrell and Chandler were never to meet, because he now decided not to go to Australia with the Fracasses, and to stay in London instead. He booked them their passage in mid-April, and moved into the Chelsea flat at 8 Swan Walk which he had found with the help of Helga Greene. His London life began again, but not at the same pace as during his previous stay. He was now badly confused both in body and mind, and was quieter than before. He spent more and more time with Helga, whom he adored. She remembered their time together fondly:

> Ray and I played darts everywhere. His favourite pub was The Saddler's Arms at Sand Marsh. We played with the locals who never seemed to resent it. 'I'm only a rabbit at this game,' he used to say. 'Not bad, but no cigar.' . . . Used to play darts against himself if I were busy. He'd come into wherever I was and say: 'You won again' and disappear to go on playing. . . . Ray used to enjoy dancing when he was young, but he didn't know the new dances so we took a few lessons in Guildford late on Saturday afternoons. He wanted to learn the new dances, but 'They must leave my waltz alone, my waltz is my own.'[23]

Chandler decided that he wanted to take Helga on holiday. Hamish Hamilton suggested Kenya, but Chandler said he would 'probably be Mau Mau'd'. (The Mau Mau rebellion of 1952, in what was then the British Crown Colony of Kenya, was a bloody campaign led by Kikuyu tribesmen to expel European settlers out of the country. It was equally bloodily crushed, by British troops, in 1954.) He thought instead of returning to Tangier, but Ian Fleming persuaded him to consider going to Naples, where he might be able to interview the exiled American gangster 'Lucky' Luciano for the *Sunday Times*, Fleming's own employer at the time.

Charles Luciano had risen within the ranks of the American Mafia during Prohibition to become a godfather and a household name. His nickname referred to his ability to avoid arrest, despite running an empire based on narcotics, extortion and prostitution. He was eventually prosecuted in 1936 on the evidence of three prostitutes and a pimp on his payroll, and sent to prison where, according to legend, he continued to run the Mob. He was released in 1946 (supposedly in return for having given to US military Intelligence information about wartime Sicily), but expelled from the United States. Initially in exile in Cuba (where he was seen with Frank Sinatra), Luciano had always denied his importance within the Mafia and maintained that his ranking had been exaggerated by the press and the FBI in order to make his arrest seem more significant than it was.

Chandler liked the idea of meeting him. Having always been ambivalent towards the way the American press portrayed celebrity mobsters, he sent a telegram to Luciano in Naples requesting an interview. The ex-mobster replied to the request unequivocally: 'Nothing to say. Don't come on my account.' Chandler decided to go anyway, and Helga agreed to accompany him. On their arrival in Naples at the end of April, he wrote to one of the members of the old London 'shuttle service' from the Hotel Royal:

> Had a rather tiring trip. Greek plane to Rome and then train to Napoli. No food on the train. The Greek plane was well flown, but the service was not up to British standards. . . . There are lovely whores in the three bars, but they are not in my line. I've never been with one in my life and don't intend to start now. . . . Helga and I are having a bit of a row. She says I organize too much and I say the same of her. She wants to see everything, I want only people and things. I don't give a damn about Pompeii or Capri or historical monuments. There is too much damn history already.[24]

Chandler was told that he should leave a message for Luciano at the California Restaurant. He left an invitation for lunch and eventually met with his subject, who now agreed to the interview. The two men, according to Helga Greene, drank 'Italian vodka which tasted like petrol' throughout their conversation, but they got on well. Chandler, she warned Fleming, took no notes. In his resulting article, he expanded on his views about the Italian Mafia in America. During the joke that was Prohibition, he said, everyone still drank, including judges and policemen. Americans still wanted to gamble and use prostitutes. Someone was going to continue supplying the nation with these commodities and services, since America still wanted them, and the Italians were the best at doing so. The growth of the Mafia into a vast nationwide organization was an embarrassing reminder of American hypocrisy, and 'every so often we seem to try and salve our conscience by selecting a highly publicised scapegoat in order to create the illusion that our laws are being rigidly enforced'.

In 1936, Chandler continued, Luciano had been chosen as such a scapegoat by the FBI and by newspaper columnists. He was tried by a jury that would have read about him already – 'and if they could not read, there was always radio'. Chandler insisted that on the whole American jury members were stupid because 'intelligent people can usually find a way of escaping jury service', and he also attacked the prosecution's use of witnesses who were themselves facing charges:

> The principal witness against Luciano was a man held on a burglary charge. If convicted he would have been a four time loser, which in New York State would have required an automatic life sentence – a real one, not a nominal one. He would probably have testified that his mother was a multiple poisoner, if immunity had been promised to him. He said that he had known Luciano for eight or nine years and that Luciano had recently offered him a job at $40 a week as a collector from houses of prostitution. If he had said $400 a week or $1,000 I might have kept a straight face. But $40 for that? Absurd. It gives me some slight pleasure to know that this witness later, after the prosecutor was out of office, recanted his testimony and said that he had only seen Luciano in some bar.[25]

Chandler concluded that 'If Luciano is an evil man, then I am an idiot', and ended his interview – which he titled 'My Friend Luco' – with a personal opinion of the gangster's character:

> He has a soft voice, a patient sad face, and is extremely courteous in every way. This might all be a front but I don't think I am that easily fooled. A man who has been involved in brutal crimes bears a mark. Luciano seemed to be a lonely man. I liked him and I have no reason not to. He is probably not perfect, but neither am I.[26]

The *Sunday Times* refused to print the article.

*

Chandler and Helga returned to London. There had been plans for further travels in Italy, but Helga refused to continue the holiday with a constantly drunk Chandler. On their premature return, he moved back into the Chelsea flat. He was now feeling bad about Jean Fracasse, to whom he was speaking regularly on the telephone. His conscience about the matter had already prompted him to give Jean the British and Commonwealth rights to *Playback,* which she had promptly sold to Helga for £2,000 cash. The gift of these rights was an extravagant gesture which did nothing to help ease Chandler's mind, however, and his guilt-driven drinking landed him back in a London clinic, on Queen's Gate in Kensington.

On his release from the clinic in May 1958, Chandler was forced to face an issue that he had been avoiding for three years. The Inland Revenue was continuing to demand $50,000 worth of taxes from him for his extended stay in 1955, a year in which he had received substantial royalty payments from *The Long Goodbye*. In happier times, he might have attacked the situation with his characteristic relish for bureaucratic battles. But he was weak now, and paid the money. 'I have never been so frustrated in all my life,' he said of the Inland Revenue, 'by the inability to get straight answers.'

The case had been complicated by the authorities' claim that Chandler was still a British citizen through his mother. This claim was eventually dropped, on condition that he pay his outstanding taxes. Though his reaction to the tax demand was not as fierce or ingenious as it might have been in earlier years, he did make some stand; although only enough to increase his costs. He hired an accountant to work with his solicitor, Michael Gilbert, on the matter and communicated with them on a weekly basis; he would, too, often meet up with Gilbert for lunch at Simpson's in the Strand. It was a wearying affair – Chandler refused to allow the treatment for alcoholism that he had been receiving in 1955 to be used as part of his defence, and insisted that his stay had been prolonged beyond the six months permitted because he was looking after Natasha Spender at the time. This was never going to be sufficient defence (as, indeed, was proved), but he was adamant, if not entirely without a sense of humour. 'I wish you would send me a bill,' he wrote to Gilbert, 'because I read a blood-curdling article about lawyers' fees somewhere lately . . . it said that even if you passed their chambers and they happened to be looking out the window, they entered a modest charge of a guinea. You realize of course that it is only curiosity that makes me want to see the bill. I haven't the remotest intention of paying for it.'

Chandler was now making serious inroads into his fortune. It was decided that any earnings he might make in the future would be paid directly into an offshore Bahamian account held in his name. Henceforth, he was to be Chairman of Philip Marlowe Ltd, Nassau. Somewhat dramatically, he began to travel around London on the underground instead of by taxi.

The prospect of there being substantial future income was in fact looking increasingly unlikely. The only real writing Chandler managed in London in 1958 was a short introduction for a book by Frank Norman called *Bang To Rights*, which had been written while the author was in prison. Having met the author at a lunch hosted by Stephen Spender at the Café Royal Chandler offered to write a foreword. 'There is no damned literary nonsense about his writing,' it read, '. . . the situation is there, the people are there, and you are there with them; and that is a rare thing.' As with his testimonial to Fleming's *Moonraker*, the introduction from Chandler helped considerably to raise the author's profile. Norman himself went on to become a successful writer of London musicals and later described his inauspicious meeting with Chandler in 1958:

> We got on very well and drank a lot of whisky and he made arrangements for the following week to go to the theatre – it was a play by Donald Ogden Stewart. We sat in the stalls, and Ray went to sleep. And at one point a machine gun suddenly went off, which woke Ray up and he said, 'It's just not good enough. You know, just letting a gun off. That's not good enough to make a play.' And we marched out and didn't see the rest of the play.[27]

Chandler continued to write letters of complaint to people who annoyed him: the telephone company; Harrods, which had miscalculated his bill; the RAC Club, which refused to let him use the swimming pool in its premises in Pall Mall because he did not know any members there. He even wrote to the producer of an American television quiz show, *The Last Word*, which had irritated him in La Jolla:

> If my memory is not at fault, and if there are no technical reasons which I do not understand, then I confess to being puzzled by your panel's attitude to the phrase 'All and everyone of the Persians

drank their sherbet.' No one, so far as I remember, made what to me seem the two essential points. The use of 'everyone' is quite incorrect, and 'each and everyone', even if correct, does not make a plural phrase. . . . I don't really know why I am writing this. . . . There is an old story about us Americans which, to the right mind, tells a great deal. At a fork in the road there are two signs. One said TO A CONCERT OF THE MUSIC OF BACH. The other said TO A LECTURE ON THE MUSIC OF BACH. Guess which way the Americans went.[28]

During this period in London, Chandler also wrote to *The Times* about a leader he had read titled 'Bombs, Tanks and Boots'. 'The context shows clearly', he wrote, referring to one passage in the editorial, 'that the use of nuclear weapons refers to an event which has not yet occurred and may never occur. The verb therefore requires the subjunctive mood.'[29] *The Times* did not publish his letter.

There were more serious writing projects to be undertaken, if Chandler had the will. Hamish Hamilton suggested that he write an autobiography, but he declined. It would only be full of lies, he told the publisher, and 'who cares how a writer got his first bicycle'. His American publishers suggested a collection of his letters, but Chandler rejected that also. He did have an idea for a book called *This Year Was My Life*, in which he would take a year at random and describe what happened, but that too came to nothing. He told Helga about his idea for an *Idiot's Cook Book*, which would tell people how to do simple tasks well, and she encouraged him to work on it. But it was hard to tell any longer how serious Chandler was about his various plans. 'My baked apples,' he promised, 'are admired by everyone who owes me money.'[30]

At one point, Chandler decided that he wanted to read some classical literature, and was presented with several volumes by Hamish Hamilton. He ended up rereading his favourite thrillers instead, which he found helped ease his depression. More often he turned to television, notably the 1958 Wimbledon tennis tournament, which he watched in its entirety.[31] His paper bill from his time at Swan Walk shows that he had *Radio Times*, *TV Times*, and a listings magazine called *What's On* delivered each week. At night, he would often fall asleep in front of the television rather than go to bed; 'Sometimes, no doubt,' Helga said, 'he would be stupefied by drink.'

Reviews of *Playback*, when they appeared in 1958, were reverent rather than ecstatic. Chandler had spoken so often to the press of his plans to retire Marlowe that the book was seen as more of an epilogue to *The Long Goodbye* than as a proper novel. Notices were valedictory, speaking warmly of Marlowe's career as a whole rather than concentrating on the book itself.

One of Chandler's original reasons for coming to London had been to write a play called *English Summer*, an 'American-in-England' story he had once drafted. Its principal theme, he said, was 'the decay of the refined character [in English society] and its contrast with the ingenuous, honest, utterly fearless and generous American of the best type'. By the summer of 1958, however, his interest in the play had waned. This was met with some relief by those close to him, since what little work he had done on *English Summer* (in prose form) had turned into a strange piece of fantasy, in which the story's American hero, who is also the narrator, goes to the country to stay with a well-bred English woman with whom he is in love. Her husband is there, drunk, and behaving unpleasantly to her.

The American goes for a walk and is seduced by a mystical lady on a horse, who takes him back to her castle. He returns emboldened to the house where he is staying, to find that his hostess, whom he still loves, has shot her husband. They embrace and the hero takes off for London with the gun, in an effort to throw the police off her scent. He is arrested and released, and realizes that his lover does not really love him at all. She has taken advantage of him. The story ends with the American doubly lonely in London: 'A chill wind blew leaves and bits of paper across the now lusterless grass of Green Park, across the trim walks, almost over the high curbing into Piccadilly itself. I stood there for what seemed a long, long time, looking after nothing. There was nothing to look after.'[32]

Although he had now abandoned his sketches, play, cook book, military history and study of legal malpractice, Chandler continued to write his private verse. Though it still lacked the originality of his prose, and now its energy as well, there was nothing pretentious or overcomplicated about his late poetry:

> But always lay the grave,
> In waiting, and the silence and the maggot (naught)
> This was at last the horror which they bought.
> Man is too often nobler than his fate.[33]
>
> Young men are vainly warned
> Yet are forever mourned.
> Old men remember well
> How sounds the passing bell.
> Lie back in lonely chairs
> Dreaming of routs and fairs. . . .
>
> Young men may die in May;
> Old men must pass away
> When winter nights are cold,
> Damp, damp the graveyard mould.[34]

Over the course of the summer, Chandler saw only the people who came to visit him at the flat in Swan Walk. One of these visitors was Maurice Guinness, Helga's cousin, who would often drop in on his way home from work in the City. The two would lie on couches and have arguments about Marlowe's welfare. ('Do let Philip earn a little money,' Guinness wrote to Chandler. 'I get so worried about his finances.') Guinness persuaded Chandler to marry Marlowe off, and he obligingly wrote ten pages of a new story, which he called 'Poodle Springs', in which the detective and Linda Loring are on their honeymoon. Ian Fleming thought the marriage a good idea, once Chandler had explained to him that he planned to have his hero drink himself to death because he could not work any more. When the *Daily Mail* found out that Marlowe was to get married, it sent a journalist to Swan Walk to interview Chandler:

> I felt like a struck-off psychiatrist as, in the dimly lit Chelsea flat, the horizontal Chandler on his couch and I in the chair beside him both refuelled our glasses with whisky to see this thing through together.

The reporter asked Chandler about Cissy, suggesting that the death of Chandler's own wife had prompted him to create a fictional marriage for Marlowe. Chandler, dressed in tweeds, was clearly in some sort of daydream:

> 'She was my one true love. . . . She was a raging beauty, a strawberry blonde with lovely skin that I used to touch. You can see her photograph.' He sat up and we both looked at the wall behind the mantelshelf. There was no photograph there. Chandler looked bewildered and then said: 'Oh, I forgot. We're not in my own house.' He sank down again upon the divan. 'I don't regard California as my house anymore. It's just a place I store furniture.'[35]

In the end, however, Chandler told Guinness that the book did not work. The idea that Marlowe should get married, 'even to a very nice girl, is quite out of character. I see him always in a lonely street, in lonely rooms, puzzled but never quite defeated.' Soon afterwards, he abandoned the project.

One of the few public appearances that Chandler made during the summer of 1958 was in an interview with Ian Fleming for BBC Radio. When Fleming arrived at Swan Court at ten in the morning to pick his subject up, he found him already drunk. Once he was being recorded, Chandler showed no interest in Fleming's questions, and instead appeared intent on explaining the ease with which, in America, he could arrange for a contract to have a person killed. The process was simple, he told Fleming. You approach someone whom you know to have petty criminal connections, give him money, and ask to be put in touch with someone more serious. Within a few days, if you in turn seem serious enough, you will meet someone in a position to order the killing. This person will ring a contact in New York, who will telephone two assassins. They will have a legitimate cover, such as running a hardware store in Denver: 'They go to wherever the man lives. They get an apartment near his rooms and they study him for day after day after day so they know exactly when he goes out, when he comes home, what he does.' They pick their moment, Chandler continued, and one of them simply walks up to the target and shoots him. The other has a car ready and they disappear back to Denver. The police, by the time they arrive at the scene, have no idea where to look. The interview continued on this sidetrack; Chandler uninterested in discussing issues that no longer concerned him, and Fleming too tickled by Chandler's deafness to his questions to try and persuade him otherwise. A heavily edited version of the interview was broadcast on the BBC's Home Service.

*

Helga Greene hired Don Santry, a male nurse, to look after Chandler, which proved to be an arrangement that worked well. The flat in Swan Walk was peaceful, situated as it was on a hidden and beautiful Chelsea street near the river. In this atmosphere of relative calm, Chandler was happy to do very little. He was even contacted by a distant Thornton cousin, Dr Loftus Bor, who traced him through his publisher and took him on a tour of Kew Gardens, where he worked as a botanist.[36]

The peace was broken in August, however, by a telephone call from Jean Fracasse. She was still in Australia, but had just heard that her husband had died. As a result, she was returning to La Jolla, and wanted Chandler to return there too. He felt obliged to do so and departed immediately, with Don Santry in tow as his medical valet. He intended to return to London, and left a suitcase in a security box at Harrods which contained a pair of dark glasses, photographs of Italy, ties (including one Old Etonian tie), evening dress, one dress shoe, and a grey flannel suit.

Once back in La Jolla with Santry, any possibility of Chandler dealing with the Fracasse situation swiftly disappeared. As he exasperatedly reported back to London, Fracasse had been disinherited:

> Her filthy rotten screwy bastard of a husband (this is one case in which I do not feel it noble to speak well of the dead – I knew him) made a holograph will four days before he died disinheriting her and the children and leaving what he had to his brother, who is a screwball too. Jean has no one to look to but me and it's becoming rather a drain.[37]

Chandler could not help himself becoming involved. Having initially intended to stay at the Hotel Del Charro in La Jolla before returning to London, he rented instead a small house on Prospect Street. He grew more and more anxious, and began drinking indiscriminately. His softened mind could no longer match his sense of duty in the matter of Jean Fracasse and her children. When the drinking got too bad, Santry would drive Chandler to a sanatorium for a week's stay. He was now vomiting blood and requiring protein injections.

Occasional visitors to the house, such as Neil Morgan, found him in a state of which he would once have been ashamed. He was drinking gimlets again, and Morgan recalls being at the house when a truck arrived to deliver a crate of Rose's lime cordial. 'Alcohol is like love,' Chandler had ominously written in *The Long Goodbye*. 'The first kiss is magic, the second is intimate, the third is routine. After that you take the girl's clothes off.' It seemed that the battle had been lost now in his head and, realizing this, Santry returned to London. He was also continuing to exhaust his fortune. 'Hardwick I need money,' he wrote to his American publisher Hardwick Moseley, in October 1958, '. . . cash money, not assets.'

Soon after Santry's departure, Chandler announced to Michael Gilbert his decision to marry Jean Fracasse, and instructed the lawyer to set up trusts for her two children. The plan was initially met with some optimism in London, but when Santry returned home with news of his former employer's condition, Greene decided to send her colleague Kay West out to La Jolla to see what she could do. West was met at San Diego airport by a suspicious Jean Fracasse and a befuddled Chandler. Within two weeks of her arrival, Chandler had proposed marriage to West as well. He asked her to take down a letter for him. It was to Michael Gilbert, and in it he explained that it was his intention to make West the beneficiary of his will: 'I was sitting next to him while he dictated the letter to me. His voice showed no sign of realizing what he was saying.' Days after the incident, she heard him tell his landlady, 'I'm going to marry you one day.' Jean was still coming to the house, but the nature of her relationship with the writer was unfathomable to West. She did not seem to mind him drinking. 'It's all very well for Jean to say that she stimulates him mentally,' West wrote to Helga Greene in London, 'but what's the good of that if he's going to collapse from lack of proper feeding?'

As Kay West also reported to Helga, Chandler was not only

drinking heavily but was experiencing regular blackouts as well. She had woken one night in the spare room of the house to find him on the landing, crawling on all fours towards the drinks cupboard. The next morning he had no recollection of the incident, and was in a good mood. Blackouts were no new thing to Chandler, but he now had witnesses in the house to see even the most private details of his alcoholic dementia. The sight of his condition was made worse for West by his occasional moments of lucidity, and even happiness:

> I remember one day he took me into town, because he said he wanted to introduce me to his friends, by which he meant the shopkeepers and so on. He needed to go to the post office, so I said that I would go shopping and meet him outside the post office in a few minutes. I got there first and saw him come out. He looked so old and lonely and then he looked up and saw me waiting for him and his face lit up like a little boy's.[38]

The atmosphere created by Chandler's condition was so warped that after four weeks in La Jolla West suffered a breakdown of her own. She was hospitalized in San Diego and had to return to London. She returned traumatized by the state into which Chandler had sunk – 'someone with authority in relation to Ray should see the situation he is in' – and half-disgusted by his relapse: 'As far as I am concerned, he's had his chances, and plenty of them,' she told Helga. 'Don't you think you'd better get out?'[39] She added that she had found him malnourished, dirty and self-destructive: his breakdown was too complete for anyone in-experienced to deal with it.

But even now, after forty years of alcoholism, Chandler refused to admit fully – either to himself or others – the cause of his condition. In a letter to Hardwick Moseley, he apologized for his recent silence by saying that he had had hepatitis: 'I had all the classic symptoms, deep depression, weakness, an aversion to food, body itching and vagueness of memory of recent things. I had all these things in London.'[40] In truth, he was now so physically weak that he was actually suffering the symptoms of several illnesses.

He was still managing to write, however. Having abandoned the idea of marrying Marlowe off, Chandler completed a short story called 'Marlowe Takes on the Syndicate' which was bought by the *Daily Mail* in London. The story centred on Chandler's fixation of this time – contract killers – and it concerns Marlowe's attempts to protect a man with a Mob contract on his head. 'Marlowe Takes on the Syndicate' is the only Marlowe story in which Chandler appears to have been more interested in the plot than in the hero. It is also the first time that Philip Marlowe had ever tried to take on the national Mafia, rather than local hoods, and it was a hopeless task. 'The guy is as good as dead,' a police friend warns Marlowe. 'The Outfit has reasons. They don't just do it for kicks anymore.' Though Marlowe saves the man, it turns out that his client is also in the Mafia, and is trying to use the detective as a fall guy in yet another Mob killing. As with Chandler's very first short story, 'Blackmailers Don't Shoot', it is possible to read 'Marlowe Takes on the Syndicate' half a dozen times without understanding exactly what has happened.[41]

*

After hearing the dismal reports of both Santry and West, Helga decided to visit La Jolla for herself. Her arrival in February 1959 cheered Chandler and he proposed marriage, suggesting that they return together to live in England. Helga accepted. She had anticipated the proposal and had discussed it with Kay West – eventually deciding that Chandler's only hope of recovery was to be in London under her care. She had grown very close to him, and believed that she could help him to a full recovery. Chandler was delighted by her acceptance and insisted on taking her into La Jolla so that he could buy her a ring. His excitement provided enough adrenalin to transform his frail physical condition. Friends in London arranged a lease for the couple on a house in Elm Park Road in Chelsea. At the beginning of March, Chandler bade a happy goodbye to Neil Morgan, giving him his dictionary and his collection of pipes.

The couple were returning to London via New York. The stopover had two purposes. Firstly, Chandler was to make a speech to the Mystery Writers of America. Having always held writers' guilds to be a waste of time, he had not been persuaded to join the MWA until 1958. He had been voted Honorary President soon afterwards, and his New York speech of acceptance saw him in high spirits. He proudly told the audience of his engagement to Helga: 'I don't really know how I got her. It must have been a sunny day. Any day without rain makes a Britisher vulnerable.'[42]

The second reason for the stopover in New York was so that he could meet Helga's father, H. S. H. Guinness, who was in America on business. It was on Chandler's insistence that they saw him, as he wanted formally to ask for Helga's hand in marriage. The three met for lunch at a New York restaurant. Chandler, said Helga, was nervous but sober.

Guinness made his disapproval so immediately apparent that it all but destroyed Chandler, who had been rehearsing the scene since La Jolla. Following the lunch, he urged Helga to carry on alone to London, saying that he would try to join her in the summer. He returned by himself to La Jolla and rented back the house on Prospect Street which, two weeks earlier, he had left with his fiancée. He started drinking and stopped eating. He rang no one, and did not leave the house.

Within a week of his return Chandler had pneumonia. On 23 March he was taken by ambulance to the Scripps Clinic in La Jolla. Three days after his admission to the hospital, Raymond Thornton Chandler died. He left no burial instructions and an estate worth $60,000. Henry Clarendon, the self-portrait he had written into his final novel, had already predicted how the moment would occur:

The starched white dragons will minister to me. The bed will be wound up, wound down. Trays will come with that awful loveless hospital food. My pulse and temperature will be taken at frequent intervals and invariably when I am dropping off to sleep. I shall lie there and hear the rustle of starched skirts, the slurring sound of rubber shoe soles on the aseptic floor, and see the silent horror of the doctor's smile. After a while they will put the oxygen tent over me and draw the screens around the little white bed and I shall, without even knowing it, do the one thing in the world no man ever has to do twice.

Epilogue

The Hell With Posterity I Want Mine Now
                                   (Letter, October 1947)

Having left no funeral instructions, Chandler was buried four days after his death at San Diego's Mount Hope state cemetery in plot number 1577-3-8. Seventeen people were present for the unglamorous interment, including a local representative of the Mystery Writers Association. The *New York Times* ran an obituary the next day:

> Raymond Chandler Dies At 70; Wrote Noted Detective Stories. Created Philip Marlowe, Hero of The Big Sleep – Won an Audience of 'Highbrows'.[1]

American literary critics were still unsure as to what to make of Chandler, confused as to how long he would be remembered. As recently as 1948, the *New York Times* had dismissed him as 'a hater of the human race'. Though the paper later conceded *The Long Goodbye* to be 'a great novel', other publications continued to doubt Chandler's importance; *The New Yorker* had written off the novel as being 'hardly worth the bother'. British critics, however, remained convinced of Chandler's potentially long-lasting appeal. *The Times* in London ran an obituary applauding the work of a man who had, 'in working the vein of crime fiction, mined the gold of literature'.

*

Chandler had written so many different wills in the last four years of his life, including one on the back of a restaurant menu, that no one – possibly including himself – knew for certain who he meant to inherit his estate. He had returned to La Jolla in March 1959 so despondent that it was unclear even to Helga Greene whether he still planned to marry her. Jean Fracasse presumed that a will he had shown her in May 1958 still stood, and telephoned Michael Gilbert on the day after Chandler's death. The solicitor informed her of a handwritten codicil he had received four weeks before his client had died, in which the latter had left everything to Greene.

Jean Fracasse insisted that the codicil had to have been written 'under duress', and filed a suit in San Diego in November 1959. By the time the case went to court in May 1960, both the American and the British press had picked up on the story. 'Two Women Start a Fight Over Raymond Chandler's Will', reported the *Sunday Express* in London. Helga was described as the 'auburn-haired former wife of Mr Hugh Carleton Greene, Director-General of the BBC', while the plaintiff was referred to as Chandler's Australian secretary. 'Both women claim sole possession of Chandler's estate,' the *Express* said, 'and both claim to hold his effective will. The hard-drinking author offered marriage to each of the women in his last years.'[2]

Jean Fracasse told the court in San Diego that Helga Greene, during her final visit to La Jolla, had isolated Chandler, got him drunk and used emotional leverage to make him change his will. She went on to say that on 20 February 1959 (when the disputed codicil to the will had been written) she recalled seeing barbiturates 'scattered all over the floor' and Chandler shaking with drink. On other occasions, according to Fracasse, Greene had pretended that Chandler was asleep when friends called, and had locked his bedroom door. Jean Fracasse also claimed that Helga Greene had tried to use sex to win her client over, and that she, Jean, had once found Chandler passed out on his bed during Helga's visit, with the bottom half of his pyjamas off. She told the court that she alone had known how to deal with Chandler:

> He was a man who needed to be occupied and he was a man with a brilliant mind and he drank because he was bored and because he was a chronic alcoholic, but by keeping him interested in things, and once getting him into a creative mood, then you had a chance.[3]

After four days, Superior Court Judge Gerald C. Thomas dismissed the suit 'with prejudice', saying that Jean Fracasse had offered no evidence for any of her allegations and that the will in Helga Greene's favour stood. The case left Jean worse off than she had been before she had met Chandler. Helga was so appalled by the case that she filed her own suit against Jean Fracasse for $4,735, money Chandler had lent Jean in the twelve months before his death. The estate, and Raymond Chandler's effects, remained with Helga Greene.

*

Chandler's death was not marked by any of the honours that would be bestowed on Ernest Hemingway (who died two years later, in 1961), William Faulkner (1962) or John Steinbeck (1968). By the start of the 1960s, none the less, his books had been translated into the following languages: Bulgarian, Czech, Danish, Dutch, Finnish, French, German, Hebrew, Slovak, Hungarian, Italian, Japanese, Norwegian, Polish, Portuguese, Romanian, Serbo-Croat, Spanish, Slovene, Catalan, Swedish and Greek. In Japan, there was a Raymond Chandler fan club, and when the popular German magazine *Der Stern* published Chandler's late short story, 'Marlowe Takes on the Syndicate', it recorded its highest ever circulation.

In the United States, a Marlowe television series called *Philip Marlowe* began on NBC in September 1959 and ran for twenty-six episodes. Helga Greene, meanwhile, commissioned two editors to make a selection from Chandler's massive correspondence. One of them, Dorothy Gardiner, wrote to Helga from New York to say she found the task of editing almost impossible: 'Did he ever write a dud line?' she asked. The selection was finally published in 1962, under the title *Raymond Chandler Speaking*, and went quickly into reprint both in Britain and America. In a book entitled *Down*

These Mean Streets a Man Must Go, which appeared the same year, the Californian critic Philip Durham argued for the acceptance of Chandler as a writer of lasting appeal. He quoted Chandler's own definition of literature as 'any sort of writing that glows with its own heat'. By the early 1970s, interest had spread to what Chandler had written beyond his seven Marlowe novels. In 1973, a collection of his boyhood prose and poetry was published by the University of South Carolina Press. Three years later, the Southern Illinois University Press published his screenplay of *The Blue Dahlia*, and this was followed by the publication of *Playback*, the unused screenplay on which he had based his last novel.

Chandler's popularity carried over into the hippie era. In 1969, MGM released a film version of *The Little Sister* called *Marlowe*, in which Chandler's hero – played by James Garner – was transplanted into late-1960s Los Angeles. The screenplay used much of the original book and featured a cameo gangster performance by the martial arts star Bruce Lee. Nor did that mark the end of the cinema's interest in Chandler's work. In 1973, Robert Altman (the director of *M*A*S*H*) filmed another modern day version of a Marlowe story, this time an adaptation of *The Long Goodbye,* starring Elliott Gould. In the film, Marlowe's Angelino neighbours are a commune of hippie girls who practise naked yoga on their balcony, high on hash brownies. Before shooting began, Altman made his cast (which included Arnold Schwarzenegger) read *Raymond Chandler Speaking* in preparation.

Perhaps unsurprisingly for a man who had worked in Hollywood, Chandler's influence on film-makers spread beyond the posthumous adaptation of his Marlowe stories. In 1974, Roman Polanski's hard-boiled movie *Chinatown* won an Oscar for best original screenplay. Set in 1930s Los Angeles, its script was written by the screenwriter Robert Towne, who said at the time that 'Chandler was more of an inspiration in terms of his feeling for the city than anyone else.'[4] Towne added that he had had the idea for *Chinatown* after reading an article about Chandler and LA.

In 1975, Robert Mitchum starred as Marlowe in a third Hollywood adaptation of *Farewell My Lovely*, which co-starred Charlotte Rampling as Velma. Then, two years later, came the publication of *The Life of Raymond Chandler*, an authorized biography by Professor Frank MacShane of Columbia University in New York (which made public the full extent of Chandler's alcoholism). 'The first thing I should like to say', the biography began, 'is that I am treating Raymond Chandler as a novelist and not simply as a detective-story writer.' American critics reviewing the book seemed for the most part to accept MacShane's tenet. Excerpts from Chandler's notebooks were also published in 1976, and in 1977, *The World of Raymond Chandler*, a collection of essays by critics, writers and film-makers was published in Britain. It included the transcript of an interview with Billy Wilder, then aged seventy:

> It's a very peculiar thing, you know, in all the forty years plus that I have been in Hollywood, when people have come up and asked questions – newspaper men, researchers, or letters from all over the place – the two people I've been connected with who everyone is most interested in are Marilyn Monroe and Raymond Chandler.[5]

Robert Mitchum played Philip Marlowe once more for Michael Winner's 1978 version of *The Big Sleep*, with Sarah Miles as co-star. The film, which was set in modern-day England, was poorly received by critics, most of whom preferred the original version. 'The 1946 film,' said *Variety*, 'takes on even more stature in light of this.' Three years later, a second volume of Chandler's letters was published, under the title *Selected Letters of Raymond Chandler*. As with *Raymond Chandler Speaking*, the writer's letters proved almost as popular as his novels: parts of the collection were serialized by newspapers in London, New York, Johannesburg and Sydney.

As the 1970s came to an end, interest in Chandler among both readers and critics continued. Two different books were published in 1982 about his influence on Hollywood, *Raymond Chandler and Film* and *Raymond Chandler in Hollywood*. 'The activity around Chandler's work during the past ten years,' said the author of the first, 'indicates a phenomenal interest in his work and in the characters, settings, and styles associated with it.' As if to confirm this, a book called *Chandlertown* appeared the following year, celebrating the people and places of Chandler's Los Angeles.

Time magazine marked the centenary of Chandler's birth in 1988 with an essay:

> Raymond Chandler was ghostwriter to the soundtrack our lives so often imitate. . . . Chandler has inspired more poses and parodies than any other American writer of the century save Hemingway. Eliot merely articulated the deepest spiritual and emotional issues of the times; Chandler put them on the sidewalk.[6]

The essayist, Pico Iyer, defended Chandler's sustained popularity and took issue with those critics who dismissed him as a transient pulp writer obsessed with similes. The simile, Iyer argued, was 'the perfect device for describing a world in which everything is like something else and nothing is itself'. He reminded readers that 1988 also marked the centenary of T. S. Eliot's birth:

> T. S. Eliot was a civil man, and a public-minded writer, so it is only right that his anniversary be marked in public ceremonies; Chandler was the laureate of the loner, and so his admirers recall him now in quieter ways, alone, unnoticed, with a light on in their darker corners.

The end of the 1980s, however, saw Raymond Chandler's critical reputation caught in a backlash. The fashion for psychological and 'political' literary criticism discovered an easy target in Chandler. Together with Ernest Hemingway, he was branded a misogynist, homophobe and a racist; a writer who had effectively created a fantastic white male hero in order to compensate for his own insecurities. The American crime novelist George V. Higgins, appearing in a profile of Chandler on British television in 1988, speculated that Marlowe's creator had in fact probably hated his mother and his wife, and that the emotion that marked his correspondence after Cissy's death was 'hogwash'. At about the same time, a rumour began circulating Hollywood that Chandler had been a secret cross-dresser. Although not, perhaps, going so far, an article by the British critic Russell Davies, in the *Listener* in 1988, surveyed Chandler's life and work in terms of what Davies analysed to be the author's instability:

> His writing career had been a kind of holding operation, a trucial

state between his idealizing, Cissy-worshipping self, which did not really belong in the world, and the dissolute self of the Twenties, whom he had successfully suppressed. In old age, with Cissy gone, that 'nuisance' self emerged again: and though Chandler had many loyal friends, particularly in London, even they could not disguise how tiresome he could be in those last years.[7]

Chandler, Davies maintained, was sexually insecure and had 'a miserable life'. Marlowe was his escape; his fantasy. The writer 'was an unhappy man', Davies insisted, and his 1958 radio interview with Ian Fleming was proof of this, 'a sad record of a fuddled and incompetent man'.

In America, the backlash centred on what was seen as Philip Marlowe's 'fascism'. Representative of this type of criticism were the accusations made against Chandler in *City of Quartz*, Mike Davies's bestselling history of Los Angeles, which was published in 1990:

Marlowe, the avenging burgher, totters precariously on the precipice of fascist paranoia. Each successive Chandler novel focuses on a new target of Marlowe's dislike: Blacks, Asians, gays, 'greasers', and, always, women.[8]

Significantly, a book called *In Search of Literary Los Angeles*, published the following year by California Classic Books, reduced mention of Chandler to two paragraphs, dismissing him as 'a misanthrope, and a bigot'. It suggested that his vision of Los Angeles had less to do with the city and its life than with 'his own alcoholic disillusionment'. Chandler was similarly omitted by the Library of America, a literary 'Hall of Fame' set up by the National Endowment for the Humanities and the Ford Foundation.

Despite these dismissals, Chandler's popular following continued to grow, similarly to the way it had done in the early 1940s when the Marlowe novels were all but ignored by the critics. The popularity of Chandleresque writers like James Ellroy, Walter Mosely and Elmore Leonard – as well as film-makers like Quentin Tarantino – pushed attention back to the American roots of hard-boiled fiction, and to Chandler in particular. In 1989, his 'unfinished' story 'Poodle Springs' – in which Marlowe marries –

was completed as a novel by the crime writer Robert B. Parker. Twelve months after the success of Tarantino's 1994 film *Pulp Fiction*, the original screen version of *The Big Sleep* was given a nationwide cinema re-release in Britain. Also in 1994, the American actor Danny Glover played the first black Marlowe in a radio adaptation of Chandler's early story 'Red Wind'. Reflecting this fresh enthusiasm for the writer, at a book fair in San Diego in 1995 a collection of Chandler's office memos to his La Jolla secretary, Juanita Messick, was offered for sale at $15,000. At the same fair, a book which he had owned (*Lost in the Horse Latitudes* by Allen Smith) was offered at $1,500 – the same price as that of a book once owned by F. Scott Fitzgerald, called *Bacon is Shakespeare*.

Then, in December of 1995, the Library of America recognized Chandler by publishing his complete works. 'Everyone here', the Library's executive editor told the press, 'has wanted to do Chandler for a long time.' The prominent writer and critic Joyce Carol Oates criticized the decision in the *New York Review*, however, saying that the Library should have prefaced its publication with 'a balanced assessment of Chandler's significance, if any, in American literature'. She maintained that Marlowe and Chandler were racist and misogynist.

*

The damaging argument that Chandler's books reveal an underlying racism in their author carries weight only if passages from them are quoted out of context. Chandler wanted Marlowe to be real, and to talk 'as the man of his age talks, that is with a rude wit, a lively sense of the grotesque, a disgust for sham, and a contempt for pettiness'. This realism inevitably included involving the LA detective in banter where words such as 'wetback' and 'nigger' were spoken. Almost all American hard-boiled crime writers (including such black champions of the genre as Chester Himes) put racial banter into the mouths of their characters, and for the same reason as did Chandler: that it would be unrealistic of them to omit it. 'Racism', by contrast, suggests hatred, and Philip Marlowe does not hate those who challenge the old white order, not least because he does so himself. He hates people who annoy him or threaten him, regardless of their colour.

The opening to *Farewell My Lovely*, sometimes cited as proof of Marlowe's racism, in fact shows this. Marlowe is intimidated because he has been dragged into a 'shine' bar by a white ex-con who is searching for his girlfriend. He does not want to be there. Tension between blacks and white police in Los Angeles was so high at this time that night curfews for black Angelinos were not uncommon. White detectives did not go into black bars alone in the 1940s, and Marlowe feels the tension as soon as he walks in: 'Heads turned slowly and the eyes in them glistened and stared in the dead alien silence of another race.' Into the same scene, however, Chandler introduces a racist white cop, Nulty, who has been detailed to deal with a homicide committed in the bar. Scarcely the great white hope, the cop is described as 'a lean-jawed sourpuss with long yellow hands which he kept folded over his kneecaps most of the time he talked to me'. Nulty is disgusted at having been given the case:

> Shines. Another shine killing. That's what I rate after eighteen years in this man's police department. No pix, no space, not even four lines in the want-ad section.

In Chandler's writing, closely observed physical description is always consistent with the morals of the character he is describing, and Marlowe finds Nulty's long yellow hands revolting. He crosses the street from the bar and goes into a run-down hotel to question the black receptionist there. By contrast to Nulty, the receptionist is almost angelic:

> . . . behind the desk a bald-headed man had his eyes shut and his soft brown hands clasped peacefully on the desk in front of him. He dozed, or appeared to. He wore an Ascot tie that looked as if it had been tied about the year 1800. The green stone in his stickpin was not quite as large as an apple. His large loose chin was folded down gently on the tie, and his folded hands were peaceful and quiet, with manicured nails, and grey half-moons in the purple of the nails.

The most loathsome character in *Farewell My Lovely*, the psychiatrist Jules Amthor, possesses all the worst attributes of cold, Anglo-Saxon megalomania, reflected in his appearance:

I looked him over. He was thin, tall and straight as a steel rod. He had the palest, finest white hair I had ever seen. It could have been strained through a silk gauze. His skin was as fresh as a rose petal. He might have been thirty-five or sixty-five. He was ageless. . . . His eyes were deep, far too deep. They were the depthless drugged eyes of the somnambulist. They were like a well I read about once. It was nine hundred years old, in an old castle. You could drop a stone in it and wait. You could listen and wait and then you would give up waiting and laugh and then just as you were ready to turn away a faint, minute splash would come back up to you from the bottom of the well, so tiny, so remote that you could hardly believe a well like that possible.

His eyes were deep like that. And they were also eyes without expressions, without soul, eyes that could watch lions tear a man to pieces and never change, that could watch a man impaled and screaming in the hot sun with his eyelids cut off.

Marlowe's bursts of 'racist' and 'misogynist' idiom have to be seen within his wider misanthropy; a kneejerk misanthropy born out of the paranoia of a gunman – which is what Marlowe is – who initially has to distrust *everyone* in order to stay alive. When his suspicions prove groundless, Marlowe is generally willing to retract. 'That would buy a whole bus load of wetbacks like you,' he hotly accuses the Guatemalan houseboy in *The Long Goodbye*. When Marlowe realizes that the houseboy has not been bribed at all, Chandler makes him return in person to apologize. Marlowe is not a saint – and nor would he be a realistic private detective if he was one – but nor is he a 'fascist'.

Marlowe's supposed hatred of the women characters he encounters was summed up in 1983 by the American critic Edward Thorpe:

Their greed and vanity are the recurring themes that either directly or indirectly motivate murder. They were the gold-diggers, social climbers, nymphomaniacs, psychopaths, monstrous matriarchs, slatternly degenerates.[9]

For every deceitful and sinful woman in Chandler's fiction, however, there are a dozen deceitful and sinful men. Marlowe has no ranking system for his prejudices: he hates 'sham and pettiness' wherever he finds it, and has seen far too much hypocrisy among LA's power-brokers to be much impressed by the concept of a male, white utopia.

A final example of Chandler's fundamental neutrality about race – and yet also an example of how easily his neutrality might be misquoted – is demonstrated in his attitude towards Mexicans. Chandler disliked the way in which California's bohemian white community eulogized traditional Mexican art and culture as if it were a decorative touchstone. 'I can't stand books about Mexico,' he once wrote, 'The Mexicans, like the Chinese, bore me s——— [Chandler's emendation].' Modern Mexico – real Mexico – interested him far more than the pre-industrial versions imagined by beatniks. In *The Long Goodbye*, Marlowe meets a man whose face has been altered by plastic surgeons in Mexico: 'They had done a wonderful job on him in Mexico City, but why not? Their doctors, technicians, hospitals, painters, architects, are as good as ours. Sometimes a little better. A Mexican cop invented the paraffin test for powder nitrates [a test used to determine whether a suspect has recently fired a gun].' Unlike many of the middle-class Californians who saw Mexico as a kind of glorious hobby, Chandler spoke Spanish. As late as 1956, he had his Olivetti typewriter customized to incorporate Spanish accents, so that his Mexican gangsters could insult Marlowe in their native tongue.

*

It seems appropriate that the posthumous reputation of Raymond Chandler should not have enjoyed an entirely smooth ride in the forty years since his death. The fact that he has attracted passionate admirers from each successive generation would none the less suggest that Chandler will outlive most other writers of this century, regardless of his critics. The period of which he wrote has disappeared, and many of the places he described are now barely recognizable, but his language retains its brilliance. Since the 1940s, so many crime writers and screenwriters have emulated Chandler's style that Marlowe has become something of a cliché outside his original stories. Within them, he has lost almost nothing at all.

Chandler was, through circumstances not always within his control or to his liking, a man of his age. Among the effects inherited by Helga Greene in 1959 were carbon copies of the thousands of letters he had written. They included the following letter to Charles Morton, editor of *Atlantic Monthly*, written from La Jolla in October 1947:

I had an idea for some time back that I should like to do an article on The Moral Status of the Writer, or more frivolously, The Hell With Posterity I Want Mine Now. Not a frivolous article really. It seems to me that in all this yapping about writers selling themselves to Hollywood or the slicks or some transient propaganda idea, instead of writing sincerely from the heart about what they see around them, – the people who make this kind of complaint, and that includes practically every critic who takes himself seriously, overlook (I don't see how they can, but they do) that no writer in any age ever got a blank check. He always had to accept some conditions imposed from without, respect certain taboos, try to please certain people. It might have been the Church, or a rich patron, or a generally accepted standard of elegance, or the commercial wisdom of a publisher or editor, or perhaps a set of political theories. If he did not accept them, he revolted against them. In either case they conditioned his writing. No writer ever wrote exactly what he wanted to write, because there was never anything inside himself, anything purely individual that he did want to write. It's all a reaction of one sort or another.

Oh the hell with it. Ideas are poison. The more you reason, the less you create.[10]

As a writer, Raymond Chandler travelled from youthful mediocrity in Britain to an inspired late middle age in America. He found the trail between those two periods in his life to be a crushingly lonely one at times. Loneliness, however, seems to have been his lot from the start, just as it was Marlowe's. 'You got a friend somewhere that might like to hear your voice?' the detective taunts himself in *The Little Sister*. 'No. Nobody. Let the telephone ring please. Let there be someone to plug me into the human race again. . . . I just want to get off this frozen star.'

However bleak his life could be, Chandler tried never to give up the possibility of happiness, or lose sight of the human comedy in his failure to find it. He felt jinxed in the struggle, but he was resolved to approach the world with something more than pessimism.

Notes

CHAPTER ONE
1. Quoted in Carl L. Degler, *Out Of Our Past*, Harper Colophon 1984, p. 8
2. Ibid., p. 20
3. Hugh Brogan, *History of the United States of America*, Penguin 1990, p. 390
4. Letter to Charles Morton, 15 January 1945. Bodleian Library, Oxford, Chandler files
5. Letter to Charles Morton, 20 November 1944. Bodleian, Chandler files
6. L. Frank Baum, *The Wizard of Oz*, Puffin 1982
7. Raymond Chandler, *The Long Goodbye*, Penguin 1959, p. 211
8. Raymond Chandler, *The Little Sister*, Penguin 1955, p. 18
9. Letter to Hamish Hamilton, 15 July 1954. Bodleian, Chandler files
10. Ibid.
11. Ibid.
12. Quoted by Frank MacShane, *The Life of Raymond Chandler*, Jonathan Cape 1976
13. Letter to Charles Morton, 1 January 1945. Bodleian, Chandler files
14. Letter to Dale Warren (publicity director at Houghton Mifflin), 14 March 1951. Bodleian, Chandler files
15. W. R. Leake (ed.), *Gilkes and Dulwich*, published by the Alleyn Club circa 1930, p. 144
16. Ibid.
17. A. Rawlins, Head of School in 1907, quoted in Leake, op. cit.
18. Letter to Wesley Hartley, 3 December 1957. Bodleian, Chandler files
19. Letter to Hamish Hamilton, 10 November 1950. Bodleian, Chandler files
20. P. G. Wodehouse, who had been a First XI cricketer while at school, would fly into London from New York to watch major Dulwich games. Another near contemporary of Chandler's, E. de Selincourt, went on to write popular cricket adventure stories
21. From the 'Wodehouse at Dulwich' Exhibition, 1995
22. Leake, op. cit., p. 125
23. Excerpted from a novel by Gilkes called *A Day At Dulwich* in Leake, op. cit., p. 177. Although not a novelist, one might add G. Wilson Knight, the famous Shakespearian scholar, to this impressive list of Old Alleynians. One should also qualify the generalizations made here about the famous authors to emerge from Dulwich by explaining that Forester and Powell arrived at the school after the departure of Gilkes in 1914. Although his effect on the way the school was run and the atmosphere within it would last well into the 1920s (when Forester and Powell were pupils) Gilkes did not teach them.
24. Letter to Helga Greene, 13 July 1956. Bodleian, Chandler files
25. Letter to Dale Warren, 4 January 1951. UCLA Special Collections, Chandler
26. Frances Donaldson, *Wodehouse*, Weidenfeld & Nicolson 1982, p. 49
27. Letter to Roger Machell, 24 March 1954. Bodleian, Chandler files

28. Neil Morgan's Chandler files at the *San Diego Tribune*
29. Letter to Dale Warren, 15 January 1950. Bodleian, Chandler files
30. Letter to Hamish Hamilton, 11 December 1950. Bodleian, Chandler files
31. The critic Jacques Barzun described Chandler's early poetry as such in Matthew Bruccoli's collection of early Chandler writing, *Chandler Before Marlowe*, University of South Carolina Press 1973
32. Date and addressee of letter unknown. Bodleian, Chandler files
33. Letter to Hamish Hamilton, 11 December 1950. Bodleian, Chandler files
34. Letter to James Sandoe, 10 August 1947. Bodleian, Chandler files
35. Letter to Hamish Hamilton, 22 April 1949. Bodleian, Chandler files
36. Raymond Chandler, 'The Remarkable Hero', *Academy*, 9 September 1911
37. Frank MacShane (ed.), *The Notebooks of Raymond Chandler*, Ecco Press 1976
38. Quoted by MacShane, *The Life of Raymond Chandler*, op. cit., p. 22

CHAPTER TWO
1. Letter to Charles Morton, 15 January 1945. Bodleian, Chandler files
2. Letter to Hardwick Moseley, 6 May 1954. Bodleian, Chandler files
3. Joe Domanick, *To Protect and to Serve*, Simon & Schuster 1994
4. Letter to Hamish Hamilton, 10 November 1950. Bodleian, Chandler files
5. Raymond Chandler, *The Little Sister*, Penguin 1955, p. 19
6. Ibid.
7. Dulwich College Chandler files
8. Frank MacShane, *The Life of Raymond Chandler*, Jonathan Cape 1976
9. Mike Davies, *City of Quartz*, Vintage 1990, p. 33
10. Domanick, op. cit., p. 33
11. Ibid., p. 46
12. 'Song of the Boatman on the River Roon'. Bodleian, Chandler files
13. Letter to Alex Barris, 16 April 1949. Bodleian, Chandler files
14. Letter to Deirdre Gartrell, 2 March 1957. Bodleian, Chandler files
15. Bodleian, Chandler files
16. Bodleian, Chandler files
17. Raymond Chandler, *Playback*, Penguin 1961, p. 34
18. Raymond Chandler, 'Bay City Blues', *Dime Detective Magazine*, June 1938
19. Quoted by MacShane in *The Life Of Raymond Chandler*, op. cit.
20. 'Lines With An Incense Burner'. UCLA Special Collections, Chandler
21. Raymond Chandler, *Playback*, op. cit., p. 78
22. 'Lines With An Incense Burner'. UCLA Special Collections, Chandler
23. Bodleian, Chandler files
24. 'Ballad to Almost Any Goddess'. Bodleian, Chandler files
25. Jules Tygiel, *The Great Los Angeles Swindle: Oil, Stocks and Scandal during the Roaring Twenties*, Oxford University Press 1994, p. 10
26. Quoted in ibid.
27. Ibid.
28. Letter to Helga Greene, 5 May 1957. Bodleian, Chandler files
29. bid.
30. Letter to Ray Stark, 28 August 1950. UCLA Special Collections, Chandler
31. Letter to Helga Greene, 5 May 1957. Bodleian, Chandler files
32. Letter to Roger Machell, 24 March 1954. Bodleian, Chandler files
33. Letter to Hamish Hamilton, 27 February 1951. Bodleian, Chandler files. This was said of J. B. Priestley
34. The suggestion that Chandler never knew Cissy's real age was made by

Dorothy Gardiner, the co-editor of *Raymond Chandler Speaking*. In a letter to Hamish Hamilton in January 1960, Gardiner wrote: 'It is probable that he never realized that she was in fact an old woman when she died.' Bodleian, Chandler files

35. Notebooks. Bodleian, Chandler files
36. Letter to Neil Morgan, 18 November 1955. Bodleian, Chandler files
37. Chandler, *The Little Sister*, op. cit., p. 5
38. Letter to Edgar Carter, 15 November 15 1950. UCLA Special Collections, Chandler
39. Tygiel, op. cit., p. 207
40. Ibid., p. 79
41. Ibid., p. 78
42. Excerpts from 'Epithalamion' and 'Envoi'. Bodleian, Chandler files
43. Ibid.
44. Raymond Chandler, *The Lady in the Lake*, Penguin 1952, p. 38
45. Letter to Roger Machell, 24 March 1954. UCLA Special Collections, Chandler
46. Professor Donald Goodwin, *Alcoholism: The Facts*, Oxford University Press 1994, p. 40
47. Raymond Chandler, 'The King in Yellow', *Dime Detective Magazine*, March 1938
48. Marlowe is knocked unconscious twice in *Farewell My Lovely*. After the first time, he comes round with a clear case of amnesia:

> The illuminated dial showed 10.56, as nearly as I could focus on it. The call had come at 10.08. Marriott had talked maybe two minutes. Another four had got us out of the house. Time passes very slowly when you are actually doing something. I mean, you can go through a lot of movements in very few minutes. Is that what I mean? Okay, better men have meant less.

Marlowe fumbles on, trying to work out how long he has been unconscious, and settles on 'twenty minutes' sleep' (an expression which Chandler once considered as a title for a short story). One hundred pages later he is hit again:

> A pool of darkness opened at my feet and was far, far deeper than the blackest night.
> I dived into it. It had no bottom.

This time the alcohol/violence parallels of the blackout come through more strongly:

> It was night. The world outside the windows was a black world. A glass porcelain bowl hung from the middle of the ceiling on three brass chains. There was light in it. It had little coloured lumps around the edge, orange and blue alternately. I stared at them. I was tired of the smoke. As I stared, they began to pop open like the heads of small dolls, but alive. There was a man in a yachting cap with a Johnny Walker nose and a fluffy blonde in a picture hat and a thin man with a crooked bow tie. He looked like a waiter in a beach-town fly trap.

The surreal imagery in this passage is poignant, since people who knew Chandler closely in the late 1950s have said that, in common with other alcoholics, he experienced hallucinations when trying to dry out. One friend recalls being with Chandler in a London restaurant in 1956 when he started 'seeing' nomadic Arabs in the corner of the room.

The link between drink and blackouts is most obvious in *The Lady in the Lake*, where Marlowe is knocked out in a hotel, only to come round to discover that someone has poured gin over him. The initial knock-out scene is typically dramatic and makes further reference to the lowest common denominator between drink and pain - vomit: 'The scene exploded into fire and darkness. I didn't even remember being slugged. Fire and darkness and just before the darkness a sharp flash of nausea.' This line marks the end of the chapter; the next starts with the line 'I smelled of gin'.

In Marlowe's next adventure, *The Little Sister*, he is doped unconscious with potassium hyprocyanide:

> A face swam to me out of the darkness. I changed direction and
> started for the face. But it was too late in the afternoon. The sun
> was setting. It was getting dark rapidly. There was no face. There
> was no wall, no desk. Then there was no floor. There was nothing
> at all. I wasn't even there.

Marlowe's first semi-conscious impulse on coming round is to look round the room for a drink ('Finally, after what seemed like four years on the road gang, my little hand closed around six ounces of ethyl alcohol. Just what the label said'). It is worth noting that, according to medical literature on alcoholism, the five chief symptoms of delirium tremens are memory disturbance, insomnia, agitation, hallucinations and illusions. DTs are not what happens when an alcoholic drinks, but what happens when he stops drinking, or tries to. This was a condition that Chandler had known all about by the time he came to write the Marlowe novels.

49. Chandler had started at Dabney's in 1919, aged thirty. Marlowe would be the same age at the start of his own fictional career and get older in each book. Chandler openly distrusted his boss Joseph Dabney, who lived in a vast mansion on South Lafayette Place and who was sued by the Lloyds in 1930 for the misappropriation of oil revenues. Marlowe would have similarly little respect for the clients he worked for

50. Domanick, op. cit., p. 59

51. Ibid., p. 55

52. Letter to Dale Warren, 27 March 1949. Bodleian, Chandler files

53. Raymond Chandler, *The Long Goodbye*, Penguin 1959, p. 45

54. Chandler, *The Lady in the Lake*, op. cit.

55. Hugh Brogan, *History of the United States of America*. Penguin 1990, p. 518

56. 'My Friend Luco' (proposed article for *Sunday Times*, unpublished). Bodleian, Chandler files

57. Hal Mohr, *Sound and the Cinema*. Quoted in Ian Hamilton, *Writers in Hollywood*, Heinemann 1990.

58. Raymond Chandler, *The Big Sleep*, Penguin 1948

CHAPTER THREE

1. Raymond Chandler, *The Big Sleep*, Penguin 1948, p. 125

2. Cissy not only had no money of her own, but Chandler would increasingly have to help Vinnie Brown, Cissy's sister, who now also lived in Los Angeles. (At one point Vinnie was so badly off that she was forced to take in needlework. 'Cheer up,' Chandler once wrote to her; 'Don't be such a goof.')

3. Letter to Hamish Hamilton, 10 November 1950. Bodleian, Chandler files

4. Bodleian, Chandler files

5. Notebooks. Bodleian, Chandler files

6. Ibid.
7. Letter to Erle Stanley Gardner, 5 May 1939. UCLA Special Collections, Chandler
8. Although Chandler (like Shaw) came to crime fiction almost by chance, he did start to become secretly obsessed by it. By the end of his life he was reading little else except mysteries. Most he claimed to find fairly awful, but that he became addicted to the genre of which he so often spoke disdainfully, is not in doubt. He even started enjoying the formulaic English school of detection that he thought so lifeless – even (almost) enjoying Sherlock Holmes. Accused once of hating Doyle's invention, Chandler replied that he had in fact only recently finished rereading *A Study in Scarlet*. He said he had been confused by precisely what 'little thing of Chopin's' Holmes is at one point so anxious to hear performed by the famous violinist Norman Neruda:

> . . . what did Chopin ever write for the violin at all? And even if in those comparatively civilized days (compared with ours) violinists had already descended to the vulgarity of arranging music for the violin which was never written for it, I find it hard to believe that so astute a lover of music as Mr Sherlock Holmes would pick out such an item out as worthy of mention, much less going to hear. Or can it be that the great Sherlock really knew as little about music as he did about the rope-climbing abilities of snakes?

Letter to James Keddie, 29 September 1950. UCLA Special Collections, Chandler
9. Letter to James Sandoe, 17 December 1944. Bodleian, Chandler files
10. Letter to James Sandoe, 2 June 1949. UCLA Special Collections, Chandler
11. Quoted in William F. Nolan, *The Black Mask Boys*, William Morrow, 1985, p. 21
12. Letter from Lester Dent to Philip Durham, 27 October 1958. UCLA Special Collections, Chandler
13. Quoted in Nolan, op. cit., p. 43
14. *Black Mask*, December 1933
15. Chandler, *The Big Sleep*, op. cit., p. 9
16. Notebooks. Bodleian, Chandler files
17. 'Improvisation for Cissy', 29 October 1935. Bodleian, Chandler files
18. Raymond Chandler, 'Smart Aleck Kill', *Black Mask*, July 1934
19. Letter to Frederick Lewis Allen, 7 May 1948. Bodleian, Chandler files
20. When the story was later anthologized, the name of the detective was changed, with Chandler's permission, to 'Philip Marlowe'. This would happen retrospectively to other *Black Mask* stories, none of which originally featured Marlowe
21. Raymond Chandler, 'Finger Man', *Black Mask*, October 1934
22. Raymond Chandler, 'Trouble is my Business', *Dime Detective Magazine*, August 1939
23. Raymond Chandler, 'Mandarin's Jade', *Dime Detective Magazine*, November 1937
24. Letter to Hardwick Moseley, February 1955. UCLA Special Collections, Chandler
25. Letter to James Sandoe, 7 December 1950. UCLA Special Collections, Chandler
26. Quoted by Edward Thorpe in *Chandlertown*, Vermilion 1983, p. 51
27. *The Lady in the Lake* was the novel in which Chandler later used aspects of

the George Dayley case
28. Joe Domanick, *To Protect and to Serve*, Simon & Schuster 1994, p. 53
29. Ibid., p. 23
30. UCLA Special Collections, Chandler files
31. Raymond Chandler, *The Little Sister*, Penguin 1955
32. Letter to Charles Morton, 12 October 1944. Bodleian, Chandler files
33. Letter to Sergeant Hays of the LAPD, March 1956. UCLA Special Collections, Chandler
34. Notebooks. Bodleian, Chandler files
35. Chandler, 'Smart Aleck Kill,' op. cit.
36. Even when he was a famous novelist in the 1950s, and in a brighter mood, Chandler could not switch off. The following letter was written in September 1951 to Hamish Hamilton:

> I don't know whether you have ever been to a dude ranch. I had never been to one before. . . . The kind of place where people who work in the office wear riding boots, where the lady guests appear for breakfast in levis rivetted with copper, for lunch in jodhpurs with gaudy shirts and in the evening either in cocktail gowns or in more jodhpurs and more gaudy shirts and scarfs. The ideal scarf seems to be very narrow, not much wider than a boot lace, and runs through a ring in front and then hangs down one side of the shirt. I didn't ask why: I didn't get to know anyone well enough. The men also wear gaudy shirts, which they change constantly for other patterns, all except the real horsemen, who wear rather heavy wool or nylon and wool shirts with long sleeves, yoked in the back, the kind of thing that can only be bought in a horsy town.

Bodleian, Chandler files
37. Raymond Chandler, 'The Simple Art of Murder', *Atlantic Monthly*, December 1944
38. Dashiell Hammett, 'The Golden Horseshoe', included in *The Continental Op*, First Vintage 1992

CHAPTER FOUR
1. Raymond Chandler, *The Big Sleep*, Penguin 1948, p. 199
2. Ibid., p. 66
3. The parallels between Carmen Sternwood and Cissy's own laudanum and modelling days in New York are obvious
4. From the essay 'The Simple Art of Murder', *Atlantic Monthly*, December 1944
5. Raymond Chandler, 'The Killer in the Rain', *Black Mask,* January 1935
6. Chandler, *The Big Sleep*, op. cit., p. 57
7. Chandler had felt justified in using his old material, but he was still uncomfortable when the publishers of *Black Mask* put out an anthology of contributors' stories called *The Hard-Boiled Omnibus*. As it turned out, he received only one letter of complaint (from an American diplomat in Mexico City). He replied at length, saying that he had a right to use his old stories because he was still the copyright owner. There was no fraud on the public, he continued, because 'the thing is re-created in a different form'. (The diplomat, by odd coincidence, was Howard Hunt, who, as one of President Nixon's aides, would later be implicated in the Watergate scandal.)
8. Sent in a letter dated 11 October 1948 from Ray Stark (a Hollywood agent) to *Screen Writer Magazine*: 'I thought you might be interested in the following

paragraphs that I received from Raymond Chandler prior to the radio dramatization of Philip Marlowe. All the men connected with the show were tremendously helped by this advice.' Bodleian, Chandler files

9. Some of Chandler's critics have suggested that every wisecrack in his books, regardless of who utters it, sounds as though it has come from Marlowe's lips, and that the former's comic credentials do not extend beyond the creation of his wry central character. This is in part accurate (Chandler certainly lacked the tonal diversity of Dickens), and in part overlooks the fact that virtually all Chandler characters come from the same milieu. Whatever side of the law they operate on, and whatever their gender, they are all of about the same age, all cynical and all from Los Angeles

10. Chandler, *The Big Sleep*, op. cit., p. 73

11. Ibid., p. 133

12. *The Five Great Novels of James Cain*, Picador 1985, p. 34

13. Letter to Alfred Knopf, 19 February 1939. Bodleian, Chandler files

14. From a letter to Natasha Spender (undated), quoted in *The World of Raymond Chandler*, ed. Miriam Gross, Weidenfeld & Nicolson 1977, p. 134

15. This is from one of the short stories that Chandler wrote after *The Big Sleep*. Called 'No Crime In The Mountains', it was published in *Dime Detective Magazine* in September 1941

16. Ibid.

17. The five crime stories that Chandler wrote after the publication of his first novel were:

    'The Lady in the Lake' (parts of which he would use in his fourth novel, including the title); 'Pearls Are a Nuisance'; 'Trouble is My Business'; 'I'll Be Waiting'; 'No Crime in the Mountains'.

    Chandler in fact used three of these stories in later novels. 'Pearls Are A Nuisance' features in *The High Window*; 'The Lady in The Lake' and 'No Crime in the Mountains' both feature in *The Lady in the Lake*. Together with 'Trouble is My Business', these stories each earned Chandler between $350 and $370. 'I'll Be Waiting' is an atmospheric story about a hotel detective written for the famous 'slick' magazine, *Saturday Evening Post*, in October 1939. It was not violent, although the threat of violence hangs over the story. Chandler received $600 for it, and the *Post* expressed interest in his doing more work for them, but did not want anything too hard-boiled. 'I didn't think much of the story,' said Chandler; 'I felt that it was artificial, untrue and emotionally dishonest like all slick fiction.'

18. Raymond Chandler, 'The Bronze Door,' *Unknown*, November 1939

19. Letter to George Harmon Coxe, 27 June 1940. UCLA Special Collections, Chandler

20. Pocket Books would pay $15,000 per million copies, but half of this went to the book's original publisher, in Chandler's case Knopf. This would infuriate Chandler when his novels finally did appear in pulp, as he once told Erle Stanley Gardner:

    You and I may never write a [hardback] best-seller, even a moderate best-seller . . . and yet there is a better continuing sale for our kind of stuff than for any kind. I think we are getting gypped on the reprints. A man whose book sells a quarter or half a million copies in any kind of edition ought to get a very substantial income out of it. We don't.

    Letter to Erle Stanley Gardner, 4 April 1946. Bodleian, Chandler files

21. Publishers like Knopf would authorize their own dollar paperback editions, but these too were almost impossible to market without press coverage

22. Raymond Chandler, 'Professor Bingo's Snuff', *Park East*, June 1951. Another non-detective short story Chandler wrote was 'A Couple of Writers', about a drunken novelist and his wife, a neurotic playwright, who live in unhappy and reclusive matrimony. It starts with the line, 'No matter how drunk he had been the night before Hank Bruton always got up very early and walked around the house in his bare feet, waiting for the coffee to brew.' The story was never published and ends dispiritingly, with Hank's wife leaving him after an argument in which she tells him that he has no life; she returns after realizing that she has no life either

23. Letter to Hamish Hamilton, date unknown. Bodleian, Chandler files

24. Letter to Erle Stanley Gardner, 29 January 1946. Bodleian, Chandler files

25. Letter to George Harmon Coxe, 19 December 1939. UCLA Special Collections, Chandler

26. The full address was 1155 Arcadia Avenue

27. Raymond Chandler, *Farewell My Lovely*, Penguin 1949, p. 149

28. Ibid., p. 92

29. Quoted by Frank MacShane in *The Life of Raymond Chandler*, Jonathan Cape 1976

30. Notebooks. Bodleian, Chandler files

31. Chandler, 'No Crime in the Mountains', op. cit.

32. Chandler (and others) believed that the reason for the genre's popularity was that 'literary' fiction had grown too introspective in the 1930s to interest the average reader. In the face of excessively intellectual fiction, readers were turning in numbers and 'with relief to the man who tells a good story'. They were not turning to such books in hardback, however

33. The actual addresses were 857 Illif Street and 12216 Shetland Lane

34. Bodleian, Chandler files

35. Letter to George Harmon Coxe, 19 December 1939. Bodleian, Chandler files

36. Letter to George Harmon Coxe, 9 April 1939. Bodleian, Chandler files

37. Letter to Alfred and Blanche Knopf, 14 June 1940 (while Chandler was living in Arcadia). Bodleian, Chandler files

38. Letter to Blanche Knopf, 27 March 1946. Bodleian, Chandler files

39. Letter to James Sandoe, 23 September 1948. UCLA Special Collections, Chandler

40. Letter to S. J. Perelman, 9 January 1952. Bodleian, Chandler files

41. Letter from Perelman to Chandler, 24 October 1951. UCLA Special Collections, Chandler

42. Included in *The Most of S. J. Perelman*, Simon & Schuster 1958

43. Raymond Chandler, *The High Window*, Penguin 1955, p. 9

44. Ibid.

45. Ibid., p. 213

46. In *The High Window*, Marlowe is constantly suffering abuse from characters who consider him to be in a low-life profession. The discrepancy between what the characters *think* private detectives are like, and what Marlowe actually *is* like, had an intended parallel for Chandler. Within their two worlds, both Marlowe and Chandler were acquiring reputations as clever operators in fields that would never allow them to fulfil their potential. Just as Chandler was asked by educated fans why he didn't write a 'proper' novel, so Marlowe has to deal with jokes about his career. 'A private detective,' says one facetious client upon entering Marlowe's shabby office. 'A shifty business, one gathers.

Keyhole peeping, raking scandal, that sort of thing.' 'You on business,' says Marlowe, 'or just slumming?'

47. Raymond Chandler, *The Lady in the Lake*, Penguin 1952
48. *Sunday Times*, 29 October 1944

CHAPTER FIVE

1. John Houseman, *Unfinished Business*, Columbus Books 1988, p. 256
2. Raymond Chandler, *The Little Sister*, Penguin 1949, p. 181
3. Raymond Chandler, 'Writers in Hollywood', *Atlantic Monthly*, November 1945
4. *Double Indemnity* was certainly not the first film since the early 1930s to have adapted a hard-boiled story. John Huston's *The Maltese Falcon*, based on Dashiell Hammett's novel and starring Humphrey Bogart, was released in 1941 and paved the way for adaptations both of Cain and Chandler. Nevertheless, however superb the film was, it was more a mystery story than a murder story. Similarly, *Casablanca* (1942) was as much a romantic and musical war drama as it was a hard-boiled thriller. *High Sierra*, which also starred Bogart, and which also came out in 1942, was another film that could claim to have set the way for *Double Indemnity* (in it Bogart plays a bank robber turned killer). What is accepted, however, is that *Double Indemnity* was the straw that finally broke the Production Code's back, for a deluge of risqué material arrived at the Code's offices after the film was released
5. Quoted from Ian Hamilton, *Writers in Hollywood*, Heinemann 1991, p. 61
6. The details of all negotiation between the Production Code Office and studios during this time are on record in the Margaret Herrick Library at the Academy of Motion Picture Art and Sciences in Los Angeles
7. Quoted in Paul Skenazy, *James M. Cain*, Continuum 1989
8. Taken from an interview with Billy Wilder which appeared in *The World of Raymond Chandler*, ed. Miriam Gross, Weidenfeld & Nicolson 1977.
9. Ibid.
10. Ibid.
11. Maurice Zolotow, 'Through a Shot Glass Darkly: How Raymond Chandler Screwed Hollywood', *LA Herald Examiner*, 20 July 1980. The piece was first published in the January–February edition of *Action*, 1978
12. Wilder confided his thoughts on Chandler to the publicity director at Paramount, Teet Carle, who repeated them in a letter to Paul McClung of Dell Publishing. The excerpt begins 'He [Wilder] told me on the phone the other day, "Raymond Chandler's talents as a writer were superb – magnificent . . ." '. Bodleian, Chandler files
13. 'The best scenes I ever wrote were practically monosyllabic,' said Chandler: 'And the best short scene I ever wrote, by my judgment, was one in which a girl said "uh huh" three times with different intonations, and that's all there was to it.'
14. Richard Schickel, *Double Indemnity*, British Film Institute 1992
15. Letter to Hamish Hamilton, 10 November 1950. Bodleian, Chandler files
16. From Frank MacShane, *The Life of Raymond Chandler*, Jonathan Cape 1976
17. This was in a note Chandler wrote to a later secretary, Juanita Messick. It is included among Messick's papers, which at the time of writing were being auctioned on behalf of her estate by several American rare-book collectors.
18. Raymond Chandler, *The Little Sister*, Penguin 1949, p. 122
19. UCLA Special Collections, Chandler
20. Twentieth-Century Fox followed RKO's example and re-made *The High*

Window, which they had bought before Chandler's sudden fame. It was released in 1947 as *The Brasher Doubloon*, with George Montgomery (an ex-stunt man who had started his career as the Lone Ranger's stunt double) starring as Marlowe. It turned out to be scarcely better than Fox's first version

21. Quoted in an interview with Dick Powell which appeared [date unknown] in the *Saturday Evening Post*
22. Letter to James Sandoe, 15 August 1949. UCLA Special Collections, Chandler
23. Letter to Lenore Offord, 6 December 1948. UCLA Special Collections, Chandler
24. Letter to Hamish Hamilton, 13 November 1953. Bodleian, Chandler files
25. From an interview with John Houseman, which appeared in *Sight and Sound*, Autumn Issue 1962
26. Margaret Herrick Library, Academy of Motion Picture Arts and Sciences, LA
27. Zolotow, op. cit.
28. H. N. Swanson, *Sprinkled with Ruby Dust: A Hollywood Memoir*, Warner 1989
29. Letter to Carl Brandt, 26 November 1948. Bodleian, Chandler files
30. Chandler, 'Writers in Hollywood', op. cit.
31. Raymond Chandler, 'Oscar Night in Hollywood', *Atlantic Monthly*, March 1948
32. Jonathan Hill and Jonah Ruddy, *Bogart: The Man and the Legend*, Mayflower Bell 1966
33. Letter to Hamish Hamilton, 30 May 1946. Bodleian, Chandler files. Both Chandler and Hawks thought the acting of Martha Vickers to be as good as anything in *The Big Sleep*, and Hawks fell out with Warner Brothers over the cutting of the film: 'The girl who played the nymphy sister was so good', said Chandler, 'she shattered Miss Bacall completely. So they cut the picture in such a way that all her best scenes were left out except one. The result made a nonsense and Howard Hawks threatened to sue.'
34. Margaret Herrick Library, Academy of Motion Picture Arts and Sciences, LA
35. Offensive lines about the police were something that the Production Code also tried to excise. The following double entendre was cut from the original shooting script of *The Big Sleep*:
    Bogart: You'd make a good cop.
    Bacall: Only if he wore smoked glasses.
36. *New York Times*, 1 September 1946
37. *Sequence,* No. 7, Spring 1949
38. Letter to Alfred Knopf, 12 January 1946. Bodleian, Chandler files

CHAPTER SIX
1. Letter to Alex Barris, 18 March 1949. Bodleian, Chandler files
2. From an interview conducted by the author with Neil Morgan in August 1994
3. Ibid.
4. UCLA Special Collections, Chandler
5. Letter to James Sandoe, 10 August 1947. UCLA Special Collections, Chandler
6. *Chimera*, 'A Special Issue on Detective Fiction', Volume V, No. 4, Summer 1947
7. Letter to Charles Morton, 7 January 1947. Bodleian, Chandler files
8. In a letter to Hamish Hamilton, Chandler added:

    A writer who accepts a certain formula and works within it is no more a hack than Shakespeare was because to hold his audience he had to include a certain amount of violence and a certain amount of low comedy.

Letter to Hamish Hamilton, September 28 1950. Bodleian, Chandler files

9. Letter to Hamish Hamilton, 17 June 1949. Bodleian, Chandler files
10. Letter to Hamish Hamilton, 4 December 1949. Bodleian, Chandler files
11. William Menard, 'Raymond Chandler and Somerset Maugham', *San Diego Magazine*, December 1986
12. Ibid.
13. Letter to Hamish Hamilton, 5 January 1949. Bodleian, Chandler files
14. Information about the Marlowe radio series is contained in the Chandler files at UCLA
15. At the time of writing (as has been said), Messick's papers were being auctioned by several American rare-book dealers
16. Letter to Erle Stanley Gardner, 29 January 1946. UCLA Special Collections, Chandler
17. Raymond Chandler, *The Long Goodbye*, Penguin 1959, p. 280
18. Letter to Paul Brooks, President of Houghton Mifflin, 28 November 1957. UCLA Special Collections, Chandler
19. Letter to James M. Fox, 16 February 1954. Fox was a crime writer, and his correspondence with Chandler was published in 1978, in a limited edition by Neville & Yellin, Santa Barbara, California
20. Letter to Charles Morton, 19 March 1945. Bodleian, Chandler files
21. From an interview conducted by the author with Albert Hernandez in August 1994
22. The waitress in question was Albert Hernandez's wife. La Plaza is now a Methodist church
23. Juanita Messick, who became Chandler's secretary in the 1940s, described Cissy as such in a magazine article called 'Philip Marlowe Slept Here', published on 18 March 1982. Neil Morgan's Chandler files, *San Diego Tribune*
24. Letter to James M. Fox, 18 January 1954 (see note 19 above)
25. Letter to Dale Warren, 7 January 1945. UCLA Special Collections, Chandler
26. Letter to James Sandoe, 27 January 1948. UCLA Special Collections, Chandler
27. Letter to Hamish Hamilton, 5 October 1951. Bodleian Chandler files
28. Letter to Hamish Hamilton, [date unknown]. Bodleian, Chandler files
29. Raymond Chandler, 'The Simple Art of Murder', *Atlantic Monthly*, December 1944
30. Chandler's other articles for *Atlantic Monthly* were 'Writers in Hollywood' (November 1945); 'Oscar Night in Hollywood' (March 1948) and 'Ten Per Cent of Your Life' (February 1952). They all echoed thoughts about which he had written in his letters, and have been quoted in Chapter Five.
31. Letter to James Sandoe, 19 November 1949. UCLA Special Collections, Chandler
32. Letter to H. F. Hose (Chandler's Classics master at Dulwich), February 1951. Bodleian, Chandler files
33. Letter to Hamish Hamilton, 22 April 1949. Bodleian, Chandler files
34. Chandler once wrote a mock obituary of the type of writer he found ridiculous:

He committed suicide at the age of 33 in Greenwich Village by shooting himself with an Amazonian blow gun, having published two novels entitled *Once More The Cicatrice* and *The Sea Gull Has*

No Friends, two volumes of poetry, *The Hydraulic Face Lift* and
Cat Hairs in The Custard, one book of short stories called *Twenty
Inches of Monkey*, and a book of critical essays called *Shakespeare
in Baby Talk*.

Bodleian, Chandler files
35. In one of his notebooks, Chandler kept an excerpt from a book called *The
Proud Walkers*:

> We moved out of Houndshell mine camp in May to the homeplace
> father had built on Shoal Creek, and I recollect fox grapes were
> blooming and there was spring chill in the air. Fern and Lark and I
> ran ahead of the wagon, frightening water thrushes, shouting back
> at the poky mare mule. We broke cowcumber branches to wave at
> baby, wanting to call him, but he did not have a name.

'What is there about this' Chandler, had written to himself below the excerpt,
'that is beyond disgust to me? Is it the nature faking or that the attitude has
been done to death so that one simply cannot feel any honesty in it? Is it that
the minor cadence, the restraint, all the words, the pseudo-simplicity of the
thought and so on, suggest a mind either too naive or too phony to be endured,
or a cynical imitation of something that might once have been good? Whatever
it is it reeks.'
Notebooks. Bodleian, Chandler files.
36. Letter to Charles Morton, [date unknown]. Bodleian, Chandler files
37. Letter to Charles Morton, 2 June 1949. Bodleian, Chandler files
38. Letter to James Sandoe, 14 October 1949. UCLA Special Collections,
Chandler
39. Letter to Hamish Hamilton, 19 August 1948. Bodleian, Chandler files
40. Raymond Chandler, *The Little Sister*, Penguin 1955, p. 179
41. Ibid., p. 78
42. The first German translations of the Marlowe novels would appear in 1950
43. An approximate translation would read:

> It goes without saying that I took great pleasure in reading what
> you had written, and I am touched by the respect you pay me in
> writing with such care about a type of fiction that is often
> considered of little significance. . . . I find your admiration for
> Agatha Christie a little hard to swallow. I shouldn't criticize her
> books just because they are of no interest to me, but I do find the
> idea that Mrs Christie fools her readers without cheating them
> impossible to believe. Is it not the case that she creates her surprises
> by simply reversing the portrait of a character that she has, up until
> that point, portrayed in colours totally different from the finished
> portrait?

Letter to Robert Campigny, 7 February 1958. Bodleian, Chandler files
44. Letter to H. N. Swanson, 9 July 1951. UCLA Special Collections, Chandler
45. Letter to Charles Morton, 22 November 1950. Bodleian, Chandler files
46. Chandler's finances were further improved in 1950 when Houghton Mifflin
published an anthology of his old *Black Mask* stories, prefaced by the essay on
crime fiction he had written for *Atlantic Monthly* in 1944 called 'The Simple
Art of Murder'.
47. Letter to Hamish Hamilton, 4 September 1950. Bodleian, Chandler files

48. The full figures for Chandler's royalties up to January 1950 are as follows (the first two numbers given in each territory are of copies sold in the editions specified):

> *USA and Canada*
> Hardback (68,933) Reprint (3,515,658) $56,355
> *Great Britain*
> Hardback (65,000) Cheap (39,580) Penguin (265,601) $17,567
> *Elsewhere*
> Total (257, 436) $14,471

49. Letter to Dale Warren, [date unknown]. Bodleian, Chandler files
50. Chandler would use the drive to Tijuana airport in *The Long Goodbye* when Marlowe takes Terry Lennox there from LA
51. Letter to Edgar Carter, 13 December 1951. Bodleian, Chandler files
52. Letter to Hamish Hamilton, 27 February 1951. Bodleian, Chandler files
53. Bodleian, Chandler files
54. Letter to Hamish Hamilton, September 1951. Bodleian, Chandler files

CHAPTER SEVEN

1. Letter to Roger Machell, 23 May 1957. Bodleian, Chandler files
2. *Sunday Times*, 21 September 1952
3. Letter to Hamish Hamilton, 2 November 1952. Bodleian, Chandler files
4. From the transcript of a BBC Radio Home Service profile of Chandler made in 1960. UCLA Special Collections, Chandler
5. Letter to Paul Brooks, 28 September 1952. Bodleian, Chandler files
6. Ibid.
7. Letter to William Townend, 11 November 1952. Bodleian, Chandler files
8. It would be another seven years before 'Empire Day', 24 May, was officially renamed 'Commonwealth Day' in Britain
9. From the BBC Radio Home Service transcript, op. cit.
10. From Dilys Powell, 'Ray and Cissy', in *The World Of Raymond Chandler*, ed. Miriam Gross, Weidenfeld & Nicolson 1977, p. 87
11. Letter to Dale Warren, 13 November 1952. Bodleian, Chandler files
12. Letter to Alex Barris, 16 April 1949. Bodleian, Chandler files
13. Letter to Charles Morton, 9 October 1950. Bodleian, Chandler files
14. Letter from Roger Machell to Chandler, 30 June 1953. Bodleian, Chandler files
15. There was a brief debate over the book's title. Chandler wanted *Summer In Idle Valley*, which Hamilton turned down in London because it sounded too much like a straightforward mystery. Chandler then suggested *The Long Goodbye*, which he had initially thought too 'pretentious', but which both publishers preferred. Chandler still took his titles very seriously. Some titles have magic, he once told Hamilton; 'something that has nothing to do with what the words in the title mean'. Chandler told him of recent titles that he had admired: '*Red Shoes Run Faster, Death in the Afternoon, The Beautiful And Damned, Journey's End, Lost Horizon, Point Of No Return.*'
16. Raymond Chandler, *The Long Goodbye*, Penguin 1959, p. 318
17. Ibid., p. 159
18. Marlowe is critical of phoney intellectualism in *The Long Goodbye*, as Chandler had been in his correspondence during the 1940s. A billionaire's mansion is described as being decorated in 'the latest sub-phallic symbolism'. A chauffeur is reading T. S. Eliot: 'I grow old I grow old. . . . I shall wear the

bottoms of my trousers rolled. What does that mean Mr Marlowe. Not a bloody thing. It just sounds good.' Chandler was conscious of not getting carried away with this topic, lest it sound incongruous coming from Marlowe. 'Too literary,' says one character to the detective. 'You're some kind of dick aren't you?'

19. Chandler, *The Long Goodbye*, op. cit., p. 152
20. Ibid., p. 64
21. Letter to H. N. Swanson, 14 March 1953. Bodleian, Chandler files
22. *Sunday Times*, 29 November 1953
23. *Saturday Review*, 23 August 1953
24. From the correspondence between William Gault and Raymond Chandler, UCLA Special Collections, Chandler
25. Letter to Leonard Russell, 29 December 1954. Bodleian, Chandler files
26. This is taken from two letters written after Cissy's death: 1) letter to Hamish Hamilton, 5 January 1955; 2) letter to Helga Greene, 19 March 1957. Both Bodleian, Chandler files
27. When the police report was released after Chandler's death, it was done so with the personal request of the local police chief that it be used with discretion, because 'Ray was one of the best'.
28. Chandler, *The Long Goodbye*, op. cit., p. 73
29. Neil Morgan, 'The Long Goodbye', *California Magazine*, June 1982
30. Letter to Roger Machell, 5 March 1955. Bodleian, Chandler files
31. Letter from Louise Loughner, 25 February 1955. UCLA Special Collections, Chandler
32. Letter to William Gault, April 1955. Bodleian, Chandler files

CHAPTER EIGHT
1. Letter to Jessica Tyndale, 19 June 1956. Bodleian, Chandler files
2. John Pearson, *The Life of Ian Fleming*, Jonathan Cape 1966, p. 255
3. Letter to Hamish Hamilton, 27 April 1955. Bodleian, Chandler files
4. Natasha Spender, 'His Own Long Goodbye', in *The World Of Raymond Chandler*, ed. Miriam Gross, Weidenfeld & Nicolson 1977, p. 129
5. The core of the Chandler 'shuttle service' was Natasha Spender, Jocelyn Rickards, Alec Murray and Alison Hooper
6. Natasha Spender in Gross, op. cit.
7. Letter to the editor of the *Evening Standard*, 30 June 1955. Bodleian, Chandler files
8. Natasha Spender in Gross, op. cit.
9. Bodleian, Chandler files
10. Letter to Wesley Hartley, 3 December 1957. Bodleian, Chandler files
11. Helga Greene in an unused introduction to *Raymond Chandler Speaking*. Bodleian, Chandler files
12. Pearson, op. cit., p. 262
13. Letter to Ian Fleming, 9 June 1956. Bodleian, Chandler files
14. Raymond Chandler, *Playback*, Penguin 1961, p. 147
15. Paradoxically, when Chandler reviewed *Diamonds Are Forever* for the *Sunday Times* (which, together with Fleming's *Doctor No*, was the only book reviewing he did in London), he thought that the author had made Bond too human. 'I don't like James Bond thinking,' he wrote, 'I like him when he is in the dangerous card game. I like him when he is exposing himself to half a dozen thin-lipped professional killers . . . I like him when he finally takes the beautiful girl in his arms and teaches her about one tenth of the facts of life she

already knew.' *Doctor No*, by contrast, Chandler considered 'masterful'.

16. Letter from Ian Fleming, 9 June 1956. Bodleian, Chandler files
17. Natasha Spender in Gross, op. cit.
18. Letter from Louise Lee, 16 April 1958. Bodleian, Chandler files
19. Letter to Louise Loughner, 15 June 1955. UCLA Special Collections, Chandler
20. Letter to Louise Loughner, [date unknown]. UCLA Special Collections, Chandler
21. *Daily Express*, 14 January 1956
22. *Daily Mirror*, 13 April 1958
23. *News Chronicle*, 1 May 1958
24. *Daily Express*, 7 July 1958
25. Letter to Roger Machell, 15 March 1958. Bodleian, Chandler files
26. *Daily Express*, 25 May 1957
27. Letter to Louise Loughner, 21 May 1955. UCLA Special Collections, Chandler
28. Letter to Paul McClung, 11 December 1951. Bodleian, Chandler files
29. Letter to Roger Machell, [date unknown]. Bodleian, Chandler files
30. Letter to Neil Morgan, [date unknown]. Bodleian, Chandler files
31. Natasha Spender, op. cit.
32. Letter to James Fox, 16 December 1955, in *Letters: Raymond Chandler and James M. Fox*, Neville & Yellin, 1978
33. Natasha Spender in Gross, op. cit.
34. Bodleian, Chandler files
35. Letter to Louise Loughner, 21 May 1955. UCLA Special Collections, Chandler
36. Letter to the editor of *The Third Degree*, April 1954. UCLA Special Collections, Chandler
37. Telegram to Louise Loughner, 29 May 1956. UCLA Special Collections, Chandler
38. Letter from Jessica Tyndale to Helga Greene, 3 June 1956. Bodleian, Chandler files
39. Bodleian, Chandler files
40. Letter to Jessica Tyndale, 12 July 1956. Bodleian, Chandler files
41. Letter to Jessica Tyndale, 20 August 1956. Bodleian, Chandler files
42. On 7 January 1957, Jessica Tyndale wrote to Chandler saying: 'I was discouraged from writing by your postcard from Chandler, Arizona which seemed to detail a series of one-night stands throughout the South West.' Bodleian, Chandler files
43. Natasha Spender in Gross, op. cit. Natasha Spender was also interviewed by the author in the spring of 1995
44. Ibid.

CHAPTER NINE
1. Bodleian, Chandler files
2. Letter to Jessica Tyndale, 3 February 1958. Bodleian, Chandler files
3. Letter from Helga Greene to Ian Fleming, date unknown, but after Chandler's death. Bodleian, Chandler files
4. From the unused introduction by Helga Greene to *Raymond Chandler Speaking*. Bodleian, Chandler files
5. Bodleian, Chandler files
6. The title and basic plot structure of *Playback* were drawn from the unused original screenplay that Chandler had written for Universal Studios in 1947. The setting, dialogue and characters were different (Marlowe had not been in the screenplay), but when Universal's lawyers discovered that Chandler was

writing a novel by the same name, they demanded part of the royalties. He therefore offered to take the matter to court, and the studio retracted its demands.

7. Marlowe sleeps with both the heroine and Umney's secretary. 'I wouldn't say she looked exactly wistful,' he says of the former, 'but neither did she look as hard to get as a controlling interest in General Motors'

8. Raymond Chandler, *Playback*, Penguin 1961, p. 68

9. Ibid.

10. Ibid., p. 28

11. Ibid., p. 35

12. Ibid., p. 38

13. Ibid., p. 111

14. Ibid., p. 121

15. Letter to Dale Warren, 9 July 1949. Bodleian, Chandler files

16. Chandler, *Playback*, op. cit., p. 156

17. Ibid.

18. *Sunday Times*, 30 March 1958

19. Letter to Deirdre Gartrell, 20 March 1957. Bodleian, Chandler files

20. Letter to Deirdre Gartrell, 25 July 1957. Bodleian, Chandler files

21. Ibid.

22. Letter to Deirdre Gartrell, 8 May 1957. Bodleian, Chandler files

23. From the unused introduction to *Raymond Chandler Speaking* by Helga Greene, op. cit.

24. Letter to Jean de Leon, 30 April 1958. Bodleian, Chandler files

25. 'My Friend Luco' (proposed article for the *Sunday Times*, unpublished). Bodleian, Chandler files

26. Bodleian, Chandler files

27. From the transcript of a BBC Radio Home Service profile of Chandler made in 1960. UCLA Special Collections, Chandler

28. Letter to Bergen Evans, 18 January 1958. Bodleian, Chandler files

29. Letter to *The Times*, 24 June 1958. Bodleian, Chandler files

30. Chandler was so appalled by what he considered the shoddiness and cost of American medicine that he considered writing a book on that subject as well.

31. That year's men's competition was won by the Australian, Ashley Cooper, and the women's by Althea Gibson, the first famous black tennis player

32. Bodleian, Chandler files

33. 'Sonnet 13'. Bodleian, Chandler files

34. 'Youth To Age'. Bodleian, Chandler files

35. *Daily Mail*, 8 July 1958

36. Dr Bor was later described in his obituary in *The Times* as 'a world authority on Asian grasses'.

37. Letter to Roger Machell, 14 October 1958. Bodleian, Chandler files

38. Kay West (now Kay Beckett) was interviewed by the author in January 1995

39. Letter from Kay West to Helga Greene, 16 February 1959. Bodleian, Chandler files

40. Letter to Hardwick Moseley, 5 October 1958. Bodleian, Chandler files

41. 'Marlowe Takes on the Syndicate' was published the month after Chandler's death by the *Daily Mail*. It was serialized in four parts, from 6 April to 10 April 1959. It has since been reprinted under the titles 'Wrong Pigeon' and 'The Pencil'

42. A transcript of Chandler's MWA speech is included in the Chandler papers at UCLA

EPILOGUE

1. *New York Times*, 27 March 1959
2. *Sunday Express*, 1 May 1960
3. The transcript of the four-day trial is on record at San Diego's County Court archives
4. Quoted in Al Clark, *Raymond Chandler and Hollywood*, Proteus 1982, p. 16
5. Miriam Gross (ed.), *The World of Raymond Chandler*, Weidenfeld & Nicolson 1977, p. 44
6. *Time*, 12 December 1988
7. *Listener*, 24 November 1988
8. Mike Davies, *City of Quartz*, Vintage 1992, p. 91
9. Edward Thorpe, *Chandlertown*, Vermilion 1983, p. 68
10. Letter to Charles Morton, 28 October 1947. Bodleian, Chandler files

Index

Academy (magazine) 25, 26, 27, 29
Agee, James: *A Death in the Family* 186
Allen, Woody 142
Altman, Robert 279
Ambler, Eric 230
And Now Tomorrow (film) 146
Arbuckle, Fatty 67
Arnold, Matthew 12
Atlantic Monthly (magazine) 160, 179, 183-4, 186, 190
Auden, W. H. x, 173, 174
Avon publishers 112, 131

Bacall, Lauren 162, 163
Bachardy, Don 246, 249
Bain, P. W. 14
Barham, Guy 64
Barrow, Jane 237, 238, 242-3
Barrow, Ralph 'Red' 55, 205, 237-8, 242-3
Baum, L. Frank: *The Wizard of Oz* 6
Baumgarten, Bernice 205, 206
Betjeman, John 184
Big Bear Lake, California 109, 118, 119,129, 158, 159
Big Sleep, The 69, 70, 82, 99-101, 103-5, 107-8, 111-12, 113-14, 119, 131, 132, 150, 250; films 150, 161-5, 280, 283
Black Mask (magazine) 71, 75-86, 90, 91, 94-5, 97, 103, 104, 114
Blakely, David 224
Bogart, Humphrey 144-5, 149, 161, 162-3
Bookseller (journal) 177
Bor, Dr Loftus 271
Bowen, Elizabeth 190
Brackett, Charles 136, 139, 161
Brackett, Leigh 161
Brandt, Carl 177, 188, 205
Brasher Doubloon, The (film) 298-9(n. 20)
'Breakfast Club' 64
Breen, Joseph 141, 142
Brown, Vinnie 293(n. 2)
Bruneman, Les 89
Bryan, Senator William Jennings 5-6
Burgess, Anthony 212
Cain, James M. 106, 108, 112, 114, 144
  Double Indemnity see under Chandler, Raymond
  Our Government 106
  The Postman Always Rings Twice 106-7, 136, 138
Campigny, Robert 190-1
Camus, Albert: *L'Étranger* 190
Cape, Jonathan 230
Capone, Al 87, 91
Carey, Phil ix
Carle, Teet 146-7, 298(n. 12)
Carson, Edward 247
Casablanca (film) 298(n. 4)
Cathedral Springs, California 119, 120, 122, 126
Chandler, Cissy (*formerly* Pascal) (wife): early life 47; courtship and marriage to Chandler 46, 47-50, 54-5, 60; appearance 48, 54, 148, 174-5; and Chandler's bingeing 61, 66, 70, 83, 148; illness 53, 61, 70, 108; reclusive life with Chandler 91, 98, 108-9, 112, 114-15; longs to live in La Jolla 115, 121-2; further illness 122; interest in films 135-6; with Chandler in Hollywood 134, 147, 158, 159, 196-7; at La Jolla 159, 167, 168-9, 174-5, 180-1, 197; her health deteriorates 178, 187; taken to England 198-201, 203-5; final illness and death 206, 211, 213; Chandler remembers 223, 239, 261, 269-70
Chandler, Florence (*née* Thornton) (mother): marriage and divorce in America 3, 4, 6; returns to Ireland 6-9; with Chandler in South London 9-10, 11, 15, 22, 24, 26, 30; joins Chandler in America 34, 40, 41; with the Pascals 46, 47; refuses to condone marriage 49-50; illness and death 49, 54
Chandler, Henry 64
Chandler, Maurice (father) 1-3, 4, 6, 33, 66, 108, 191
Chandler, Raymond: birth 3; childhood 1, 4-11; at Dulwich College, London 10, 11-20; a year on the Continent 20-4; in Civil Service 24-5; early writing 24-32; emigrates to USA 30, 33-41; war experiences 41-5; to Seattle, San Francisco and back to LA 45-7; meets

and marries Cissy 47-50, 54-5; at Dabney Oil co. 50, 51-4; lost years 61-4, 68, 69; decides to be a writer 71-5; writes for *Black Mask* 75-6, 77, 79-86, 90, 91, 94-5, 97, 103, 104; in Santa Monica 71, 83, 91-3, 98, 99, 108-9; writes first novel 99 (*see Big Sleep*); and more pulp fiction 109; and the Second World War 111, 118, 130; finishes second novel 115 (*see Farewell My Lovely*); not drinking and depressed 120-2; compulsive letter-writing 123-5; completes third novel 126, (*see High Window*); writes fourth novel 129 (*see Lady in the Lake*); invited to Hollywood 132-6; co-scripts *Double Indemnity* 136, 138-46; works as 'dialogue doctor' 146-7, 152; plans fifth novel 148 (*see Little Sister*); sacrifices himself for *The Blue Dahlia* 153-7; leaves Hollywood 158-61, 165-6; at La Jolla 159, 167-9, 176, 177-8, 180-1; screenplay abandoned 170-1; friendship with Maugham 174-6; works with Hitchcock 192-4; begins sixth novel 195 (*see Long Goodbye*); party for Priestley 195-6; and Cissy's deterioration in health 187, 196-7; takes Cissy to England 197, 198-205; and Cissy's death 213-18, 221, 222; returns to drinking 220-1; female 'shuttle service' in London 220-8, 235-6; and Fleming 221-2, 228-30; condemns Ellis hanging 224, 234; and Louise Loughner 231-2, 242, 244; in Italy 237; back to La Jolla 237-8; to Spain and Tunisia with Natasha Spender 238-40; collapse and psychiatric treatment 242-5; in USA with Natasha Spender 245-6, 249; completes seventh novel 252 (*see Playback*); relationships with Jean Fracasse and Helga Greene 250-2, 259-62, 264-5, 271-2, 273; interviews Luciano in Naples 262-4; writing projects 267, 268; BBC interview 270-1; back in La Jolla 271-3; last Marlowe story 273-4; engagement to Helga 274-5; death 275; funeral 276; obituaries 276-7; lawsuit over will 277-8

alcoholism ix, 61-4, 66, 68, 69, 70, 117, 122-3, 128, 140-1, 154-5, 156-8, 221, 222, 224, 273

appearance 11, 22, 24, 34, 37, 47, 54, 148, 201, 260

on the Catholic Church 8-9, 151, 182

love of cats 124, 158, 175-6, 179

earnings and finances 52, 56, 71, 82-3, 91, 97, 108, 109, 112, 117, 129, 132, 152, 154, 156, 157, 159, 167, 217, 231, 238, 242, 265-6, 275

house-moving x, 50, 56-7, 71, 108-9, 119, 159, *see also* London

interest in language 21-2, 73, 117

letter-writing 123-5, 183, 266-7, 278, 279, 280

and Marlowe ix-x, 63, 64, 99-100, 101-3, 104, 128, 131, 178, 182, 246-9, 258-9, 287

and misogynism 100, 283, 285

nationality and identity 23-4, 42, 178-9

political views 181-3

and racism and anti-Semitism 254-5, 282, 283-5, 286

reputation and critical recognition 107-8, 113-14, 117-18, 128-9, 131-2, 150, 151, 165, 171-4, 190, 212-13, 278-83

on science fiction 211-12

and sex 61, 62, 141-2, 148, 220-1, 227-8, 246-7

interest in television 191-2, 267-8

on writers and writing 72-5, 122, 151-2, 173, 174, 184-8, 200, 205-6

non-fiction:
'Hollywood and the Screenwriter' 159-60
'Oscar Night in Hollywood' 160-1
'Realism and Fairyland' 27-8
'The Remarkable Hero' 27
'The Simple Art of Murder' 183-4
'Ten Per Cent of Your Life' 184
'Trench Raid' 44, 45

novels see The Big Sleep; *Farewell My Lovely*; *The High Window*; *The Lady in the Lake*; *The Little Sister*; *The Long Goodbye*; *Playback*

poetry 24, 25-6, 60, 268-9 *and see below*
'Ballad to Almost Any Goddess' 48-9
'Free Verse' 30-2
'Improvisation for Cissy' 83
'Lines with an Incense Burner' 46, 47
'Nocturne from Nowhere' 60
'Song at Parting' 60
'Song of the Boatman on the River Roon' 40-1
'Sonnet 13' 269
'The Unknown Love' 24
'Youth to Age' 269

screenplays and screenwriting:
And Now Tomorrow 146
The Blue Dahlia 46, 63, 153-8, 279
Double Indemnity 132, 136, 138-46, 150
Playback 44, 45-7, 170-1, 245, 279
The Unseen 147, 152

short stories:
'Bay City Blues' 45
'Blackmailers Don't Shoot' 79, 80-2, 274
'The Bronze Door' 28, 109-10, 113
'A Couple of Writers' 296(n. 22)
'The Curtain' 103
'Do You Terribly Mind Being Seduced'

225-6
'English Summer' (unpub.) 28-9, 268
'Finger Man' 84, 85
'How To Ruin Doctor' 243
'I'll Be Waiting' 296(n. 17)
'Killer in the Rain' 103
'The King in Yellow' 62-3, 96-7
'The Lady in the Lake' 296(n. 17)
'Mandarin's Jade' 70, 86
'Marlowe Takes on the Syndicate' 273-4, 278
'No Crime in the Mountains' 109, 118-19, 296(n. 17)
'Pearls Are a Nuisance' 296(n. 17)
'Poodle Springs' (unfinished) 269, 282-3
'Professor Bingo's Snuff' 113
'Red Wind' 95, 283
'Smart Aleck Kill' 82, 83-4, 94
The Smell of Fear (anthology) 90
'Trouble is My Business' 85-6, 296 (n. 17)
Chaplin, Charlie 59
Chase, James Hadley: Blonde's Requiem 176-7
Chicago 2, 3-4, 78
Chimera (journal) 172
Chinatown (film) 279
Christie, Agatha 87, 190, 191
Chula Vista Sanatorium 216-17, 256
Churchill, Winston 183
Clark, Al: Raymond Chandler and Hollywood 280
Clift, Montgomery 165
Cody, 'Buffalo Bill' 2
Connolly, Cyril 174, 206
Cornford, Frances 241
Coxe, George Harmon 114
Crosby, Bing 145
Cukor, George 174, 175, 198

Dabney, Joseph 51, 57, 293(n. 49)
Dabney Oil Syndicate 50, 51-4, 55, 57, 69, 82
Dahl, Roald 252
Daily Express 30, 46, 232, 234
Daily Mail 269-70, 274
Daily Mirror 233
Daly, Carroll John 78-9
Davies, Mike: City of Quartz 282
Davies, Russell 281-2
Davis, Police Chief James Edgar 64, 65, 88-90
Dayley, Dr George 88
De Mille, Cecil B. 59
Dent, Lester 77
Depression, the 64-5, 69, 83, 87, 90, 120, 121
DeVoto, Bernard 212-13
Dime Detective Magazine 97

Domanick, Joe: To Protect and to Serve 88-9
Double Indemnity (film) see under Chandler, Raymond
Douglas, Norman: South Wind 82-3
Doyle, Sir Arthur Conan 29, 75, 293-4(n. 8)
Dulwich College, London 10, 11-20, 34, 41, 44, 99, 118
Durham, Philip: Down These Mean Streets a Man Must Go 278-9

Einstein, Albert 20, 183
Eliot, T. S. x, 31, 173, 174, 281
Ellis, Ruth 224, 234
Ellroy, James 282
Encounter (magazine) 266
Esquire (magazine) 228
Evening Standard 224

Falcon Takes Over, The (film) 137, 138
Farewell My Lovely 114, 115-18, 122, 131, 195, 247-8, 254, 284-5, 291-2(n. 48); films 279, see Falcon Takes Over, The; Murder My Sweet
Faulkner, William 80, 152, 153, 161, 278
FBI 78, 181, 262, 264
Fisher, Steve 159
Fitt, Ernest 4, 6, 35, 127
Fitt, Grace (née Thornton) 3, 4, 6, 35, 127
Fitt, Harry 4, 35
Fitzgerald, F. Scott 75, 152, 153, 283
Fleming, Ian 221-2, 228-30, 243, 258, 262, 269, 270-1, 282
  Casino Royale 221, 228, 229
  Live and Let Die 228, 230
  Moonraker 229, 266
Flint, Motley 59
Flint, R. W.: 'A Cato of the Cruelties' 171
Foch, Marshal Ferdinand 42
Ford, Henry 51
Forester, C. S. 18, 93, 290(n. 23)
Forster, E. M. 29
Fracasse, Dr 250-1, 261, 271
Fracasse, Jean 250-1, 259, 260, 261, 264-5, 271, 272, 277-8
Francis, F. J. 201
Frank, Alvin 57

Gardiner, Dorothy 278, 291(n. 34)
Gardner, Erle Stanley 74-5, 79, 80, 94, 107, 112, 114, 116
Garner, James 279
Garrick Club, London 230
Gartrell, Deirdre 260-1
Gault, William 213
Geisel, Theodor 180
George VI, King 165
Gilbert, Michael 222, 244, 265, 272, 277

Gilkes, A. H. 13-15, 16-18, 19, 21, 44
  A Day At Dulwich 19
Glover, Danny 283
Glyn, Elinor: The Reason Why 26-7
Going My Way (film) 145
Goldwyn, Samuel 159
Goodwin, Prof. Donald: Alcoholism 62
Gould, Elliott 279
Granger, Farley 193
Grant, Cary 149
Greene, Graham 171
  The Heart of the Matter 173
Greene, Helga 251-2, 259, 260, 261-5, 271,
  272, 273, 274-5; wins lawsuit over will
  277-8; commissions Raymond Chandler
  Speaking 278; on Chandler ix, 228, 230,
  267, 268
Greene, Hugh Carleton 251
Guinness, H. S. H. 275
Guinness, Maurice 269, 270

Haig, Field Marshal Sir Douglas 42
Hamilton, Hamish 107, 176-7, 195, 199,
  200-1, 203, 206, 207, 221, 251, 262,
  267; Chandler's correspondence with
  113, 161-2, 176, 179, 183, 187-8, 201,
  222, 239, 254, 294(n. 36), 294-5(n. 36);
  publishing house 203, 204, 230
Hammett, Dashiell 20, 75, 77, 79-80, 94,
  101, 106, 107, 112, 114, 182, 184, 190,
  212
  'The Golden Horseshoe' 95
  The Maltese Falcon 80, 298(n. 4)
  The Thin Man 80, 108
Harper's 212
Hawks, Howard 161, 163
Hays Office 68, 136
Hearst, William Randolph 64
Heflin, 'Van' 177
Hemingway, Ernest x, 74, 123-4, 278, 281
  Across the River and Into the Trees 205-6
Henderson, Donald: Mr Bowling Buys a
  Newspaper 235
Herbert, Hon. David 239, 247
Hernandez, Albert 180
Higgins, George V. 281
High Sierra (film) 298(n. 4)
Highsmith, Patricia: Strangers on a Train
  192
High Window, The 99, 126-9, 132, 137,
  139, 254, 296 (n. 17); see Brasher
  Doubloon, The; Time to Kill
Himes, Chester 283
Hitchcock, Alfred 192, 193-4, 257
  Strangers on a Train 192-3
Hitler, Adolf 111
Holding, Elizabeth Sanxay: The Innocent
  Mrs Duff 159

Hollywood 67-8, 87, 90, 108, 132-66, 169-
  71
Hollywood-Citizen News 117-18
Hollywood Reporter 155
'Hollywood Ten' 182-3
Hooker, Edward 245, 246, 249
Hooker, Evelyn 245, 246, 249
Hooper, Alison 223
Hoover, J. Edgar 181
Hose, H. F. 15, 25, 118, 203
Houghton Mifflin 177, 206
Houseman, John 134, 147, 148, 153, 154-
  5, 157
Hughes, Howard: Scarface 87
Hunt, Howard 295(n. 7)
Huston, John: The Maltese Falcon 298(n. 4)

I'm No Angel (film) 136
Ireland 1, 3, 7-9
Isherwood, Christopher 245, 246, 249
Iyer, Pico x, 281

Jacobson, Carl 65
James, Henry 46
Julian, C. C. 58-9
Julian Petroleum Company 58, 59

Kennedy, Robert 233
Kipling, Rudyard 12, 160
Knight, G. Wilson 290(n. 23)
Knopf, Alfred 80, 98, 105-6, 107, 112, 117,
  118, 126, 129, 131, 132, 176-7;
  Chandler's correspondence with 107-8,
  111, 123-4, 126, 130, 166
Knopf, Blanche 123

Ladd, Alan 146, 153, 154, 156, 157, 162
Lady in the Lake, The 61, 66, 129-32, 247,
  292(n. 48), 296(n. 17); film 158-9
La Jolla, California 115, 121-2, 159, 167-9,
  174-5, 177-8, 180, 181, 197, 217, 238,
  243-4, 250, 271-3, 275
Lake, Veronica 154, 156, 157
Latimer, John 180, 181, 195
Lee, Bruce 279
Legman, G. 246
Leonard, Elmore 152, 282
Listener (magazine) 281-2
Little Sister, The 36-7, 56, 90-1, 148, 149,
  171, 176, 187-91, 287, 292(n. 48); film
  see Marlowe
Lloyd, Estelle 39, 40
Lloyd, Dr Warren 34, 36, 38-9, 40, 49, 50,
  57, 71
London 130, 183, 200-2; Bloomsbury 28-9,
  30; Carlton Hill 240-2; Connaught Hotel
  199, 218, 221, 225; Eaton Square 235;
  Forest Hill 26; Streatham 24; Swan Walk

261-2, 264, 267-8, 269, 271; Upper Norwood 9-10, 11
Long Goodbye, The 51, 56, 66, 195, 197, 205, 206-11, 212-13, 216, 221, 246-7, 248-9, 252, 254, 256, 257-8, 259, 265, 272, 276, 285, 286; film 279
Los Angeles 34, 38, 39-40, 47, 50-1, 55-9, 64, 66, 67-9, 86-7, 90, 94, 120-1; Creamery 38, 40, 60; Police Department 51, 64-5, 67, 87-91, 93
Los Angeles Daily News 58, 145
Los Angeles Times 64, 93, 108
Loughner, Louise 218, 231-2, 235, 241, 242, 243, 244, 256
Luciano, Charles 'Lucky' 262-4
Luhr, William: Raymond Chandler and Film 280
Lummis, Charles Fletcher 36

MacCarthy, Desmond 132
McCarthy, Senator Joseph 182
Macdonald, Dwight 186
Machell, Roger 199, 204, 207, 220, 236
MacMurray, Fred 142
MacShane, Frank: The Life of Raymond Chandler 280
Mannix, Edgar 158-9
Marlowe (film) 279
Mason, A. E. W. 18
Masters, John: Bhowani Junction 220
Maugham, W. Somerset 174-6, 229
  Ashenden 174
Mayer, Louis B. 59, 64
Mellon, Andrew 50
Mencken, H. L. 76-7
Messick, Juanita 177, 181, 215, 283
MGM 158-9, 279
Miles, Sarah 280
Miller, Max 180, 181
Mitchum, Robert 279, 280
Mohr, Gerald 177
Montgomery, George 298-9(n. 20)
Montgomery, Robert 159
Moral Rearmament movement 92
Morgan, Neil 167-8, 169, 180, 181, 214, 216, 217-18, 237, 272, 274
Morton, Charles 183; Chandler corresponds with 179, 184-7, 191, 196, 287
Moseley, Hardwick 272, 273
Mosely, Walter 282
Munro, Hector Hugh ('Saki') 25
Murder My Sweet (film) 150-1, 152
Mystery Writers of America 274-5, 276

Nathan, George Jean 76-7
News Chronicle 233-4
Newsweek (magazine) 151, 171
New Yorker, The (magazine) 125, 171, 276

New York Herald Tribune 145
New York Review (magazine) 283
New York Times 107-8, 146, 165, 212, 276
Norman, Frank: Bang To Rights 266
Nye, Senator Gerald 59

Oates, Joyce Carol 283
Observer 183, 221
O'Neill, Eugene 173
Ormonde, Czenzi 193
Orwell, Sonia 222

Paramount Studios 132, 134, 136, 138-51, 153-8, 159, 163, 169
Parker, Robert B. 283
Partisan Review (journal) 171, 173
Pascal, Gordon 41, 46
Pascal, Julian 46, 47, 49, 50, 198
Penguin Books 200
Penn, William 1-2
Perelman, S. J. xi, 114, 124-5, 229
Phileo, Milton 55, 61, 63
Picture Post (magazine) 172
Pinkerton, Allan 78
Place in the Sun, A (film) 165
Plattsmouth, Nebraska 3, 4-5, 6-7, 33, 35
Playback 170-1, 245, 251, 252-9, 265, 268
Pocket Books 111, 112, 131, 152
Polanski, Roman: Chinatown 279
Porcher, Leon 47
Pound, Ezra 173
Powell, Dick 150
Powell, Dilys 174, 203-4
Powell, Michael 18, 290(n. 23)
Presnell, Robert 147, 148
Priestley, J. B. 174, 195-6
'Production Code' censorship 136-8, 139, 141-2, 143, 145, 146, 147, 150, 157, 161, 163, 164-5
Prohibition movement 4, 35, 66-7, 78, 263
Proust, Marcel: Remembrance of Things Past 20
Publisher's Weekly (magazine) 105-6

Quakers 1-2, 3, 8, 11, 231

radio adaptations 104, 177
Rampling, Charlotte 279
Raymond, Henry 87, 88
Revue-Critique, La (journal) 190
Rickards, Jocelyn 222, 240
RKO Pictures 137, 150
Robinson, Edward G. 143
Roosevelt, Franklin D. 66, 120
Russell, Bertrand 183
Russell, Leonard 203-4

St Louis, Missouri 34-5

Saki *see* Munro, Hector Hugh
Salinger, J. D.: *Catcher in the Rye* 186
Sanders, George 138
Sanders, Sydney 98, 137, 176, 177
San Diego Daily Journal 169
San Diego Tribune 250
San Diego Union 216
Sandoe, James 124, 170, 171, 183, 187
San Francisco 36-8, 46
Santa Monica 71, 83, 91-3, 99, 108, 119
Santry, Don 271, 272, 274
Saturday Evening Post 296(n. 17)
Saturday Review (magazine) 213
Schwarzenegger, Arnold 279
Selincourt, E. de 290(n. 20)
Sequence (magazine) x-xi, 165
Shackleton, Ernest Henry 19
Shaw, 'Cap' Joseph 77-8, 79, 80, 81, 84-5, 97
Shaw, Bernard 25
Shaw, Mayor 87-8
Sheppard, J. T. 21
Shortridge, Senator Samuel 64
Siegel, Bugsy 88, 89
Simenon, Georges 20, 190
Sinatra, Frank 262
Sistrom, Joe 132, 139, 140, 141
Sitwell, Edith 222
Sitwell, Osbert 173
Smart Set (magazine) 75, 76
Smith, Allen: *Lost in the Horse Latitudes* 283
Spender, Elizabeth 241
Spender, J. A. 25
Spender, Matthew 241
Spender, Natasha 221, 222-3, 224-5, 228, 230-1, 236, 237, 238-41, 245-6, 248, 249, 265
Spender, Stephen 25, 174, 221, 236, 240, 265
Stanwyck, Barbara 142
Stein, Gertrude 173
Steinbeck, John 114, 278
Stern, Der (magazine) 278
Stevenson, Robert Louis 93
Sunday Express 277
Sunday Times 132, 174, 200, 212, 221, 228, 232, 262, 264
Swanson, H. N. 152-3, 158, 159, 161, 170, 191, 192, 193, 196, 211-12

Tarantino, Quentin 282
  Pulp Fiction 283
Tatler (magazine) 190
Taylor, Elizabeth 165
Thomas, Judge Gerald C. 278
Thornton, Ernest 7, 9, 10, 11, 15, 20, 24, 25, 26, 30

Thornton, Ethel 9, 10, 15
Thornton, Mrs 7, 10
Thorpe, Edward: *Chandlertown* 280, 285
Time (magazine) x, 171, 190, 212, 281
Times, The 267, 276-7
Times Literary Supplement (journal) 128
Time to Kill (film) 137, 138
Tit-Bits (magazine) 29
Todd, Thelma 88
Towne, Robert 279
Townend, Will 19, 37, 235
Twentieth-Century Fox 136, 137, 298(n. 20)
Tygiel, Jules: *Swindle* 57
Tyndale, Jessica 220, 228, 242, 243, 244-5, 251

Universal Studios 170-1
Unknown (magazine) 109
Unseen, The (film) 147, 152

Variety (magazine) 145, 280
Vincent, Arthur 203
Voules, Horace 32

Walker, Robert 193
Warner Brothers 150, 163, 165, 192
Waterford, Co. 1, 3, 7-9, 11
Waugh, Evelyn x, 29, 190
Welles, Orson 136
Wells, H. G. 13
West, Kay 272-3, 274
West, Mae 68, 136
West, Nathaniel: *Day of the Locust* 187
Westminster Gazette 25-8
Wilde, Oscar 25, 247
  The Importance of Being Earnest 9
Wilder, Billy 132, 136, 139-41, 142, 143, 144, 280
Williams, Tennessee: *A Streetcar Named Desire* 186
Wilson, Edmund x, 171, 185
Winner, Michael 280
Wodehouse, P. G. 12, 14, 17, 18, 19, 37, 289(n. 20)
World of Raymond Chandler, The 280
World War, First 41-5, 63
World War, Second 111, 118, 119-20, 130, 147, 153, 154, 202

Young, Loretta 146

Zola, Emile 28
Zolotow, Maurice: 'How Raymond Chandler Screwed Hollywood' 156-8